Mikael Forslund

Colour profiles
Andrzej M. Olejniczak

Saab 37
Viggen

Published in Poland
in 2022
by STRATUS sp.j.
27-600 Sandomierz 1
e-mail: office@mmpbooks.biz
www.stratusbooks.pl

for
MMPBooks,
e-mail: office@mmpbooks.biz
© 2022 MMPBooks.
http://www.mmpbooks.biz

ISBN
978-83-66549-72-2

Editor in chief
Roger Wallsgrove

Editorial Team
Bartłomiej Belcarz
Robert Pęczkowski
Artur Juszczak

Scale Plans
Dariusz Karnas

Colour Plates
Andrzej M. Olejniczak

Text
Mikael Forslund

Translation
Jan Forsgren

Proofreading
Roger Wallsgrove

DTP
Bartłomiej Belcarz

Printed by
Drukarnia Diecezjalna,
ul. Żeromskiego 4,
27-600 Sandomierz
www.wds.pl

PRINTED IN POLAND

Table of contents

Saab 37 *Viggen*
Introduction

In this book, I have consistently chosen to use the acronym Saab. Until 1965, the company name was written as SAAB (Svenska Aeroplan Aktiebolaget). Regarding missiles, I have elected to use the abbreviation *RB*, even if the pre-1965 designation was *Rb*. Additionally, the designation SK (*Skol-flygplan*, i.e. Training Aircraft) appears in capital letters (after 1965). Sk, is written about Training Aircraft manufactured before 1965. Written Squadron (English) or Division (Swedish), is "the same".

The name *Viggen* comes from the lightning (*viggen*) produced by the Norse God Thor's hammer *Mjölner*. Apart from prototypes, the *Viggen* was built/modified in the following variants: AJ, AJS, SK, SK 37E, SF, AJSF, SH, AJSH, JA, JA 37D and JA 37Di. The Saab 37 *Viggen* was originally intended as a multi-role combat aeroplane. The idea of using a single type of aircraft for different roles, such as fighter, bomber and aerial reconnaissance can be traced to the 1930s. However, it was not until the introduction of the Saab JAS 39 *Gripen* (JAS = *Jakt, Attack, Spaning* = Fighter, Attack, Reconnaissance), during 1996 (first flight 9 December 1988, prototype 39-1) that *Flygvapnet* (Swedish Air Force) received a true multi-purpose combat aircraft.

Following the initial development in the late 1950s of what would become the *Viggen*, a "cooperation" with the USA became a reality through a 1960 treaty. President Eisenhower provided Sweden with access to advanced US aviation technology, with US engineers supporting the *Viggen* development at Saab at Linköping. In all likelihood, the selection of a Pratt & Whitney engine in 1961 could have been a part of this, as well as the subsequent selection of the *RB 24*, *RB 27* and *RB 28* missiles.

The deal was that the future *Viggen* would provide protection to US atomic submarines armed with nuclear Polaris missiles which could be patrolling off the Swedish west coast.

With the *Viggen* (first flight 8 February 1967, prototype 37-1), Saab and *Flygvapnet* almost reached the intended goal of producing a multi-role combat aeroplane.

But it was not a clear-cut thing that the Saab 37 *Viggen* would be selected by *Flygvapnet*.

The 37-1 prototype taking off with two dummy RB 04Es beneath the wings. (Via Archives of Swedish Aviation Historical Society)

Some foreign aircraft were considered to replace, mainly, the Saab 35 *Draken*. In April 1964, an Aviation Equipment Commission, led by the politician Karl Frithiofson, was appointed by the government. The task was to compare existing foreign aircraft with the projected Saab 37 *Viggen*. Aircraft considered included the British Hawker Siddeley Buccaneer and BAC TSR 2, as well as the US General Dynamics F-111 and McDonnell Douglas F-4 Phantom II. The latter, in particular, was of particular interest.

The result of the Commission's work, presented on 31 March 1965, showed among other things, that the Phantom II had a higher load capability and longer range than the *Viggen*. However, this was not considered to be of importance for Sweden. The foreign aircraft were deemed to be too expensive. The operational requirements also appeared to be better suited for the projected *Viggen* than any of the foreign types of aircraft considered. Work on the Saab 37 *Viggen* could continue. By the end of 1965, some 2,000 Saab employees were involved in the 37 *Viggen* programme.

Before the first 37 *Viggen* prototypes had been completed, a few Saab 32 *Lansen* (Lance) were used as *Viggen* electronics test beds. On 10 February 1965, A 32A s/n 32080, known as *32 alfa*, made an initial flight fitted with *Viggen* electronics. Another A 32A, s/n 32280, known as *32 gamma*, was fitted with a *Viggen* nose and Ericsson PS 37/A radar for flight tests commencing on 14 December 1965. Beginning in March 1966, the second Saab J 32B *Lansen* prototype, s/n 32502, was used to test the *Viggen* rescue system, including ejection seat. Among other things, the aim was to make it possible for the pilot to eject safely from an aircraft standing on the ground. This was not completely achieved, as it was necessary to have a forward speed of at least 75 km/h for a safe ejection. Later on, with the generation 3 ejection seat, the initial goal was finally achieved. A total of 79 test ejections were made using s/n 32502.

Further tests of various kinds were performed at Saab for the 37 *Viggen*. These included a test rig for the fuel system, with a *Viggen* cockpit for vibration tests by pilots (for high speed flights at low altitude) as well as an HS-rig (Hydraulic Control System) being constructed.

There were numerous contractors for the *Viggen* project:
Main contractor:
Saab, aircraft, *RB 04, RB 05* and computer (*CK 37*)
Other major contractors:

Volvo Flygmotor:	Engine
AGA:	Radio
Bofors:	Armament
Arenco,	
SATT,	
SRA:	Counter measures

Equipment contractors:

Honeywell:	Auto pilot
LME (Ericsson):	Radar
SRA:	Indicators
AGA:	Gyro platform
SRT:	Radar altitude instruments

Subcontractor/s:

Vendor, with other companies supplying components to Vendor

During 1966, the future *Viggen* configuration was set. To a large extent, the airframe was built-up from light metal alloys on an aluminium base. Many of the sheet metal plates were glued! In order to save weight, titanium was also used to a certain extent. The airframe was calculated to have a strength of 12 Gs! The *Viggen* was designed to be easy to operate, both from a pilot's and technician's point of view. The engine could be changed in six hours. In order to use the *Flygvapnet* low-ceiling hangars, the fin could be folded, thus reducing the height of the aircraft from 5.6 m to 4.0 m. The fin could folded manually by a technician in three minutes. The nose section could be slid forward on two rails, thus easing radar maintenance. The canopy and front screen were built from strengthened acrylic glass. The curved front screen could withstand a bird collision at 1,000 km/h.

The Defence Committee proposed that 831 *Viggens* were to be ordered for *Flygvapnet*. Due to economic and other causes, this quantity was substantially reduced to 337 aircraft. From the mid-1960s, the *Viggen* project was the target of harsh criticism, being hotly debated in newspapers, TV and radio. One point of view was that the *Viggen* was far too expensive for Sweden. The cost of the *Viggen* was put against child care, child benefits and state pensions. On 19 March 1973, the documentary "*Viggen* 37, a movie on how to spend 30 billions of tax money", premiered.

In October 1966, the 37-1 prototype was ready for testing. On 24 November, the aircraft was shown to the public for the first time. Despite the fact that no radar was fitted, the nose section was painted Black. Initially, the *Kungliga Flygförvaltningen (KFF)* (Royal Air Board) had ordered seven prototypes. In the event, trials were also performed using other *Viggens* than those built as prototypes. Although the *Viggen* had been built to withstand 12 G, this was limited to seven G during exercises.

The *Viggen* engine could be started without an external power source. A powerful battery provided power for the Auxiliary Power Unit (APU). The *Viggen* was the world's first combat aircraft

SK 37 Viggen s/n 37806, coded F 7-64, seen taxiing to its parking space at F 7 Såtenäs, under the guidance of a conscript mechanic. (Leif Fredin, via Archives of Mikael Forslund)

that had a completely new wing shape, consisting of two codependent delta wings. Much foreign interest was shown in this aerodynamic solution. The advantages of the double delta configuration included a short take-off and landing run (500 m). This meant that the *Viggen* could operate from damaged runways, as well as utilizing simple highway bases within the road network, thus ensuring less vulnerability to the air base system. The double delta also resulted in exceptional stability in all speed envelopes as well as excellent manoeuvrability. Another innovation was that the *Viggen* had reverse thrust following landing. Three lids closed the nozzle, guiding the jet slightly upwards/forwards. This system, along with heavy braking from the pilot, resulted in a landing run of less than 500 m (900 m without thrust reverse). There was an additional advantage when operating from road bases. Using the thrust reverse, the aircraft could taxi backwards on the ground!

The undercarriage along with the brakes were of rugged construction. The main undercarriage consisted of two relatively thin tandem wheels. This made it possible for the *Viggen* to land at a steeper angle than with a more conventional undercarriage. Another advantage was that when retracted, the undercarriage took up a relatively small amount of space, based on the thickness of the wheels.

Road bases had been used prior to the introduction of the *Viggen*. This base system was still active, being increased as time went on. The *Bas 90* (Base 90) system included a large extension of many Swedish air bases. A road base often consisted of a main runway, connected with two or three short runways 800 m in length and 16 m wide. The runways were connected with taxi runways, and parking areas. This system was created for *Viggen* operations. During a crisis, an enemy would have found it impossible to destroy the Swedish system of air bases. Regarding maintenance, see below.

The 50th Anniversary of Flygvapnet at F 4 Östersund on 6 June 1976. SH 37 s/n 37904, coded F 7-08, stands nearest the camera, being finished in the then recently introduced splinter camouflage. In the background, a few AJ 37 Viggen of F 7 Såtenäs in overall Natural Metal and Saab J 35D Drakens from F 4 Östersund can be seen. (Leif Fredin, via Archives of Mikael Forslund)

Initial plans called for making the first *Viggen* variant, the AJ 37, a two-seater. This was due to concerns about the pilot's work load, with some things to be allocated to a rear-seat navigator/systems operator. However, development of computers progressed so much during the 1960s, that it was decided that the *Viggen* was to be a single-seater (apart from 18 SK 37 conversion trainers). For its time, the *CK 37* (*Centralkalkylator 37* = Central Calculator) was ahead of its time, assisting the pilot in navigation, maintaining altitude during low level sorties and maintaining speed during short landing approaches. Initially, the *CK 37* had a capacity of eight Kb. Apart from the *Viggen*, only the US Grumman A-6 Intruder was equipped with a similar computerized system at this juncture.

Different components in the *Viggen* computer system were supplied by the following companies: AGA (*Aktiebolaget Gasaccumulator*) supplied the flight attitude transmitter and voice communication system, Arenco the air data system, Philips the navigation equipment, L M Ericsson the entire radar system, SRA (*Svenska Radioaktiebolaget*) for the radar altimeter, central and aiming line instruments, with Honeywell Inc. supplying the analogue autopilot.

Some cockpit indicators presented important information to the pilot. The position of the aircraft was presented on a numeric indicator, providing longitude and latitude. Presentation of radar and control information was provided by the *Centralindikator (CI)* (Central Indicator), which was fitted

to the AJ 37 and SH 37s (the SF 37 and SK 37 lacked radar). In the JA 37, the *CI* was replaced by a *Målindikator (MI)* (Target Indicator) and a *Taktisk indikator (TI)* (Tactical Indicator).

An SF 37 of F 17 seen taxiing out for take-off at F 17 Kallinge on 11 June 1994. (Mikael Forslund)

The *Siktlinjesindikator (SI)* (Aiming Line Indicator) was fitted to the AJ 37, SK 37, SF 37 and SH 37 variants. This system was upgraded for the JA 37. The *SI* was the most sophisticated indicator. The *SI* presented electronically generated symbols for control and aiming reflected in a transparent surface on the pilot's eye level (HUD, i.e. Head Up Display). In the air, the pilot could keep an eye on the terrain while at the same time receive adequate information without having to look down onto the instrument panel. Apart from the flight attitude, information such as barometric altitude, radar altitude, estimated time to selected target, possible speed errors and coordinates of preselected turning points were presented.

The JA 37 pilot had an acoustic (tonal) *Gränsvärdesvarnare (GVV)* (Limit Warning device). Among other things, the pilot could obtain a rising warning signal at increasing G-loads (the limit was seven G), or similar when the angle of attack increased. The pilot also received a tonal warning (as well as a visual warning) when his aircraft was struck by outside radar. When this occurred, the pilot was able to perform electronic radar jamming or drop chaff.

The fuel system consisted of eight (seven for the SK 37) integral tanks, and an external fuel tank (which could be released in an emergency). The JA 37 external fuel tank was fitted with four tail fins, as opposed to the external fuel tank carried by the other *Viggen* variants, which had three tail fins. Four of the integral tanks were located in the wings, three (two for the SK 37) in the front fuselage and one in the rear fuselage. The *Viggen* could be refuelled with the engine running (something which was performed by the author on the AJ 37 during his national service in 1979/80). As for fuel consumption, this was of course different during different situations. For instance, at maximum thrust and at low level, the engine consumed ten litres of kerosene per second.

When maintaining the aircraft on the ground, a huge variety of equipment and vehicles were at hand. When preparing the aircraft for the next sortie during active service, which for the AJ 37 took between 15 to 20 min, this was performed by a technician and six conscripts.

The first *Viggen* variant introduced into service was the AJ 37 *Viggen* (AJ being short for *Attack/ Jakt*, i.e. Attack/Fighter), which had a primary attack role, with a limited secondary fighter role. The AJ 37 entered service with Wing F 7 at Såtenäs in 1973. Dedicated photo reconnaissance variants of the basic AJ 37 airframe were developed as the SF 37 (*Spaning Foto*, ie Reconnaissance Photo) and SH 37 (*Spaning Hav*, i.e. Reconnaissance Sea) *Viggen* respectively. A two-seat conversion trainer, designated SK 37 (*Skol*, ie Trainer), was produced in 18 examples. In the latter part of its active service, a number of SK 37s were modified to SK 37E (E being short for "Electronics"). (Please refer to the table and relevant chapter).

The JA 37 prototype (*Jakt/Attack*, ie Fighter/Attack), s/n 37-8, first flew on 15 December 1975. Five years later, F 13 at Norrköping became the first *Flygvapnet* Wing to receive JA 37s. Many of the AJ 37s, SF 37s and SH 37s were subsequently modified as multi-role combat aircraft as the AJS 37, AJSF 37 and AJSH 37 respectively (please refer to the tables), with the designations signifying their respective roles. Some JA 37s were modified as the JA 37D (Modification No.4, i.e. D) and JA 37Di (*D-Interoperabel*, i.e. D-Interoperational, being fitted with the colour tactical indicator) (please refer to the table and relevant chapter).

The final *Flygvapnet Viggens* were withdrawn from use in 2005. Some 20 million engineering hours had been invested in the *Viggen* project.

In 1982, the Hollywood movie star/director Clint Eastwood wanted to borrow a *Viggen* for his forthcoming movie Firefox. The *Viggen* was supposed to play the role of a modern Russian fighter. Unfortunately, Eastwood's request was declined, with Hollywood having to resort to models.

Today (2022) only two *Viggens* are airworthy (at Swedish Air Force Historic Flight), SwAFHF, at Såtenäs: AJS 37098 and SK 37E 37809.

Saab 37 *Viggen* Production

Prototypes/test:	8
AJ 37:	108
JA 37:	149
SF 37:	28
SH 37:	28
SK 37:	18

Quantity built: 337 (AJ s/n 37003 was rebuilt as SH 37 s/n 37900 and AJ 37 s/n 37033 as SF 37 s/n 37950).

The first series aircraft (AJ 37) was delivered to *Flygvapnet* on 21 June 1971 and final one (JA 37) on 29 June 1990. The last official flight of a *Flygvapnet Viggen* took place on 25 November 2005. Some 614,000 hours had been accumulated.

The final cost of the *Viggen* project was estimated at around 100 billion SEK.

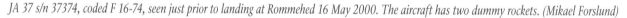

JA 37 s/n 37374, coded F 16-74, seen just prior to landing at Rommehed 16 May 2000. The aircraft has two dummy rockets. (Mikael Forslund)

Chapter 1

The Choice of Engine

Several different designs were investigated before the Saab 37 *Viggen* began to take shape. It was intended that the new combat aeroplane would replace the Saab 32 *Lansen* and Saab 35 *Draken*. Among the various types of engines discussed were the Bristol Olympus, Bristol Orpheus, Rolls-Royce RB 153 and Rolls-Royce Medway. On 2 December 1961, the Royal Air Board declared that the Pratt & Whitney JT8D would power the future aircraft. Among the aircraft using this engine was the Boeing 727. It was intended that the JT8D would be built under licence by *Svenska Flygmotor AB* (SFA) at Trollhättan. The SFA-built JT8D was designated *RM 8* (*RM = Reamotor* = Jet Engine), being fitted with a Swedish-designed afterburner. The engine was a so-called turbofan. Two variants of the basic *RM 8* were built, the first being the *RM 8A* which powered the first production *Viggen* variants AJ 37, SK 37, SF 37 and SH 37.

The *RM 8B* was seven cm longer in length, having one additional fan stage up front, with a corresponding reduction in length of the low pressure compressor (which was attached to the fan). The *RM 8B* also had a different burn chamber and modified afterburner. The engine chosen was largely responsible for the final production variant, the JA 37. The somewhat lengthened *RM 8B* meant that the JA 37 was longer than previous variants. The fuselage was lengthened just ahead of the front end of the engine, with the front fuselage being sloped slightly downwards, also becoming 13 cm longer.

As the engine was mounted on rails, changing the engine was fairly easy. The engine also powered the generator, hydraulic pumps and the fuel pumps. The thrust was provided from the high pressure supercharger via a gear box, reaching 445 kW, of which the fuel pump of the afterburner consumed 245 kW. This was due to the high fuel consumption when the afterburner was lit. A stand-by reserve, in the shape of a wind-driven generator, was activated during engine failures. This provided an effect of six kW, enough to power a hydraulic pump. For safety reasons, the wind-generator was released prior to emergency landings. The engine also supplied air pressure to the pilot's climate system, as well as cold or hot air to the electronics.

A squadron of JA 37s lined-up at F 21 Luleå on 9 June 1991. A fuel pump unit (known as PUGG) can be seen behind the aircraft. (Mikael Forslund)

The tail section of AJS 37 s/n 37108, coded F 10-55, on display at Flygvapenmuseum *in Linköping, Sweden, on 1 October 2016. This particular AJS 37 was the last production AJ 37. (Mikael Forslund)*

	RM 8A	RM 8B
Quantity built:	207 (s/ns 9001–9207)	173 (s/ns 9401–9573)
Weight (kg):	2,100	2,220
Length (m):	6.16	6.23
Inlet diameter (m):	1.03	1.03
Impeller delivery:	16.5:1	16.5:1
Combustion chambers:	9	9
Idle thrust (kp):	330	325
Thrust (kp):	6,690	7,350
Thrust with afterburner (kp):	11,790	12,750

Former F 6 *Viggen* pilot Alf Ingesson-Thoor from F 6 Karlsborg explains the performance of the RM 8A engine, originally published in "*System 37 Viggen*":

"*When flying on the basic engine, i.e. max turned off (MS), the aircraft wasn't that particularly impressive, even under-powered. During check flights on hot days, when take-offs were performed using only the basic engine, the aircraft barely got airborne. The afterburner's Zone 1 was used to retain a speed of M 0.9 at low altitude when carrying a heavy load. Zone 2 was an increase of speed zone and a take-off zone. Zone 3 was where things began to happen. The word accelerate really is insufficient, the Viggen simply runs off.*"

Chapter 2

The Prototypes/Test Aircraft

One of the requirements was that the new aeroplane would be able to take-off and land on 500 m long runways. In order to achieve this, the *Viggen* was fitted with a delta wing as well as a canard wing. Compared with the Saab 35 *Draken*, the *Viggen* had 50 percent higher lifting power when flying at the same angle of incidence. A strong twin-wheel main undercarriage made sure that landings could be performed at speeds of five m/s against the more normal three m/s. Perhaps the biggest novelty was the ability to almost reverse the engine thrust following landing, ensuring a braking movement which made the aircraft stop completely after 400 m! The thrust during this manoeuvre was about 3,500 kp. Literally hundreds of road bases were found across Sweden. Such a road base usually had a runway of 1,000 m (forming part of the Swedish public road network).

On 6 December 1962, Saab publicly displayed a model of the 37 *Viggen* (37-0). During the spring of 1964, a 1:1 scale wooden mock-up had been finished. Before the flight of the first *Viggen* prototype, trials of the electronic systems were made in a few modified Saab 32 *Lansens*.

On 8 February 1967, the first prototype, 37-1, took to the air for the first time. The test pilot was Captain Erik Dahlström. Apart from national insignia and the text Saab 37-1 on the fin, the aircraft was overall Natural Metal. On both sides of the air intakes, a symbol in the shape of Thor's hammer (Thor being a Norse God) from which three flashes emanated. The three flashes symbolized the three intended roles of fighter, attack and reconnaissance. Some 700 control points were fitted to the aircraft, registering rudder positions, pressure and vibrations.

On 31 May 1968, a tragic fatal accident occurred when the test pilot Lennart Fyrö accidentally ejected while 37-1 was on the ground.

Following repairs, spin trials were performed with 37-1 during 183 flights. In order to enhance visibility, the upper section of the nose was painted Black, the lower section Red while the left side of the fin was painted Black. A pod containing a anti-spin parachute was fitted to the tail cone. 37-1 was also used to test different armament options. Its final role in active service was to investigate the aircraft's performance when taxiing into end of runway nets, using runway 08-26 at Malmen airfield (Malmen-Malmslätt/Linköping).

Linköping during April 1969. At the time, the fifth prototype, 37-5, was undergoing trials with FC. Note that 37-6 is fitted with a camera pod (known as FUNK-pod) for photographing the release or firing of external loads. The first prototype, 37-1, has been fitted with the new dorsal spine. (Åke Andersson, Saab)

11

The 37-1 prototype caught during a high altitude sortie. (Via Archives of Mikael Forslund)

The 37-1 prototype ready for start at Saab. (Via Archives of Peter Kempe/Mikael Forslund)

The 37-1 prototype. Note the Viggen insignia on the air intake. (Via Archives of Veteranklubben Saab)

The 37-2 prototype taxiing out for take-off. Note that the national insignia on the front fuselage (on this aircraft only), were differently shaped than usual. (Both via Archives of Mikael Forslund)

A rare photograph of the second and third prototypes, 37-2 and 37-3 respectively. Note that 37-3 lacks national insignia, also carrying a measurement and camera pod (known as MUNK-pod). (Via Archives of Veteranklubben Saab)

The third prototype, 37-3, coded 53, seen taxiing and landing at F 6 Karlsborg on 1 June 1969. The aircraft is carrying a MUNK-pod (measurement and camera pod) as well as a FUNK-pod (camera pod for photographing the release or firing of external loads). Also of note is the saw tooth wing leading edge. (Aviation Photo Scandinavia, via Archives of Mikael Forslund)

The final fight took place on 27 June 1979. It was transferred to *Flygvapenmuseum* (Swedish Air Force Museum in Malmslätt/ Linköping), but was scrapped in 2013 due to heavy corrosion.

The second prototype, 37-2, flew on 21 September 1967 with Saab's test pilot Jon Ertzgaard at the controls during the 65 min flight. During the development of the JA 37, s/n 37-2 was modified to JA 37 status, being used for armament and control systems trials. The first flight occured on 4 June 1974. The bigger fin of the SK 37 and JA 37 variants was fitted to s/n 37-2. The serial number was subsequently amended from 37-2/52 to 37-21/52.

The aircraft was used for engine and aerodynamic stability trials while carrying dummy armament. The aircraft was fitted with the world's first digital autopilot. It was discovered that roll performance was poor. Before the introduction of the autopilot on the JA 37, roll performance had been improved considerably through the inner and outer rudders of the wings being mechanically connected, with more powerful servos also being fitted. These efforts resulted in considerably better roll performance for the JA 37 series.

In late 1982, this *Viggen* prototype was fitted with an electronic control system (ESS) intended for the Saab JAS 39 *Gripen* project. Flight trials lasted 50 hours. The regular mechanical/hydraulic control system was retained during these trials. The aircraft was grounded in 1991, and eventually scrapped.

The third prototype, 37-3, took to the air on 29 March 1968. The different electronics systems on the *Viggen* were tested, as were the gun sight indicator and radar. The aircraft was modified to partial JA 37 status, although neither the Oerlikon cannon nor *RM 8B* engine were fitted. A Ericsson PS 46/A pulse doppler radar was fitted for trials. The aircraft was later reserialled as s/n 31/53.

The fourth prototype, 37-4, was flown on 28 May 1968, being mainly used for engine trials.

The fourth prototype, 37-4, seen over the Lapland mountains sometime during the early 1970s. A FUNK-pod (camera pod for photographing the release or firing of external loads) is fitted to a right wing attachment point. A rearview camera pod for documenting the firing of missiles is fitted beneath the nose. Note the sawtooth wing leading edges. (Via Archives of Veteranklubben Saab)

Saab 37-1 (prototype)

1/72

The fifth prototype, 37-5, on display at an air show at F 15 Söderhamn in June 1970. Orange stripe around the nose (FS 22510) denotes it as an FC trials aircraft. The Olive-Green (FS 34092) surfaces are a colour test for the future camouflage. A FUNK-pod (camera pod for photographing the release or firing of external loads), is mounted on the centre attachment point. Among other aircraft in the background is a Saab Sk 35C Draken. (Leif Fredin, via Archives of Mikael Forslund)

The fifth prototype, 37-5, seen taxiing at Halmstad airfield on 31 August 1969. The Orange-painted (FS 22510) surface on the nose denotes this Viggen as being used for trials by FC. (Via Archives of Mikael Forslund)

The 37-5 prototype landing at F 17 on 8 June 1969. Note the unpainted nose section and the rearview camera pod mounted beneath the nose. The Orange-painted (FS 22510) surface denotes the aircraft's trial use by FC. A FUNK-pod (camera pod for photographing the release or firing external loads) is fitted on the centre attachment point. (Via Archives of Mikael Forslund)

The 37-6 prototype on display at the Paris Air Show on 2 June 1969. The numerals 752 on the rear fuselage and the text/painting on the nose section were applied especially for the Air Show. This occasion marked the first time that the Viggen had been displayed abroad. (Via Archives of Mikael Forslund)

This included afterburner, air intake configurations and the ejector nozzle. The wing was also fitted with a sawtooth, which improved the airflow across the wing when carrying a full armament load. The wing sawtooth modification was later also fitted to s/ns 37-1, 37-2 and 37-3.

On 7 May 1969, s/n 37-4 crashed on landing at Linköping during thrust reverse trials. This was the first *Viggen* crash. The aircraft flipped over, trapping test pilot Milton Mobärg. In the event, Mobärg was uninjured. The front fuselage was only lightly damaged, subsequently being used in the construction of the seventh *Viggen* prototype, s/n 37-7.

The fifth prototype, s/n 37-5, first flew on 15 April 1969. It was used to test handling characteristics when carrying an external fuel tank and a full armament load (eg rockets, missiles and bombs), as well as weapons delivery. A camera, mounted in a small pod beneath the nose, was used to document the trials.

The 37-6 prototype on display at the Paris Air Show on 2 June 2969. The numerals 752 on the rear fuselage and the test/painting on the nose section were applied especially for the Air Show. This occasion marked the first time that the Viggen had been displayed abroad. (Via Archives of Swedish Aviation Historical Society)

For the majority of its test career, 37-5 was used by *Försökscentralen (FC)*. It was marked FC-05, with national insignia being applied along with a 50 cm wide Orange (FS 22510) stripe behind the radar cone. After some time, 37-5 was rebuilt to partial JA 37 status, albeit retaining the *RM 8A* engine. The code was 51, later changed to 55. Between 1987 and 1992, the fifth prototype was also used to test the PS-05 radar intended for the Saab JAS 39 *Gripen*. Cannon and missile trials were also performed.

The sixth prototype, s/n 37-6, was flown on 24 January 1969. It was used for a wide variety of trials, including armament. Initially coded 56, it was displayed at Le Bourget in 1969, when it was marked as 752 (exhibition serial) on the rear fuselage and Saab *Suede 37 Viggen* on the nose. This was retained following the return to Sweden. 37-6 was subsequently used for engine trials, with the code being changed to 61. Following the loss of s/n 37-7 in a crash on 27 August 1975, s/n 37-6 was modified for continued use in engine trials originally performed with the former prototype.

37-6 ended its days with the *Kungliga Tekniska Högskolan (KTH)* (Royal Technical College) in Stockholm, eventually finding its way into preservation at *Västerås Flygmuseum* (2022).

Due to the crash of 37-4, a seventh prototype, 37-7, was constructed, flying for the first time on 20 November 1969. As mentioned above, the forward fuselage of 37-4 was reused on 37-7. At speeds of Mach 1.1 with a full armament load, the nose had a tendency to pitch upwards. The solution was to fit a bulbous section to the upper centre fuselage. Additionally, the forward fuselage was modified to point 1° upwards. With the flap of the canard wing being set at -4°, and at some alternate weapons loads -7°, the nose pitch problem was resolved. The remaining six prototypes were all modified in this manner. 37-7 was later converted to JA 37 status, being marked 71/57. It was lost on 27 August 1975 following take-off from Wing F 6. The pilot, Per Pellebergs, ejected safely. The cause of the crash was compressor blade failure.

The eighth prototype, s/n 37-8, first flew on 15 December 1975, being marked as 8/58. It was flown by Ulf Frieberg. This was the first *Viggen* flight after the grounding order following the wing failures had been rescinded (please refer to the AJ 37 chapter). Essentially a JA 37, s/n 37-8 was fitted with the enlarged fin. Due to the larger *RM 8B* engine, the fuselage was longer than previous *Viggen* prototypes. An additional elevator maneuvering cylinder was fitted, as was a fixed 30 mm Oerlikon cannon. The electronics had been much upgraded, with an effective doppler radar being mounted in the nose section.

The 37-7 prototype, coded 57, fitted with a rearview camera pod beneath the nose. (Via Archives of Swedish Aviation Historical Society)

The aircraft was written off in a crash at Åtvidaberg on 22 August 1978. The cause was an engine fire which spread to the w hole aircraft. The control system was destroyed, with the pilot, Gösta Sjöström, ejecting at an altitude of 900 m and a speed of 450 km/h. Sjöström was not injured. S/n 37-8 was replaced by the first series production JA 37, s/n 37301, which was never delivered to *Flygvapnet*.

The SK 37 prototype was s/n 37800 (see SK 37 chapter).

The 37-8 prototype on display at a 4 June 1978 air show at F 10 Ängelholm. This was the JA 37 prototype. The aircraft is fitted with MUNK and FUNK pods, as well as dummy RB 24 Sidewinder and RB 71 Sky Flash missiles. Note the FC badge on the fin. Flown for the first time on 15 December 1975, 37-8 was written off on 22 August 1978. As a result of the loss of 37-8, the first series production JA 37 (s/n 37301) was used to complete the flight test schedule. (Leif Fredin, via Archives of Mikael Forslund)

Variant	S/n	Code/s	First flight	Struck of charge	Remarks	Hrs flown in Sweden
Test	37-1	-1, 1/51	8 Feb 1967		SF 37 camera nose trials. Last flight 27 Jun 1979. Preserved Flygvapenmuseum, Linköping, Sweden. Scrapped 2012	800 h
Test	37-2	-2, -2/52, -21/52, ESS/52	21 Sep 1967	25 Sep 1985	Scrapped	1,099 h 09 min
Test	37-3	-3, -3/53, -31/53, F 14-53	29 Mar 1968		Modified as JA 37 prototype. Currently (2022) preserved at Nyköping-Skavsta, Sweden	
Test	37-4	-4, -4/54	28 May 1968		W/o Saab Skavsta, Sweden 7 May 1969	
Test	37-5	-5, FC-05, -51/55	15 Apr 1969		Modified as JA 37 prototype. Last flight in Jan 1992. Scrapped	
Test	37-6	-6, -6/56, -61/56	24 Jan 1969		Modified as JA 37 prototype. Last flight in 1998. Currently (2022) preserved at Västerås Flygmuseum, Sweden	
Test	37-7	-7, -7/57, -71/57	20 Nov 1969		Included parts from 37-4. Modified as JA 37 prototype. W/o 27 Aug 1975 at Mölltorp, W Karlsborg, Sweden	
Test	37-8	-8/58	15 Dec 1975		JA 37 prototype. W/o 22 Aug 1978 at Åtvidaberg, Sweden	

The 37-1 prototype fitted with a sheet metal nose similar to that of the future SF 37. Among other things, this configuration was used to test the aerodynamic characteristics. (Via Archives of Mikael Forslund)

The 37-1 prototype in 1967. The aircraft is mostly overall Natual Metal, with part of the dorsal spine being Black (FS 27040).

The 37-5 prototype at F 15 Söderhamn in 1970. Although the aircraft is mostly overall Natural Metal, part of the fin/rudder and the fuselage is Dark Green 326 (FS 34092), the band around the nose section is Orange (FS 22510) with part of the dorsal spine being Black (FS 27040).

a.m.olejniczak '22

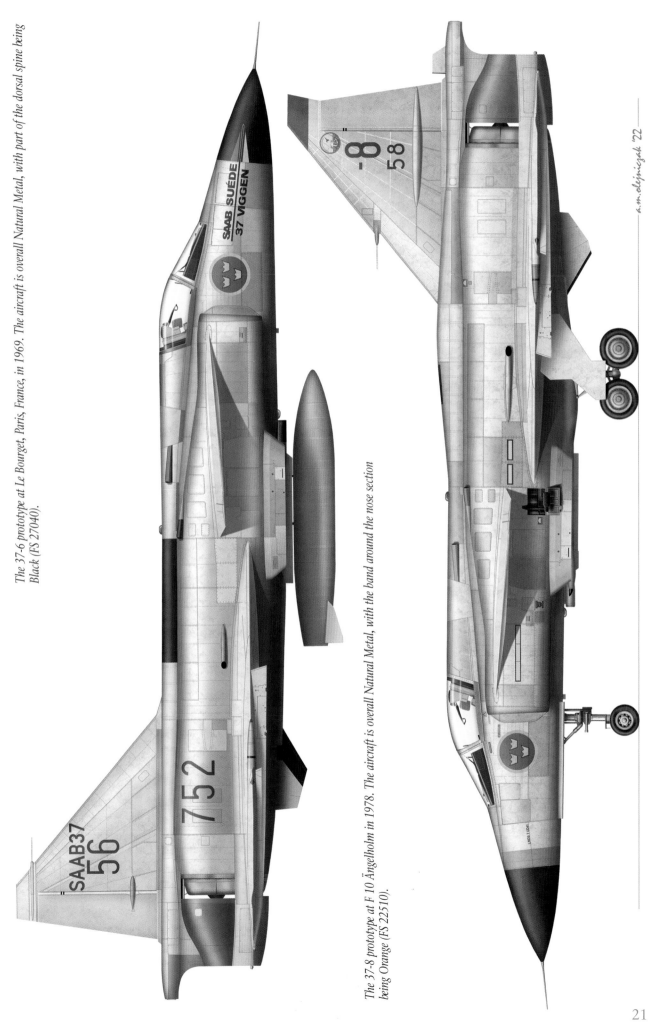

The 37-6 prototype at Le Bourget, Paris, France, in 1969. The aircraft is overall Natural Metal, with part of the dorsal spine being Black (FS 27040).

The 37-8 prototype at F 10 Ängelholm in 1978. The aircraft is overall Natural Metal, with the band around the nose section being Orange (FS 22510).

a.m.olejniczak '22

21

Chapter 3
AJ 37

The first *Viggen* production variant was the AJ 37. A total of 108 AJ 37s were built (s/ns 37001–37108), with s/n 37001 taking to the air with on 23 February 1971. The pilot on this occasion was Ingemar Rasmussen. S/n 37001 was marked as FC-51. As indicated by the AJ designation, this variant was primarily an Attack (A) aircraft, with a secondary Fighter (J) capability. On 14 September 1971, s/n 37001 was written off on landing at Malmen airfield at Malmslätt/Linköping due a faulty engine thrust reverse. The pilot, Lars Bandling, was unhurt.

The second and fourth production AJ 37s, s/ns 37002 and 37004, were coded FC-02 and FC-04 respectively and used for trials. Other early production AJ 37s were also temporarily used for various trials, including s/ns 37005 (FC-15), 37006 (FC-16) and 37007 (FC-17). Additionally, s/n 37003 was eventually rebuilt as the SH 37 prototype, being allotted the new s/n 37900. S/n 37033 was subsequently rebuilt as the SF 37 prototype, receiving a new s/n, 37950, in the process.

For the *Viggen* conversion training, two Flight Instructor groups were formed in 1972:

The *TIS:Ä* (Conversion Training: Older) and *GFSU: Ä (Grundläggande flygslagsutbildning äldre*, ie Primary Type Conversion Training: Older). Older indicated primarily older Saab A 32A *Lansen* pilots. The first pilots, of No.2 Sqn/F 7, began conversion training on 8 January 1973. The *TIS:Ä* training schedule consisted of 30 flight hours, both in the SK 37 and AJ 37, as well as 15 hours of simulator training. The following *GFSU:Ä* added another 70 flight hours and 15 hours in simulators.

In 1973, No.2 Sqn/F 7 initiated operations with the new AJ 37 *Viggen*. In late 1974, all three squadrons of Wing F 7 had re-equipped with the AJ 37, replacing the Saab A 32A *Lansen*.

The F 7 exercises with the AJ 37 began in earnest, using as many aircraft as possible. At this time, the attack squadrons operated in groups of four aircraft. During attacks, one or several groups were engaged, with almost simultaneous attacks taking place from different directions against the same target. The *CK 37* central calculator handled the processing of time and distance to the target. Prior to the sortie, this information had been fed into the *CK 37* following careful planning together with the other pilots and commanding officers. During approach to the target, more often than not at

AJ 37 s/n 37005, coded FC-15, was initially used by FC for flight testing. The band around the nose section is Orange (FS 22510). The photograph was taken in 1972 at F 10 Ängelholm. (Via Archives of Mikael Forslund)

AJ 37 s/n 37068, coded F 7-68, photographed at F 7 Såtenäs on 3 July 1980. At this juncture, several AJ 37s had yet to receive camouflage. To the left, a PUGG jet fuel pump unit can be seen. (Leif Fredin, via Archives of Mikael Forslund)

AJ 37 s/n 37068, coded F 7-68, taxiing out for take-off at F 7 Såtenäs during the mid-1970s. (Leif Fredin, via Archives of Mikael Forslund)

A pair of AJ 37s, s/ns 37017, coded F 7-17 and 37021, coded F 7-21, seen at low altitude. The aircraft are fitted with two 30/55 cannon pods each. Each pod contained one 30 mm ADEN Mk. 4 cannon. (Saab)

extreme low level, complete radio silence was common practice. Looking out for enemy anti-aircraft defences was of course important. The attack was then carried out using suitable resources. The return flight to the base was carried out at extreme low level. The design of the *Viggen* made it possible to even out air turbulence. During low level attack sorties, this meant that it was relatively simple to observe enemy targets despite turbulence. The construction of the wings resulted in a relatively large induced air resistance during dogfights. Because of this, the afterburner was used on such occasions. Even when flying straight ahead at high speeds, the induced air resistance was great. Thus, the high speed capabilities for all *Viggen* variants was not that great...

During Quick Reaction Alert readiness, the AJ 37s often carried two *30/55* cannon pods (with one 30 mm Aden cannon each) loaded with live ammunition in case of such a need arising.

During the development phase of the *Viggen*, built-in cannon armament for combat aircraft was deemed unnecessary, which from the Swedish point of view turned out to be a mistake. As a result, the 30 mm Aden cannon (identical to that of the Saab 35 *Draken*) could be carried in a pod on the *Viggen*.

With the introduction of the cannon pod, the mistake of not installing a built-in cannon in the aircraft was almost fixed. (During the JA 37 development, a built-in 30 mm Oerlikon cannon was added. More information can be found in the JA 37 chapter).

The analogue PS-37/A radar was also valuable. The PS-37/A was pulse radar optimized for reconnaissance and use against anti-shipping targets, but could also be used to present the terrain ahead as a map image. The radar was integrated with the *CK 37* central calculator. The pilot could feed information about the target and terrain directly into the radar image. The position was then automatically fed into the *CK 37* for navigation and arms delivery calculations. To a certain extent, the radar could also be used against aerial targets.

Various telecommunications counter measures, such as a built-in radar warning device, was fitted to the AJ 37.

The *KA* pod (later known as *U 22*) contained a jamming transmitter for active jamming of fighter radars and fire guidance radars. The pod's equipment could be programmed to jam most of the

AJ 37 s/n 37053, coded F 7-53, being cleared for flight at F 7 Såtenäs on 12 May 1974. (Leif Fredin, via Archives of Mikael Forslund)

AJ 37 s/n 37053, coded F 7-53, on display at a mid-1970s air show. Two RB 04Es and two dummy RB 05As have been placed near the aircraft. (Leif Fredin, via Archives of Mikael Forslund)

threat systems in operational use. The *KB* pod contained chaff and flare dispensers. Broad strips of chaff could be released, with enemy radar locking on to these instead of the aircraft. Infra-red flares could also be released as protection against the enemy's IR-missiles.

If these jamming pods were carried, this meant that the armament load was reduced during a large-scale attack. Using jamming pods during a large-scale attack demanded the use of more aircraft than otherwise.

In order to keep the aircraft in the air, a certain amount of ground work is required. *Flygvapnet* created the motto: "It is the men on the ground that keeps the aircraft flying!" During regular between-sortie maintenance at the respective Wings, a technician and conscript mechanic were responsible for one *Viggen*. All the necessary gear, fluids and fuel were located near the aircraft. Several sorties were flown each day, with the aircraft being thoroughly checked following each flight.

AJ 37 s/n 37072, coded F 7-341 (F 7-04), took part in the 14 June 1975 air show at Rygge, Norway. A few days earlier, the aircraft had been displayed at Le Bourget, Paris, France, hence the numerals 341 which had been applied for that Air Show. (Leif Fredin, via Archives of Mikael Forslund)

AJ 37 s/n 37005, coded F 7-05, taking off at full afterburner without external load. (Leif Fredin, via Archives of Mikael Forslund)

During field exercises, on wartime airfields or road base, this work was somewhat different. A so-called movable readiness troop handled all the ground maintenance. One vehicle with a trailer, one towing vehicle carrying the electrical readiness *BRAGG* gear *(Beredskapsaggregat)*, one ammunition vehicle with trailer and one fuel bowser were part of the operational field equipment.

One commander was responsible for sharing the workload between the men, as well as checking the landings and take-offs. As early as possible, the movable readiness troop was informed about which weapons should be carried by the aircraft during the next sortie. A technician was responsible for two aircraft, having a troop of six conscript mechanics for each aircraft. Everyone was assigned a special task. Refuelling from the bowser began. Simultaneously, oxygen (for the pilot) and compressed air (for the radar) were topped up. The cockpit, ejection seat, engine oil, radome, undercarriage, tyres and many other things were checked, mostly by the technicians.

Many AJ 37s of F 7 lined-up at one of the Wing's runways in the mid-1970s. Applying camouflage lasted for quite some time. (Leif Fredin, via Archives of Mikael Forslund)

AJ 37 s/n 37046, coded F 7-46, prior to landing on 3 July 1980. (Leif Fredin, via Archives of Mikael Forslund)

AJ 37 s/n 37005, coded F 7-05, taking off on full afterburner without any external load. (Leif Fredin, via Archives of Mikael Forslund)

AJ 37 s/n 37067, coded F 7-67, equipped with 16 m/71 Virgo high explosive fragmentation bombs, each weighing 120 kg, and an external fuel tank. (Via Archives of Veteranklubben Saab)

AJ 37 s/n 37004, coded F 7-04, photographed on the runway at F 7 Såtenäs on 31 August 1975. (Leif Fredin, via Archives of Mikael Forslund)

Everything was finished within 20 min. After that, the readiness gear for electrical power and air coolant for the electronics was connected. Even though the *Viggen* could take-off using power from its own battery, this was rarely done. While waiting for take-off, two men remained in close proximity to the *Viggen*. The others went off to prepare the next sortie. Apart from the readiness, other things that required attention could be performed. For instance, changing the radio took five min, changing a wheel six min, changing the *CK 37* seven min, changing the canopy 25 min, the *RS 37* ejection seat two hours and the engine, four hours.

To show off the *Viggen's* capabilities to the Swedish tax payers during air shows, the Team *Viggen* was formed in 1973. Initially, two AJ 37s of F 7, flown by Captains Rolf Andersson and Anders Lefvert, were used. A third AJ 37, flown by Lieutenant Christer Hjort, was added in 1974.

Unfortunately, three AJ 37s were lost in crashes, the causes initially being undetermined. The first crash occurred on 11 July 1974, involving s/n 37011 (code F 7-11). The cause of the crash was later found to be wing failure. The pilot, Sergeant Ola Gynäs, ejected at an altitude of 2,500 m, landing unscathed. At the time, Gynäs was unaware of the how the ejection seat had been activated. This was probably due to Gynäs suffering from black-out. The second, at the time inexplicable, crash took place on 6 October 1975. Lieutenant Göte Pettersson was flying s/n 37014 (code F 7-14), firing rockets at the F 7 target range at Hattefuran in Lake Vänern. At an altitude of 200 m, Pettersson

AJ 37 s/n 37085, coded F 6-43, equipped with 16 m/71 Virgo high explosive fragmentation bombs, each weighing 120 kg, as well as an external fuel tank. An RB 04E and an air to ground rocket pod are displayed next to the Viggen. *Note the small White (FS 27925) insignia on top of the fin. (Tor Karlsson, via Archives of Mikael Forslund)*

AJ 37 s/n 37090, coded F 6-11, photographed on 5 June 1976. The aircraft is fitted with two 30/55 cannon pods, each fitted with one 30 mm ADEN Mk.4 cannon, two dummy RB 05As, and an external fuel tank. (Leif Fredin, via Archives of Mikael Forslund)

AJ 37 s/n 37091, coded F 6-14, taking off without any external load and on full afterburner on 7 September 1976. (Leif Fredin, via Archives of Mikael Forslund)

had the feeling that the aircraft exploded, ejecting immediately. Pettersson descended into the lake, landing safely. About ten days later, many parts of the aircraft were recovered. The engine in particular was of great interest, as this was thought to have been the cause of the crash.

Four days later, on 10 October 1975, s/n 37005 (code F 15-05) was written off in a crash. When flying at low altitude over the sea north east of Hornslandet, the pilot, Lieutenant Harald Gatel, heard a loud bang. Gatel ejected more or less instinctively. Suffering minor injuries, Gatel was rescued from the sea some 20 min after ejecting. Following this third crash, all *Viggens* were grounded until March 1976. The pilots had to resort to flying the Sk 50 (Saab *Safir*), SK 61 (Beagle B 125 Bulldog = Scottish Aviation Bulldog) and the *Viggen* simulators.

A pair of AJ 37s, s/ns 37092, coded F 6-12 and 37090, coded F 6-11, taking off on 29 August 1976. (Leif Fredin, via Archives of Mikael Forslund)

Much interest was shown in recovering the remains of s/n 37005 from a depth of about 70 m. The submarine recovery vessel *Belos* was used in the recovery operation.

In November 1975, *Försökscentralen* (FC) engineers at Malmen airfield outside Linköping were able to establish the cause for the three crashes: Wing failure.

On s/n 37014, fatigue cracks were discovered on the inner attachment point of the left wing spar. The cracks had been caused by high stress during high speed flights at low level. The spar was too weak.

The post-crash reconstruction of s/n 37014's crash showed that the left wing had broken off, smashed the fin and then struck the right wing. The resulting airframe stress was so great that the aircraft had broken apart.

Prior to the three crashes Saab had constructed a reinforced wing spar, due to the demand for higher airframe utilization, the limit having increased from 2,000 to 2,800 hours. The old wing spar, fitted to the first production AJ 37s (until s/n 37027), had a thickness of twelve mm. The new wing spar was 41 mm thick, being fitted from s/n 37028 onwards. The remaining 21 AJ 37s (three aircraft, s/ns 37001, 37015 and 37018 had been written off to other causes than spar failure) from the 37001 to 37027 production block were retrofitted with strengthened wing spars.

On 1 July 1977, No.3 Sqn/F 7 was disbanded, with its AJ 37s being transferred to F 15 at Söderhamn.

The next Wing to receive AJ 37s was F 15, with No.1 Squadron receiving its first aircraft on 2 December 1974. In the event, all of the SK 37s were transferred from Wing F 7 to Wing F 15.

From the summer of 1976, all of the SK 37s were transferred to No.2 Sqn/F 15, which also had an attack aircraft group of AJ 37s. (No.3 Sqn/F 15 had been disbanded on 30 June 1967). When F 6 at Karlsborg was disbanded in 1993, some of its AJ 37s were transferred to F 15.

The SK 37s of F 15 were used to establish a *TIS*-Group (*TIS* being short for conversion training). At the same time, it was decided that F 15 would also undertake reconnaissance sorties, resulting in a number of AJSF 37 and AJSH 37 *Viggen* being transferred to the Wing (please refer to the relevant chapters).

On 30 June 1998, F 15 was disbanded, with its *Viggens*, AJ 37s, AJS 37s, AJSF 37s and AJSH 37s, being transferred to F 10 at Ängelholm and F 21 at Luleå. In fact, the transfer of the aircraft had already been initiated in early 1997. The SK 37s were transferred to F 4 at Östersund-Frösön.

The third AJ 37 Wing was F 6, with the first aircraft arriving on 7 November 1977. Nos.1 and 2 Squadrons operated AJ 37 *Viggens* until disbandment in 1994.

On 27 October 1981, a Soviet submarine, armed with nuclear weapons (!), known as *Ubåt 137* in Sweden and *S-363* in the USSR, ran aground in the Karlskrona archipelago at the inlet of Gåsefjärden in a military protected zone. This caused great consternation, with No.2 Sqn/F 6, commanded by Leif Åström, being assigned the task of dispatching a group of four AJ 37s, armed with live ammunition. This was due to fear of a Soviet attempt to liberate the submarine, which was to be stopped by *Flygvapnet*. The aircraft were armed with weaponry intended for warning, limited attack and all-out attack:

Warning: 16 High-explosive bombs with brake parachute and impact fuse. The bombs would be dropped in front of the naval vessels of the force attempting to free the submarine. (It was thought that a diving attack would provoke return fire from the naval vessels). The intention was for the bombs to explode on impact with the water surface, sending a shock wave towards the vessels.

Limited attack: Attack rockets and flash bombs.

All-out attack: *RB 04E.*

AJ 37 s/n 37067, coded F 6-01, on display at a 1984 air display. The aircraft is fitted with one RB 04E and an external fuel tank. A 30/55 cannon pod, containing one 30 mm ADEN cannon, one RB 75 Maverick and an underwing attachment point with four m/71 Virgo high explosive fragmentation bombs are displayed next to the aircraft. (Leif Fredin, via Archives of Mikael Forslund)

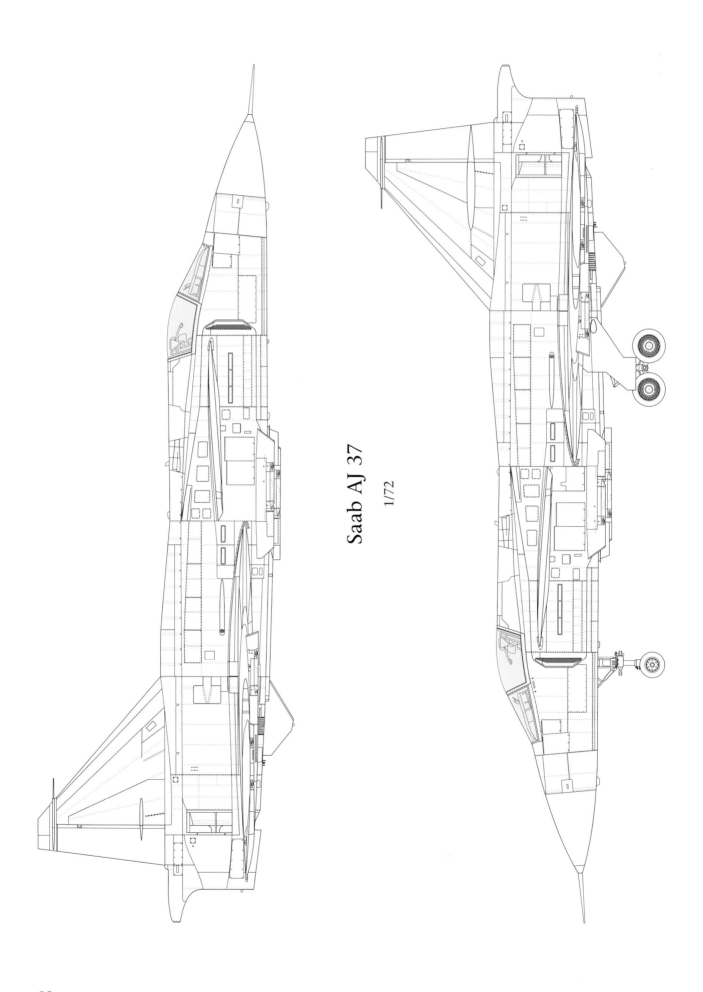

Saab AJ 37

1/72

Saab AJ 37

1/72

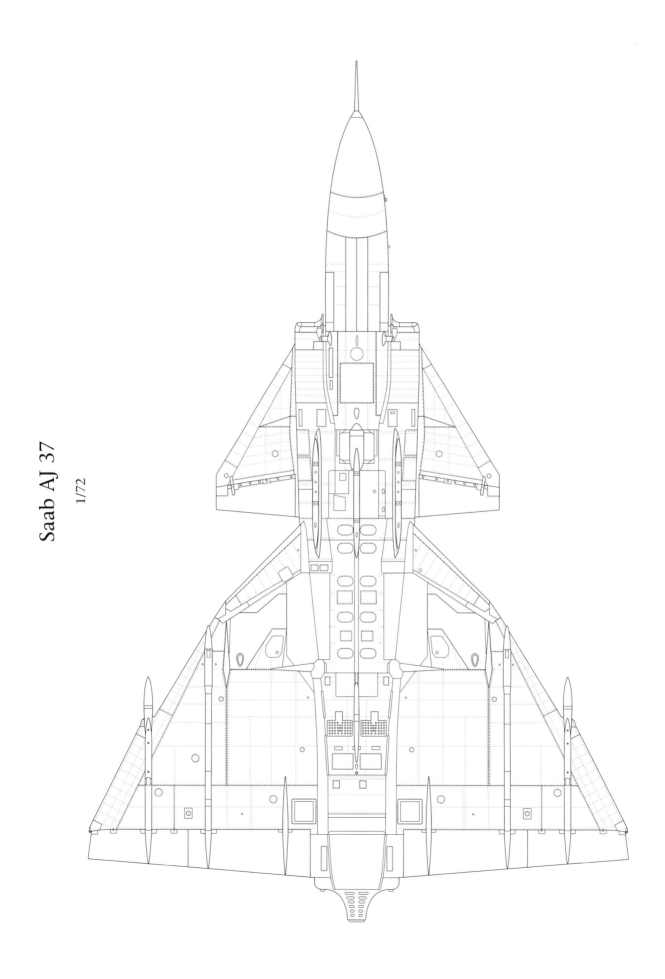

Saab AJ 37

1/72

AJ 37 s/n 37056, coded F 7-56, undergoing maintenance at F 17 Kallinge on 11 June 1994. (Mikael Forslund)

Changing the engine on AJ 37 s/n 37004, coded F 15-04, at F 15 Söderhamn on 15 May 1993. (Mikael Forslund)

AJ 37 s/n 37005, coded F 15-05, seen at F 15 Söderhamn on 25 May 1975. The aircraft carries an RB 04E as well as an external fuel tank. Beside the Viggen, two 30/55 cannon pods, each containing one 30 mm ADEN cannon, four air to ground rockets and two dummy RB 05As can be seen. A few Saab A 32A Lansen, the AJ 37s immediate predecessor at F 15, sits in the background. (Leif Fredin, via Archives of Mikael Forslund)

The F 15 Söderhamn air show on 31 August 1980 included a HKP 4A (Boeing Vertol 107) and AJ 37, s/n 37099, coded F 15-32. (Mikael Forslund)

A pair of AJ 37s, s/ns 37081, coded F 15-26 and 37054, coded F 15-14, taking off on 4 June 1978. (Leif Fredin, via Archives of Mikael Forslund)

AJ 37 Viggen s/n 37075, coded F 15-69, in the F 15 Söderhamn workshop on 28 May 1994. (Mikael Forslund)

During the night of 28-29 October 1981, four AJ 37s of No.2 Sqn/F 6 flew two sorties in close proximity to about ten Soviet naval vessels. Although the *Viggens* carried live ammunition, they did not fire their guns in anger. The vessels, including a *Kasjin*-Class destroyer, were in international waters, very close to Swedish territorial waters. The vessels awaited orders to enter Swedish territorial waters, to free a stranded Soviet submarine! Several other AJ 37 Wings flew a number of sorties during this crisis, as well as the Quick Reaction Alert reconnaissance unit with their SH 37/ SF 37s (please refer to the relevant chapters). After a couple of days, the submarine was pulled free by Swedish vessels, steaming eastwards on 6 November 1981.

In February 1984, the *Viggen* fleet was grounded once again. The reason was that some of the *RS 37* ejection seat cartridges had been fitted upside down. The aircraft had to be x-rayed, and modified as necessary.

When, during the early 1990s, the AJ 37 was developed into the AJS 37, tactics and systems development was the responsibility of No.1 Sqn/F 6. However, F 6 never received any AJS 37s, as the Wing disbanded in 1993. The aircraft were instead handed over to F 15 at Söderhamn and F 10 at Ängelholm. Please refer to the AJS 37 chapter below.

AJ 37 Viggen s/n 37006, coded F 15-06, seen during a visit to F 7 Sätenäs in 1975. (Leif Fredin, via Archives of Mikael Forslund)

A 4 June 1978 air show at F 10 Ängelholm. AJ 37 s/n 37050, coded F 15-10, is carrying an external fuel tank and two RB 04E anti-shipping missiles. Note the unpainted forward section of the left air intake, and the 37-8 prototype in the background. (Leif Fredin, via Archives of Mikael Forslund)

Type	S/n	Code/s	Taken on charge (ToC)	Struck off charge (SoC)	Remarks	Hrs flown
AJ 37	37001	FC-17, -51 F 7-51		16 May 1972	W/o 14 Sep 1971 Wing F 3, Sweden. Pilot unhurt	74 h 55 min
AJ 37	37002	FC-02, -05 F 7-02	12 Jan 1972	17 Apr 1998	Last flight 17 Jun 1997. Scrapped	1,248 h 31 min
AJ 37	37003	FC-03	24 Jan 1972	17 Aug 1973	Last flight 28 Sep 1972 as AJ 37. Rebuilt as SH 37 prototype s/n 37900	137 h 47 min
AJ 37	37004	FC-04 F 7-04 F 15-04	19 Jun 1972	1 Jul 1996	Last flight 14 Jun 1993. Scrapped	1,679 h 36 min
AJ 37	37005	FC-15 F 7-05 F 15-05	15 Mar 1972	17 Nov 1977	W/o 10 Oct 1975 NE Hornslandet, Sweden. Pilot ejected	283 h 04 min
AJ 37	37006	FC-16 F 7-06 F 15-06	15 May 1972	10 Nov 1995	Last flight 23 Apr 1992. To Flygvapnets Tekniska skolor at Halmstad, Sweden, as ground instructional airframe. Scrapped	1,622 h 56 min
AJ 37	37007	FC-17 F 7-07 F 15-07	1 Jun 1972	10 Nov 1995	Last flight 29 Jul 1992. To Flygvapnets Tekniska skolor at Halmstad, Sweden, as ground instructional airframe. Scrapped	1,640 h 21 min

AJ 37 s/n 37099, coded F 15-32, sits at the runway threshold, ready for take-off. (Via Archives of Peter Kempe/Mikael Forslund)

Type	S/n	Code/s	Taken on charge (ToC)	Struck off charge (SoC)	Remarks	Hrs flown
AJ 37	37008	FC-38 F 7-08 F 15-08	19 Jun 1972	5 Aug 1981	W/o 18 Dec 1980 Alfta, Sweden. Pilot killed	560 h 02 min
AJ 37 AJS 37	37009	F 7-09 F 6-09, -39 F 10-09 F 15-09, -39	4 Dec 1972	4 Mar 1998	Modified 26 Mar 1992 as AJS 37. Last flight 19 Mar 1997. Currently (2022) preserved at Söderhamn/F 15 Flygmuseum, Söderhamn, Sweden	1,688 h 04 min
AJ 37	37010	FC- F 7-10 F 6-10	14 Apr 1975	21 Aug 1995	Last flight 31 Jan 1994. Scrapped	1,755 h 57 min
AJ 37	37011	FC-35 F 7-11 F 15-11	18 Oct 1973	21 Apr 1976	W/o 11 Jul 1974 N Skara, Sweden. Pilot ejected	152 h 33 min
AJ 37	37012	FC- F 7-12 F 6-12	28 Sep 1972	14 Feb 1996	Last flight 31 Jan 1994. Scrapped	1,797 h 07 min
AJ 37	37013	FC- F 7-13 F 6-16, -13	11 Oct 1972	31 Jan 1995	Last flight 14 Jun 1993. Scrapped	1,798 h 42 min
AJ 37	37014	FC- F 7-14		21 Apr 1976	W/o 6 Oct 1975 Lake Vänern, Sweden. Pilot ejected	272 h 12 min
AJ 37	37015	FC-15	4 Jan 1973	23 May 1973	W/o 6 Mar 1973 four km S Wing F 3, Sweden. Pilot killed	54 h 24 min
AJ 37	37016	FC-16 F 7-16 F 15-16	4 Jan 1973	25 Oct 1995	Last flight 12 Jan 1993. 2,179 flights. To Flygvapnets Tekniska skolor at Halmstad, Sweden, as ground instructional airframe	1,575 h 02 min
AJ 37	37017	FC- F 7-17 F 6-02 F 15-17	4 Jan 1973	2 Apr 1996	Last flight 23 Jun 1993. Scrapped	1,642 h 56 min
AJ 37	37018	FC-02	15 Dec 1972	20 Dec 1974	W/o 31 Jul 1974 Wing F 3, Sweden. Pilot killed	232 h 07 min
AJ 37	37019	FC-01 F 7-19 F 6-04, -19	2 Feb 1973		W/o 8 Jun 1986 Torsby, Sweden. Pilot unhurt	944 h 25 min
AJ 37	37020	F 7-20	10 Apr 1973	14 Feb 1996	Last flight 20 Oct 1993. Scrapped	1,664 h 57 min
AJ 37	37021	FC- F 7-21 F 6-21	27 Feb 1973	9 Dec 1996	Last flight 12 Aug 1993. To Flygvapnets Tekniska skolor at Halmstad, Sweden, as ground instructional airframe	1,627 h 06 min
AJ 37	37022	F 7-22 F 6-22	20 Mar 1973	30 jun 1994	Last flight 25 May 1992. Scrapped	1,525 h 55 min
AJ 37	37023	F 7-23 FC-23 F 6-23	30 Mar 1973	5 Aug 1981	W/o 10 Feb 1981 eight km NNW Wing F 6, Sweden. Pilot ejected	660 h 57 min
AJ 37	37024	F 7-24 F 6-24	2 Aug 1973	2 Apr 1996	Last flight 23 Jun 1993. Scrapped	1,689 h 11 min
AJ 37	37025	F 7-25, -02 F 6-25 F 15-25 F 10-25	25 Apr 1973	1 Jul 1996	Last flight 26 Sep 1995. Scrapped. Cockpit to Wing F 16, Sweden, for exercises	1,656 h 56 min
AJ 37	37026	F 7-26 F 15-26 F 6-26	25 Apr 1973	12 Feb 1979	W/o 6 Sep 1978 ten km W Wing F 6, Sweden. 359 flights. Pilot ejected	241 h 09 min
AJ 37 AJS 37	37027	F 7-27 FC-27 F 6-27 F 10-57	2 Aug 1973		Modified 28 Sep 1993 as AJS 37. Finished overall Red colour scheme in anticipation of last flight 11 Jun 2001. Currently (2022) preserved at Stenbäcks Flygmuseum, Skurup, Sweden.	2,657 h 40 min
AJ 37 AJS 37	37028	F 7-28, -68 F 10-68, -60	11 May 1973	21 Jun 2000	Modified 13 Sep 1993 as AJS 37. Last flight 8 Dec 1999. Scrapped	2,684 h 49 min
AJ 37	37029	F 7-29 F 6-29 F 21-42	2 Aug 1973	14 Nov 1997	Last flight 12 Jun 1997. To Vidsel, Sweden, for exercises	2,729 h 55 min
AJ 37 AJS 37	37030	F 7-30 F 6-30 F 15-20, -30, -40 F 21-20, -30 F 10-	19 Sep 1973	8 Feb 1999	Last flight 28 Oct 1998. Modified 16 Aug 1994 as AJS 37. Scrapped	2,478 h 25 min
AJ 37	37031	F 7-31 F 6-31 F 15-10, 54 F 21-41	12 Jun 1973	10 Nov 1995	Last flight 9 Mar 1995. Currently (2022) preserved on pole outside Söderhamn, Sweden	2,999 h 59 min

Type	S/n	Code/s	Taken on charge (ToC)	Struck off charge (SoC)	Remarks	Hrs flown
AJ 37	37032	F 7-32 F 6-32	2 Aug 1973	18 Nov 1977	W/o 21 Mar 1977 Grebbestad, Sweden. Pilot killed	302 h 22 min
AJ 37	37033				Rebuilt 1972–73 as SF 37 prototype s/n 37950	
AJ 37	37034	F 7-34, -37 F 6-34	4 Sep 1973	3 Oct 1995	Last flight 1 Jun 1995. Currently (2022) preserved at Karlsborg, Sweden (former Wing F 6)	2,757 h 52 min
AJ 37 AJS 37	37035	F 7-35, -53 F 6-35	4 Feb 1974	12 May 1999	Modified 7 Aug 1992 as AJS 37. Last flight 11 Nov 1997. Scrapped	2,977 h 25 min
AJ 37	37036	F 7-36	27 Sep 1973		W/o 26 Jan 1978 Hattefuran firing range, Lake Vänern, Sweden. Pilot killed	326 h 32 min
AJ 37	37037	F 7-37 F 6-37	27 Sep 1973	30 Dec 1982	W/o 1 Jun 1982 NW Nynäshamn, Sweden. Pilot ejected	1,036 h 49 min
AJ 37	37038	F 7-38 F 6-38	18 Oct 1973		W/o 8 Sep 1982 ten km N Gällivare, Sweden. Pilot killed	1,085 h
AJ 37	37039	F 7-39 F 6-39	18 Oct 1973	12 Feb 1979	W/o 11 Jan 1979 Ranstad, Sweden. Pilot killed	417 h 56 min
AJ 37 AJS 37	37040	F 7-40 F 6-40 F 7-40	1 Nov 1973	17 May 1999	Modified 30 Mar 1993 as AJS 37. Last flight 11 Nov 1997. Scrapped	2,798 h 41 min
AJ 37	37041	F 7-41 FC-01 F 6-14 F 10-41	19 Nov 1974	5 Feb 1997	Last flight 25 Jul 1996. Scrapped	2,626 h 41 min
AJ 37	37042	F 7-42		28 Mar 1974	W/o 9 Oct 1973 at Saab's airfield, Linköping, Sweden (pre-delivery to Flygvapnet). Parts used to construct mock-up	2 h 15 min
AJ 37 AJS 37	37043	F 7-43 F 10-43	3 Jan 1974	28 May 1997	Modified 9 Aug 1993 as AJS 37. Last flight 21 Oct 1996. Scrapped	2,798 h 32 min
AJ 37	37044	F 7-44 F 6-44	16 Jan 1974	1 Apr 1986	W/o 26 Feb 1986 Hattefuran firing range, Lake Vänern, Sweden. Pilot ejected	1,547 h 21 min
AJ 37	37045	F 7-45	18 Jan 1974	19 Feb 1975	W/o 30 Oct 1974 S Linköping, Sweden. Pilot ejected	135 h 54 min
AJ 37	37046	F 7-46 F 10-46	4 Feb 1974	11 Nov 1997	Last flight 26 Nov 1996. Scrapped	2,573 h 47 min
AJ 37 AJS 37	37047	F 7-47 F 15-47	6 Jun 1974	11 Nov 1997	Modified 16 Dec 1991 as AJS 37. Last flight 27 Aug 1997. Scrapped	2,916 h 07 min
AJ 37 AJS 37	37048	F 7-48	20 Mar 1974	12 May 1999	Modified 7 Apr 1994 as AJS 37. Last flight 11 Nov 1997. Scrapped	2,960 h 42 min
AJ 37	37049	F 7-49 F 10-49	28 Feb 1974	22 Oct 1997	Last flight 27 May 1997. To Wing F 16, Sweden for fire and rescue exercises	2,647 h 58 min
AJ 37	37050	F 7-50 F 15-10, -09 F 6- F 21-	25 Mar 1974	12 Feb 1997	Last flight 13 Mar 1996. Currently (2022) preserved at F 7 Gårds- och Flottiljmuseum, Såtenäs, Sweden	2,514 h 40 min

AJ 37 s/n 37098, coded F 15-31, equipped with two ground to air rocket pods and on the right wing attachment point, an U 22 ECM pod.
(Tor Karlsson, via Archives of Mikael Forslund)

Type	S/n	Code/s	Taken on charge (ToC)	Struck off charge (SoC)	Remarks	Hrs flown
AJ 37 AJS 37	37051	F 7-51 F 15-11 F 6-14 F 21-51		24 Jan 2000	Modified 13 Nov 1991 as AJS 37. Last flight 23 Sep 1999. Scrapped	2,774 h 23 min
AJ 37 AJS 37	37052	F 7-52 F 15-12 F 10-11	6 Jun 1974	31 Aug 1999	Modified 22 Aug 1994 as AJS 37. Last flight 6 May 1999. Scrapped	2,684 h 37 min
AJ 37 AJS 37	37053	F 7-53 F 15-13 F 10-13	6 Jun 1974	23 Jun 1997	Modified 6 Dec 1994 as AJS 37. Last flight 26 Feb 1997. To Wing F 10, Sweden, for fire and rescue exercises. Scrapped	2,599 h 26 min
AJ 37 AJS 37	37054	F 7-54 F 15-54, -14 F 21-41, -41	6 Jun 1974	8 Feb 1999	Modified 22 Apr 1994 as AJS 37. Scrapped	2,563 h 59 min
AJ 37 AJS 37	37055	F 7-55 F 15-55, -15 F 10-15	6 Jun 1974	1 Jul 1998	Modified 30 Nov 1992 as AJS 37. Last flight 7 Apr 1998. Scrapped	2,440 h 19 min
AJ 37	37056	F 7-56 F 15-16	6 Jun 1974	4 Mar 1998	Last flight 14 Jan 1997. Currently (2022) preserved at Söderhamn/F 15 Flygmuseum, Söderhamn, Sweden	2,543 h 25 min
AJ 37 AJS 37	37057	F 7-57	25 Jul 1974	10 Jun 1997	Modified 4 Oct 1993 as AJS 37. Last flight 11 Mar 1997. To Flygvapnets Halmstadsskolor at Halmstad, Sweden, as ground instructional airframe	2,618 h 23 min
AJ 37 AJS 37	37058	F 7-58 F 6-58	25 Jul 1974	1 Oct 1999	Modified 18 May 1992 as AJS 37. Last flight 24 Nov 1997. Currently (2022) preserved at Volvo Museum, Gothenburg, Sweden	3,099 h 11 min
AJ 37 AJS 37	37059	F 7-59 F 10-59	12 Aug 1974	17 Apr 1998	Modified 27 Apr 1993 as AJS 37. Last flight 26 Aug 1997. Scrapped	2,766 h 49 min
AJ 37 AJS 37	37060	F 7-60 F 6-60 F 15-60	12 Aug 1974	25 Aug 1997	Modified 26 Nov 1991 as AJS 37. Last flight 4 Apr 1997. Scrapped	3,006 h 27 min
AJ 37 AJS 37	37061	F 7-61, -46 F 10-61	23 Sep 1974	8 Feb 1999	Modified 4 Jan 1992 as AJS 37. Last flight 8 Sep 1998. Scrapped	2,642 h 35 min
AJ 37 AJS 37	37062	F 7-62	23 Sep 1974	4 Jun 1997	Modified 13 Oct 1992 as AJS 37. Last flight 19 Dec 1996. To Flygvapnets Halmstadsskolor at Halmstad, Sweden, as ground instructional airframe. Scrapped	2,768 h 56 min
AJ 37 AJS 37	37063	F 7-63	18 Oct 1974	12 May 1999	Modified 11 Nov 1992 as AJS 37. Last flight 11 Nov 1997. Scrapped	2,644 h 29 min
AJ 37 AJS 37	37064	F 7-64, -01 F 6-64, -01	18 Oct 1974	10 Jun 1997	Modified 3 Feb 1992 as AJS 37. Last flight 21 Oct 1996. Scrapped	2,799 h 14 min
AJ 37	37065	F 7-65 F 21-65	19 Nov 1974	12 May 1999	Last flight 14 Aug 1997. Scrapped	2,787 h 09 min
AJ 37 AJS 37	37066	F 7-66 F 6-07	19 Nov 1994	22 May 1997	Modified 17 Dec 1992 as AJS 37. Last flight 24 Jan 1997. Scrapped	2,540 h 20 min

Four AJ 37 Viggens, *consisting of three of F 15 Söderhamn and one of F 6 Karlsborg, photographed on 8 May 1995. (Mikael Forslund)*

Type	S/n	Code/s	Taken on charge (ToC)	Struck off charge (SoC)	Remarks	Hrs flown
AJ 37	37067	F 7-67, -06 F 6-01, -07 F 10-67 F 15-37	2 Dec 1974	4 Mar 1998	Last flight 25 Nov 1996. To AMT-Skolan at Söderhamn. Currently (2022) preserved at Söderhamn/F 15 Flygmuseum, Söderhamn, Sweden	2,609 h 27 min
AJ 37 AJS 37	37068	F 7-68, -53	23 Jan 1975	31 Aug 1999	Modified 7 Jul 1992 as AJS 37. Last flight 1 Oct 1998. Currently (2022) preserved at Trollhättan, Sweden	2,914 h 28 min
AJ 37	37069	F 7-69 F 6-03	2 Dec 1974	9 Mar 1989	W/o 16 Feb 1989 NW Vänersborg, Sweden. Pilot ejected	1,745 h 01 min
AJ 37	37070	F 7-01	23 Jan 1975		W/o 5 Feb 1990 SW Lidköping, Sweden. Pilot killed	1,564 h 14 min
AJ 37 AJS 37	37071	F 7-02, -71	23 Jan 1975	13 Nov 1997	Modified 31 Jan 1992 as AJS 37. Last flight 7 Aug 1997. Scrapped	2,975 h 25 min
AJ 37 AJS 37	37072	F 7-04, -72 FC-58	20 Mar 1975	28 May 1997	Marked as 341 for 1975 Le Bourget Air Show, Paris, France. Modified 23 Nov 1993 as AJS 37. Last flight 27 Feb 1997 or 8 Aug 1987. To Flygvapnets Halmstadsskolor at Halmstad, Sweden, as ground instructional airframe	2,798 h 50 min
AJ 37	37073	F 15-17	5 Mar 1975	12 Feb 1979	W/o 8 Aug 1978 Wing F 15, Sweden. 453 flights. Pilot killed.	301 h 37 min
AJ 37 AJS 37	37074	F 7-18 F 15-18 F 10-18	20 Mar 1975	24 Feb 2000	Modified 20 Mar 1992 as AJS 37. Last flight 9 Nov 1999. Currently (2022) preserved at Museo del Aire, Madrid, Spain	2,674 h 02 min
AJ 37 AJS 37	37075	F 15-19, -69, -49 F 6- F 21-43	14 Apr 1975	25 Oct 2000	Modified 29 Sep 1992 as AJS 37. Last flight 25 May 2000. Scrapped	2,653 h 37 min
AJ 37 AJS 37	37076	F 15-21 F 10-76	14 Apr 1975	12 May 1999	Modified 29 Apr 1994 as AJS 37. Last flight 11 Dec 1998. Scrapped	2,915 h 58 min
AJ 37 AJS 37	37077	F 15-21 F 7-67, -77 F 21-47	6 Jun 1975	19 Jan 1999	Modified 19 May 1994 as AJS 37. Last flight 30 Nov 1998. To Wing F 4, Sweden, for fire and rescue exercises. Scrapped	2,692 h 41 min
AJ 37 AJS 37	37078	F 15-23 F 7-56 F 10-78	6 Jun 1975	3 Jun 1999	Modified 28 Sep 1994 as AJS 37. Last flight 24 Mar 1999. Scrapped	2,461 h 49 min
AJ 37 AJS 37	37079	F 15-24 F 10-24	6 Jun 1975	12 May 1999	Modified 21 Jun 1994 as AJS 37. Last flight 30 Nov 1998. Scrapped	2,486 h 48 min
AJ 37 AJS 37	37080	F 15-25, -35	18 Aug 1975	6 Mar 1998	Modified 27 May 1993 as AJS 37. Last flight 26 Jan 1998. To Hässlögymnasiet at Västerås, Sweden. Currently (2022) preserved at Västerås Flygmuseum, Västerås, Sweden	2,660 h 02 min
AJ 37 AJS 37	37081	F 15-26 F 7-76 F 10-76	18 Aug 1975	8 Sep 2000	Modified 15 Dec 1992 as AJS 37. Last flight 29 Mar 2000. Cockpit preserved at Söderhamn/F 15 Flygmuseum, Söderhamn, Sweden	2,592 h 16 min
AJ 37	37082	F 15-27	18 Sep 1975	14 Feb 1997	Last flight 6 Sep 1996. To Flygvapnets Halmstadsskolor at Halmstad, Sweden, for battle damage repair training. Scrapped	2,793 h 44 min
AJ 37	37083	F 15-28 F 6-28, -42 F 7-05, -07 F 10-07	11 May 1976	2 Dec 1996	Fin painted Red, White ghost on right side, White Santa Claus on left side in anticipation of last flight 13 Feb 1996. Scrapped	2,634 h 44 min
AJ 37	37084	F 6-42	11 May 1976	13 Nov 1984	W/o 5 Sep 1983 Kristinehamn, Sweden. 1,307 flights. Pilot killed	972 h 22 min
AJ 37 AJS 37	37085	F 6-43 F 15-43 F 7-65, -76 F 21-	11 May 1976	17 Mar 2000	Modified 23 Nov 1993 as AJS 37. Last flight 2 Dec 1999. Scrapped	2,950 h 11 min
AJ 37 AJS 37	37086	F 6-44 F 15-44	17 May 1976		Modified 10 Mar 1994 as AJS 37. W/o 5 Aug 1996 E Ulvön, Gulf of Bothnia, Sweden. Pilot killed	2,365 h 19 min
AJ 37 AJS 37	37087	F 6-45 F 15-45	17 May 1976	12 Jun 1997	Modified 17 Feb 1993 as AJS 37. Last flight 3 Apr 1997. To Wing F 17, Sweden, for fire and and rescue exercises	2,408 h 54 min
AJ 37 AJS 37	37088	F 6-46 F 7-44 F 21-44	23 Jul 1976		Modified 10 Feb 1994 as AJS 37. W/o 19 Aug 1998 Norströmsgrund, Gulf of Bothnia, Sweden. Pilot ejected	2,651 h 31 min
AJ 37 AJS 37	37089	F 6-03 F 21- F 7-69	23 Jul 1976	11 Nov 1998	Modified 19 Nov 1992 as AJS 37. Last flight 22 Jun 1998. Scrapped	2,684 h 34 min
AJ 37 AJS 37	37090	F 6-11 F 15-11, -31 F 21-45	15 Jun 1976	12 May 1999	Modified 13 Dec 1991 as AJS 37. Last flight 3 Feb 1999. Scrapped	2,464 h 53 min
AJ 37	37091	F 6-14 F 7-14 F 10-14	18 Jan 1977	18 Oct 1997	Last flight 1 Apr 1996. To Flygvapnets Halmstadsskolor at Halmstad, Sweden, for battle damage repair training. Scrapped	2,622 h 20 min

Type	S/n	Code/s	Taken on charge (ToC)	Struck off charge (SoC)	Remarks	Hrs flown
AJ 37	37092	F 6-12	21 Sep 1976	12 Feb 1979	W/o 21 nov 1978 E Hudiksvall, Gulf of Bothnia, Sweden. 446 flights. Pilot killed	339 h 03 min
AJ 37	37093	F 6-33 F 7-45, -05 F 21-45	21 Sep 1976	12 Nov 1998	Last flight 5 Mar 1997. To Wing F 21, Sweden, for fire and rescue exercises	2,638 h 23 min
AJ 37	37094	F 6-05 F 21-57 F 10-57	14 Oct 1976	12 May 1999	Last flight 15 May 1997. To 3.Helikopterbatajonen at Säve, Sweden for exercises. Currently (2022) preserved at Aeroseum, Säve, Sweden	2,597 h 50 min
AJ 37	37095	F 6-06	17 Nov 1976	12 Feb 1979	W/o 11 Jan 1979 Ranstad, Sweden. Pilot killed	242 h 48 min
AJ 37	37096	F 15-46 F 6-07 F 7-46	17 Nov 1976	12 May 1999	Last flight 2 Jul 1997. Scrapped	2,428 h 10 min
AJ 37	37097	F 15-29 F 6-29	28 Jan 1977	2 Oct 1997	Last flight 2 Jul 1997. Currently (2022) preserved at Teknikland, Optand, Sweden	2,586 h 36 min
AJ 37 AJS 37	37098	F 15-31 F 7-52 F 21-	3 Mar 1977		Modified 28 Feb 1994 as AJS 37. Currently (2022) preserved in airworthy condition with SwAFHF at Såtenäs, Sweden. Registered as SE-DXN and coded F 7-52	
AJ 37 AJS 37	37099	F 15-32 F 7-72 F 17-		30 Jun 1998	Modified 9 Sep 1993 as AJS 37. Last flight 27 Apr 1998. To Flygvapnets Halmstadsskolor at Halmstad, Sweden, for battle damage repair training. Scrapped	2,457 h 14 min
AJ 37 AJS 37	37100	F 7-33 F 15-33 F 10-33	15 Aug 1977	31 Aug 1999	Modified 14 Feb 1994 as AJS 37. Last flight 26 Apr 1999. Scrapped	2,660 h 58 min
AJ 37 AJS 37	37101	F 15-34 F 21-46	15 Aug 1977	8 Feb 1999	Modified 17 Mar 1993 as AJS 37. Last flight 30 Sep 1997. To Wing F 21, Sweden, for fire and rescue exercises. Scrapped	2,492 h 02 min
AJ 37	37102	F 6-15	15 Aug 1977		W/o 22 Sep 1977 N Kedum, Sweden. Pilot ejected	60 h 46 min
AJ 37	37103	F 6-16, -18 F 15-36	15 Aug 1977	20 Nov 1984	W/o 5 Sep 1983 Kristinehamn, Sweden. 1,185 flights. Pilot killed	947 h 49 min
AJ 37 AJS 37	37104	F 6-17, -47 F 15-17, -47 F 7-77	17 Oct 1977	30 Jun 1998	Modified 9 Nov 1993 as AJS 37. Last flight 26 May 1998. To Flygvapnets Halmstadsskolor at Halmstad, Sweden, for rescue training. Scrapped	2,697 h 10 min
AJ 37 AJS 37	37105	F 6-18 F 15-18, -38	2 Jan 1978	11 Nov 1998	Modified 22 Feb 1993 as AJS 37. Last flight 18 Jun 1998. Scrapped	2,497 h 25 min
AJ 37	37106	F 6-19 F 10-19	20 Feb 1978	12 May 1999	Last flight 10 Apr 1997. Scrapped	2,712 h 52 min
AJ 37 AJS 37	37107	F 6-20 F 7-49 F 21-49	23 May 1978	8 Feb 1999	Modified 23 Oct 1992 as AJS 37. Last flight 2 Nov 1998. Scrapped	2,569 h 23 min
AJ 37 AJS 37	37108	F 6-21 F 7-55 F 15-55 F 10-55		16 Oct 1997	Modified 5 Apr 1993 as AJS 37 (AJS 37 prototype). Last flight 10 Apr 1997. To Flygvapenmuseum, Linköping, Sweden. Currently (2022) preserved	2,462 h 52 min

Four SK 37s and four AJ 37s of F 15 Söderhamn on 31 August 1980. Note that the aircraft coded F 15-08 has the Yellow Wing numeral to the left of the national insignia. Additionally, a Black Wing numeral appears on the air intake. (Leif Fredin, via Archives of Mikael Forslund)

Saab AJ 37 Viggen s/n 37027, coded F 7 Black 27, of F 7 Sätenäs in overall Natural Metal scheme at Säve/Gothenborg in 1974.

Saab AJ 37 Viggen s/n 37092, coded F 6-Red 12, photographed at Malmen/Linköping during the late 1970s. Camouflage colours for the upper surfaces: svart (Black) 093M (FS 34031), ljusgrön (Light Green) 322M (FS 34138), mörkgrön (Dark Green) 326M (FS 34092) and brun (Brown) 507M (FS 30117), lower surfaces blågrå (Blue Grey) 058M (FS 36314).

a.m.olejniczak '22

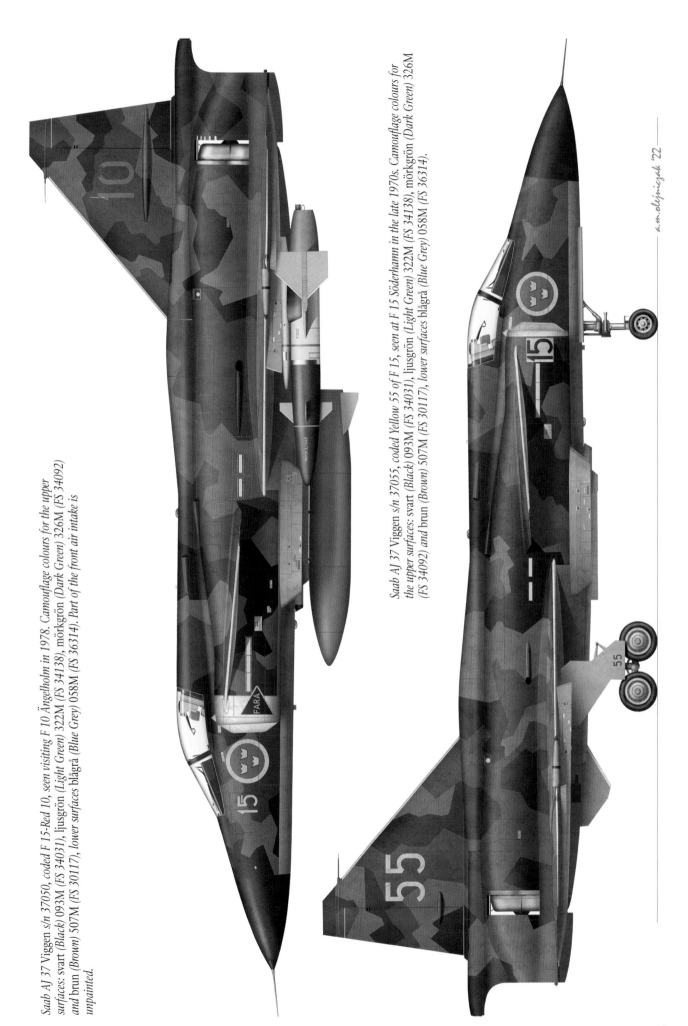

Saab AJ 37 Viggen s/n 37050, coded F 15-Red 10, seen visiting F 10 Ängelholm in 1978. Camouflage colours for the upper surfaces: svart (Black) 093M (FS 34031), ljusgrön (Light Green) 322M (FS 34138), mörkgrön (Dark Green) 326M (FS 34092) and brun (Brown) 507M (FS 30117), lower surfaces blågrå (Blue Grey) 058M (FS 36314). Part of the front air intake is unpainted.

Saab AJ 37 Viggen s/n 37055, coded Yellow 55 of F 15, seen at F 15 Söderhamn in the late 1970s. Camouflage colours for the upper surfaces: svart (Black) 093M (FS 34031), ljusgrön (Light Green) 322M (FS 34138), mörkgrön (Dark Green) 326M (FS 34092) and brun (Brown) 507M (FS 30117), lower surfaces blågrå (Blue Grey) 058M (FS 36314).

a.m. olejniczak '22

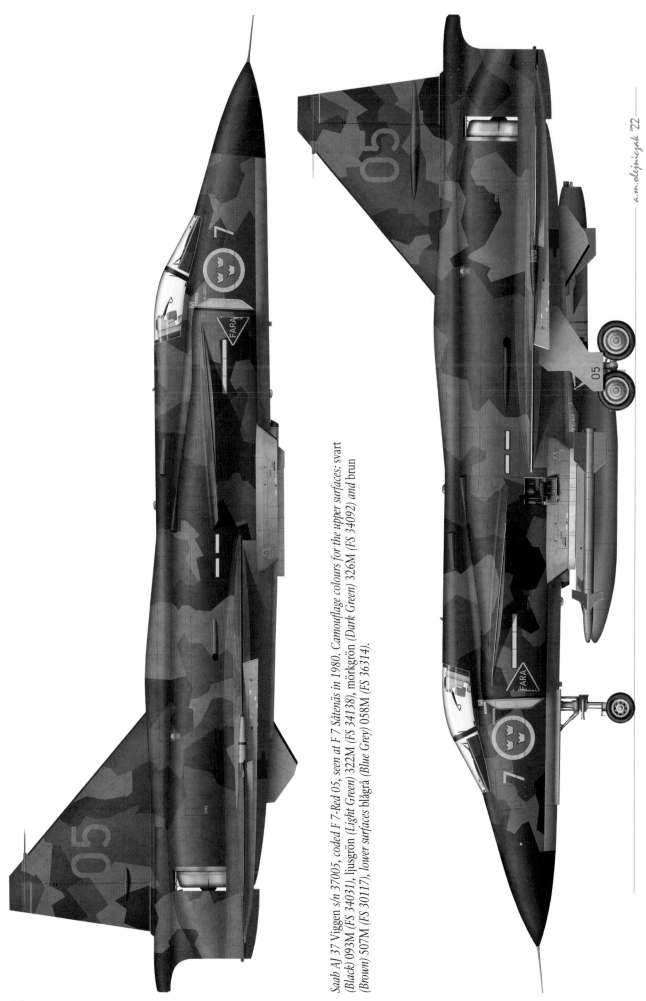

Saab AJ 37 Viggen s/n 37005, coded F 7-Red 05, seen at F 7 Såtenäs in 1980. Camouflage colours for the upper surfaces): svart (Black) 093M (FS 34031), ljusgrön (Light Green) 322M (FS 34138), mörkgrön (Dark Green) 326M (FS 34092) and brun (Brown) 507M (FS 30117), lower surfaces blågrå (Blue Grey) 058M (FS 36314).

a.m.olejniczak '22

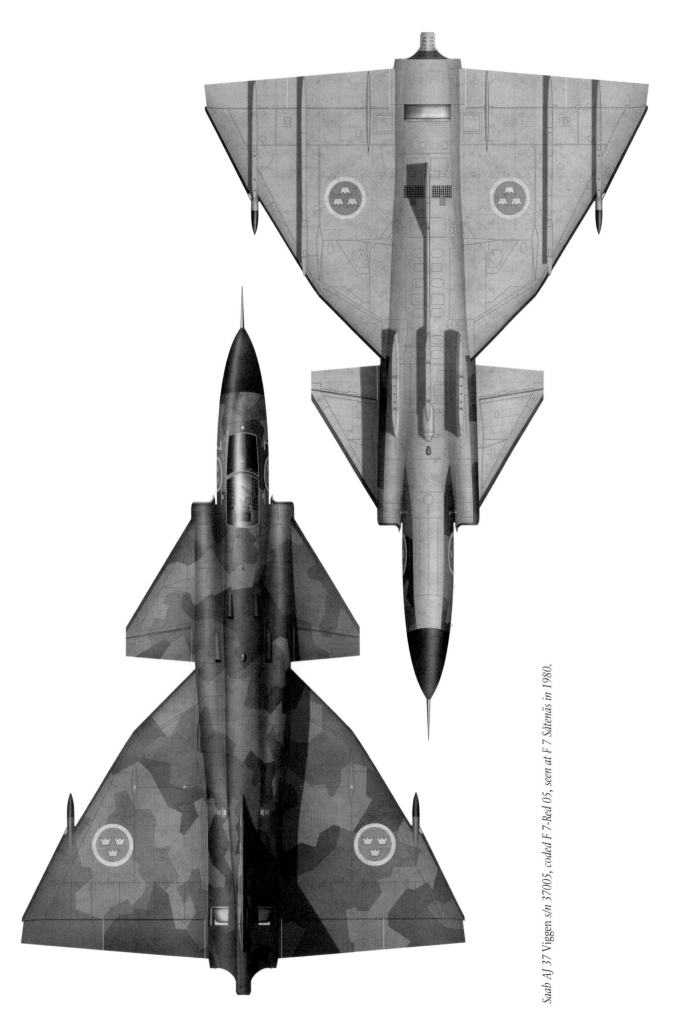

Saab AJ 37 Viggen s/n 37005, coded F 7-Red 05, seen at F 7 Såtenäs in 1980.

Saab AJ 37 Viggen s/n 37083, coded F 10-Yellow 07, seen at F 10 Ängelholm 1995. Camouflage colours for the upper surfaces: svart (Black) 093M (FS 37038), ljusgrön (Light Green) 322M (FS 34082), mörkgrön (Dark Green) 326M (FS 34079) and brun (Brown) 507M (FS 30051), with the lower surfaces being blågrå (Blue Grey) 058M (FS 35237). Red (FS 11350) fin. White (FS 17925) ghost and Santa Claus.

With the ability to carry out attack, fighter and reconnaissance sorties, the designation of the new variant became AJS 37.

In 1992, a modification programme that involved providing the AJ 37, SF 37 and SH 37 variants with a limited multi-role (fighter, attack and reconnaissance) capability was initiated. This programme was started when it became clear that the service entry of the Saab JAS 39 *Gripen* would be delayed. The computer capacity of the AJ 37 was increased, along with the ability to carry the new anti-shipping *RB 15F*, which had been developed as part of the JAS 39 *Gripen* armament. The *RB 15F* had twice the range and increased capability to withstand electronic counter measures than its predecessor, the *RB 04E*. To handle the *RB 15F*, additional computer power than was available in the AJ 37 was required. As a result, the *CK 37* (central calculator) in the AJS 37 had a multi-processor unit (*MPE*) installed. The so-called Data-bus (1553B) was also installed to increase the communication ability. The Data-bus also made it possible for armament intended for the JAS 39 *Gripen* to be adapted for the AJS 37.

Powered by a jet engine, the *RB 15F* was designed by Saab/Bofors, initially being intended for the Swedish Navy's *Spica*-class vessels for use against shipping targets. The missile was later adapted for the AJS 37 and JAS 39 *Gripen*. Acquiring the target was by means of a monopulse radar, which had the ability to select the biggest target within a target consisting of different naval vessels. The missile was able to withstand different counter measures. It was fired off at low level, after which the aircraft could immediately leave the target area.

The *m/90* bomb pod (*Mjölner/DWS 39*), initially intended for the JAS 39 *Gripen*, was from 1995 also used by the AJS 37. Designed by MBB in Germany in cooperation with *FMV* (*Försvarets Materielverk*, i.e. Defence Material Administration), the *Mjölner* demanded additional computer power than that originally available in the AJ 37. The 3.51 m long and 650 kg heavy pod was released at a distance of between eight and 22 km (depending on the altitude), then glided toward the target by means of a preprogrammed GPS and radar altimeter. Course alterations were made using the pod's four short tail fins. When the pod reached the target, a number of small charges were ejected from 24 openings on the sides of the pod.

The *RB 74* Sidewinder air-to-air missile was also added to the AJS 37 armament options. The 120 kg *RB 24J* Sidewinder could also be carried by the AJS 37 on the outer wing pylons. This air-to-air missile had previously only been carried by the JA 37. The outer wing pylons were initially intended for the 80 kg *RB 28* Falcon, but this missile was never carried by the AJS 37.

AJS 37 Viggen *s/n 37078, coded F 10-78, pictured on 7 september 1997 during Saab's 60th Anniversary Air Show at Linköping. The No.1 Squadron badge can be seen on the fin. The aircraft carries four* RB 74 Sidewinders, two BK 90 Mjölner *bomb pods and an external fuel tank. An SK 37 can be seen in the background. (Mikael Forslund)*

AJS 37 Viggen s/n 37105, coded F 15-38, seen at the F 15 Söderhamn air show on 10 June 1995. Beginning on 22 February 1993, the aircraft was modified from AJ 37 to AJS 37 status. Four RB 74 Sidewinders can be seen on the external hardpoints. (Mikael Forslund)

AJS 37 s/n 37076, coded F 10-76, photographed at F 10 Ängelholm on 22 May 1997. Beginning on 19 May 1994, the aircraft was modified from AJ 37 to AJS 37 status. Among the armament, a dummy RB 15E anti-shipping missile and one dummy RB 24J can be seen. (Leif Fredin, via Archives of Mikael Forslund)

AJS 37 s/n 37076, coded F 10-76, being towed from its hangar to the tarmac before being readied for take-off from F 10 Ängelholm om 22 May 1997. Note the badge of No.1 Squadron on the fin. Two dummy RB 15E anti-shipping missiles, two dummy RB 24J and an external fuel tank are hung from the wing/fuselage hardpoints. (Leif Fredin, via Archives of Mikael Forslund)

50

The primary task of the AJS 37 was maritime reconnaissance, with the aircraft's radar registering the relevant information. It was possible to review the sortie by means of the so-called *Planering och Analys (PLA)* (Planning and Analysis) available through the *CK 37*. Added to this was the *Video Registrering System (VRS)* (Video Registration System), which video-taped the *Siktlinjesindikatorn (SI)* (Aiming Line Indicator) throughout the sortie. The previously mentioned data rod was also available for the AJS 37.

When the AJS 37 was introduced the AJ 37s (see below) were modified at the respective workshops of Wings F 6 Karlsborg, F 7 Såtenäs, F 15 Söderhamn and F 21 Luleå. Further training was required, primarily for the pilots. The development of tactics and systems was assigned to No.1 Sqn/F 6. The last production AJ 37, s/n 37108 (coded F 6-21), was used as the AJS 37 test vehicle. Pilots from F 7 and F 15 underwent aerial reconnaissance training at F 21, with the latter pilots receiving training in flying attack sorties at F 7 and F 15. Included in this training was firing the *RB 04E* missile. Tactical training on the *RB 15F* was conducted at No.2 Sqn/F 7. With F 6 disbanding in 1994, its tasks were transferred to F 15. Trials and evaluation was performed in close cooperation between the squadron, Saab and *FMV (Försvarets Materielverk*, Defence Material Administration).

With further reorganisation and down-sizing of *Flygvapnet*, No.1 Sqn/F 10 was also equipped with the AJS 37 (as well as AJSH 37 and AJSF 37) transferred from other Wings. Personnel from disbanded Wings was transferred to F 10. After 1997, the AJS 37 remained in service only at F 10 and F 21. On 1 June 1998, the *TIS-37* (equipped with SK 37s) was transferred from F 15 to F 4. During the autumn of 1998, the JAS 39 *Gripen* replaced the last AJS 37s at F 7, with the *Viggens* being transferred to F 10 and F 21. Since 1973, some 76,000 flight hours had been accumulated at F 7 on the AJ 37/AJS 37 *Viggen*. In 2000, F 10 handed over its final AJS 37s to F 21.

A total of 48 AJ 37s were modified to AJS 37 status: s/ns 37009, 37027, 37028, 37030, 37035, 37040, 37043, 37047, 37048, 37051–37055, 37057–37064, 37066, 37068, 37071, 37072, 37074–37081, 37085–37090, 37098–37101, 37104, 37105, 37107 and 37108. The AJS 37s were operated by four Wings: F 7, F 10, F 15 and F 21.

Saab AJS 37 Viggen s/n 37078, coded Red 78 of F 10 Ängelholm, seen at its home base sometime in the late 1990s. The camouflage colours on the upper surfaces are: svart (Black) 093M (FS 34031), ljusgrön (Light Green) 322M (FS 34138), mörkgrön (Dark Green) 326M (FS 34092) and brun (Brown) 507M (FS 30117), with the lower surfaces being blågrå (Blue Grey) 058M (FS 36314).

AJS 37 Viggen s/n 37078, coded F 10-78, photographed at F 10 Ängelholm during a late 1990s air show. Beginning on 28 September 1994, the aircraft was modified from AJ 37 to AJS 37 status. Note the No.1 Squadron badge on the fin. Beneath the left wing are a BK 90 Mjölner bomb pod and one RB 24J Sidewinder. The armament on the ground includes one RB 74 Sidewinder and one 30/55 cannon pod. (Leif Fredin, via Archives of Mikael Forslund)

AJS 37 Viggen s/n 37027, coded Yellow 57 of F 10 Ängelholm, seen at its home base in 2001. The aircraft is painted overall röd (Red) (FS 11350). The fin, and lower rear fuselage are vit (White) (FS 17925).

a.m.olizniczak '22

AJS 37 Viggen s/n 37027, coded Yellow 57 of F 10 Ängelholm, seen at its home base in 2001. The aircraft is painted overall röd (Red) (FS 11350). The fin, and lower rear fuselage are vit (White) (FS 17925).

Chapter 5

AJ 37 and AJS 37 Armament

The AJ 37 had nine pylons for carrying external loads. However, only five were used:

The centre fuselage pylon (1, for a maximum load of 2,250 kg), often had a 1,400 l capacity fuel tank fitted.

The side pylons (2 and 3, beneath the fuselage, each having a load capacity of 500 kg).

Wing pylons (6 and 7, each having a maximum load capacity of 1,350 kg).

The inner wing pylons (4 and 5, hydraulic, each having a maximum load capacity of 500 kg) were not used, apart for the JA 37, which carried chaff dispensers on these pylons. The outer missile pylons (8 and 9, with a maximum load capacity of 180 kg), were intended for the *RB 28* Falcon (designed by the US company Hughes). However, for the *Viggen*, the *RB 28* was only used for initial trials, having previously been used on the Saab J 35F and J 35J *Draken*. However, this pair of pylons were used when the AJ 37s were modified as AJS 37s as well as on the JA 37s.

The AJ 37 armament consisted of:

- *RB 04E*: Swedish anti-shipping missile
- *RB 05A*: Swedish multi-target missile
- *RB 15F*: Swedish anti-shipping missile. **Only on AJS 37**
- *RB 24B*: US Air-to-air missile: AIM-9B (AIM = Air Interception Missile) Sidewinder, Infra Red
- *RB 24J*: US Air-to-air missile: AIM-9J Sidewinder, Infra Red
- *RB 74*: US Air-to-air missile: AIM-9L Sidewinder, Infra Red (earlier designated *RB 24L*)
- *RB 75*: US (Hughes) Air-to-air and ground target missile: AGM-65 Maverick, tv-operated
- *BK 90*: German/Swedish ground target bomb pod: *Mjölner (DWS 39)*. **Only on AJS 37**
- *Akankapsel 30/55*: Swedish automatic cannon, Air-to-air and ground targets: 1 x 30 mm Aden Mk.4 (*m/55*) 150 rounds. (For practice: 1 x 12.7 mm *m/39* machine gun)
- *Bomb Virgo m/71*: Swedish 120 kg high explosive bomb against ground targets. (For practice 15 kg *m/71* bomb)
- *Bomb Lepus m/71*: Swedish 80 kg flash bomb against ground targets
- *ARAK m/70*: Swedish multi-purpose rocket: 6 x 135 mm pod-mounted rockets

AJ 37 s/n 37089, coded F 6-03, on display at F 6 Karlsborg during a 4 June 1989 airshow, surrounded by different kinds of armament. Among these are two 30/55 cannon pods, each containing one 30 mm ADEN cannon, the m/71 Virgo bomb container containing four 120 kg bombs, an RB 04E and two U 22 ECM pods. (Mikael Forslund)

AJ 37 s/n 37066, coded F 7-66, on display at F 7 Såtenäs during a June 1990 air show. A total of eight dummy missiles can be seen below the wings and beside the aircraft. These include two RB 24Js, two Rb 24Bs, two RB 05As (on the fuselage attachment points), and two 30/55 cannon pods (on the wing attachment points), each containing one 30 mm ADEN cannon. RB 24Js hangs from the outward wing attachment points. (Tor Karlsson, via Archives of Mikael Forslund)

Flygvapnet used even numbers for IR-missiles and uneven numbers for radar-guided missiles. (AIM = Airborne Intercept Missile and AGM = Air Ground Missile).

RB 04 built by Saab between 1950 and 1978 as the world's first airborne independent tactical anti-shipping missile (the *RB 04C* was carried by the Saab A 32A *Lansen*). Developed as the *04E* for the AJ 37 for use against shipping targets. Deliveries began in 1974. Three *RB 04Es* could be carried by the AJ 37, but this was often reduced to two. Initially the pilot aimed the 616 kg and 4.45 m long missile against the target by using the aircraft's radar. Following release, the missile searched independently for the target by means of an active radar target seeker (data from the aircraft's radar was used). Powered by a solid fuel rocket engine (non-liquid fuel), the missile flew at low altitude at a speed slightly below Mach 1, having a range of 32 km. Following release, the aircraft could immediately leave the target area. The tactic involved a whole squadron performing the attack (two *RB 04Es* on each aircraft).

RB 05A was built by Saab, beginning in 1961. The idea was that the 3.6 m long 305 kg missile would be used by the AJ 37 *Viggen* and SK 60B (Saab 105), with each aircraft carrying two missiles each. However, only the AJ 37 was armed with the *RB 05A*. The missile was carried on the two fuselage pylons. It was intended for use against slow aerial targets, such as helicopters, and naval and ground targets. The liquid fuel rocket engine was built by Volvo Flygmotor. The fuel load was carried by the engine. The engine was of a two-stage type, being fitted with an afterburner. The initial stage accelerated the missile after it had been fired, with the second stage sustaining the Mach 1+ speed. The missile had a diameter of 0.3 m, being controlled by the pilot via a telecommunications link from transmitter to receiver. The control signals were scrambled, thus being difficult to jam. Tracer made it easy for the pilot to track the missile, which had a range of nine km. The pilot controlled the missile by means of a right-hand joy stick, during which time the AJ 37 auto-pilot was engaged. A proximity fuse was fitted in the nose section of the missile, which made it possible for it to detonate close to the target, if it should not strike the target head-on. Due to the high work-load for the pilot, the *RB 05A* was only to be used if the threat from anti-aircraft defences were slim. Initially intended for ground targets, the missile was later seen as an alternative for attacking aerial targets such as transport and bomber aircraft, which could be attacked head-on when visibility was adequate.

A simulator was used to train firing the *RB 05A*. Much training was required, up to 1,000 firings, before the pilot had accumulated the necessary capability. Training was also conducted using the SK 61 (Beagle B 125 Bulldog = Scottish Aviation Bulldog) and *RB 53 Bantam*.

RB 15F was a Swedish development by Saab and Bofors of the *RB 04E*. Powered by a jet engine, the *RB 15F* was initially intended for the Swedish Navy's *Spica* vessels against naval targets. Subsequently it was developed for Saab JAS 39 operations. However, the 600 kg missile was ready before the JAS 39 *Gripen*. As a result, the AJ 37 (AJS), SF 37 (AJSF) and SH 37 (AJSH) variants were modified to carry the *RB 15F*. Target acquisition was made through a mono pulse radar, which had the ability

AJS 37 Viggen *s/n 37054, coded F 15-14, seen at F 15 Söderhamn on 10 June 1995. Beginning on 22 April 1994, the aircraft was modified from AJ 37 to AJS 37 status. The aircraft is armed with two* BK 90 Mjölner *bomb pods, one* RB 15F, *and one* RB 74. *In front of the aircraft an* RB 05A, RB 75 *and a m/70 rocket pod can be seen. (Mikael Forslund)*

to pick the largest target within a target area consisting of several naval vessels. Compared to the *RB 04E*, the *RB 15F* had twice the range, better ability to withstand electronic counter measures, and avoid dummy targets as well as increased maneouvering ability to avoid being shot down by the enemy. It was fired off at extreme low level. Immediately after firing the missile, the aircraft could leave the area.

RB 24B was an American IR-missile (heat sensitive), originally designated AIM-9B Sidewinder. This missile was fired for the first time on 11 September 1953. The missile's capability meant that it had to be fired at the target from behind. The IR-seeker then searched for the hottest part of the aircraft, i.e. the nozzle of the jet engine(s). On each of the trailing edges of the four fins, a rotating gyro was fitted in order to stabilize the missile.

RB 24J was a development of the *RB 24B*, being originally designated AIM-9J. The missile had an improved range and maneouvering performance, also being more resilient against electronic counter measures than the *RB 24B*.

RB 74 The Sidewinder AIM-9L, earlier designated *RB 24L* by *Flygvapnet*, was an IR-missile driven by a solid fuel rocket engine, which gave it a speed of Mach 2 for about one minute. Weighing 85.3 kg,

AJ 37 s/n 37046, coded F 7-46, at the 26 August 1990 F 7 Såtenäs air show. The armament in front of the aircraft include 120 kg bomb containers, flash bombs, and a 30/55 cannon pod. The aircraft is armed with an U 22 ECM *pod and one* RB 74 Sidewinder. *(Mikael Forslund)*

AJ 37 Viggen s/n 37007, coded F 15-07, on display at F 15 Söderhamn during a 24 May 1992 air show. Among the armament seen beside the aircraft are an RB 04E (part view), RB 05A (part view), 13,5 air-to-ground rocket (part view), m/70 rocket pod, four 120 kg m/71 Virgo high explosive fragmentation bombs, two m/71 Lepus flare bombs (all dummies), and two bomb containers. (Mikael Forslund)

RB 15F (anti-shipping missile), RB 05A (part view), dummy armament, alongside an AJ 37 Viggen (which is fitted with an external fuel tank) at F 15 Söderhamn on 15 May 1993. (Mikael Forslund)

AJS 37 Viggen s/n 37081, coded F 15-26, beside SF 37 s/n 37950, coded F 13-10, photographed on 11 June 1994 during an F 17 Kallinge air show. Beginning on 15 December 1992, s/n 37081 was modified from AJ 37 to AJS 37 status. A wide variety of armament can be seen next to the aircraft. Among these are the 30/55 cannon pod, RB 15F, m/70 rocket pod, BK 90 Mjölner bomb pod, RB 04E, RB 75 Maverick and RB 05A. (Mikael Forslund)

the missile was a development of the *RB 24J* Sidewinder (AIM-9J). The thin (0.127 m in diameter) *RB 74* could be fired off at a greater angle from the target's heat source (usually the engine) than had been the case with the *RB 24J*. The firing distance at low altitude was one km and at high altitude three km at the most. The thinner air at higher altitudes meant lower air resistance.

RB 75 was purchased from Hughes in the USA, where it was designated AGM-65 Maverick. The missile was built for operations against tanks and other hard targets. The missile was bought primarily for use against ships and bridges. Modified for operations in Swedish conditions/weather, it had a range of 16 km at supersonic speed. Weighing 210 kg, the 2.49 m long *RB 75* had a television tracking device, being completely autonomous. The pilot directed the television tracking device

AJ 37 Viggen *s/n 37010, coded F 7-10, at the 26 August 1990 air show at F 7 Sätenäs. The various types of armament carried by the AJ 37 can be seen on the attachment points and beside the aircraft. Nearest the camera is a RB 04E (anti-shipping missile). On the inner attachment point of the left wing its RB 15F development can be seen. RB 24Js hangs from the outward wing and fuselage attachment points.*

The lower picture shows the RB 75 (White, FS 17925) and RB 05A (Green) by the same aircraft. (Both Mikael Forslund)

using the radar handle, with the television image being presented on an indicator mounted above the instrument panel. Approach to the target was made at low level, using its solid fuel rocket engine. Just before firing, the pilot climbed in order for him to see the target and then turned the aircraft in an approximate direction of the target. He then observed the image in the television screen, directed a hairline cross against the target, locked onto the target and fired. The missile did the rest of the job, with the aircraft leaving the area immediately.

BK 90 was a bomb pod (*DWS 39*) made by MBB (Messerschmitt-Bölkow-Blohm) in Germany in cooperation with the Swedish *FMV (Försvarets Materielverk*, i.e. Defence Material Administration), which named it *Mjölner* (after the Norse God Thor's hammer). The pod weighed 650 kg, being 3.51 m long, 0.63 m wide and 0.32 m high. It was released at speeds between Mach 0.6 and 0.9. It had a range of eight to 22 km. For guidance, the pod's GPS and radar altimeter were preprogrammed. The pod was released a long distance away from the target, after which it glided towards the target. Four short tail fins controlled the flight. Upon arriving over the target, a number of small charges were released from 24 openings on the sides of the pod.

Deliveries began in 1995, with the *BK 90* being carried by the AJS 37 *Viggen* and the JAS 39 *Gripen*.

Akankapsel 30/55 was a British 30 mm Aden Mk.4 *m/55* cannon carried in a pod designed by FFV (*Förenade Fabriksverken*). It had a capacity of 150 rounds. The rate of fire was 25 rounds/sec. The muzzle velocity was 790 m/sec. For training the 30 mm cannon could be replaced with a 12.7 mm *m/39* machine gun. The pod could be used against air or ground targets. When the AJ 37 was responsible for Quick Reaction Alert sorties, two pods armed with live ammunition were usually carried.

Virgo m/71 was a high explosive fragmentation bomb, weighing 120 kg. Up to 16 such bombs could be carried by the AJ 37. The bombs could be fitted with an impact fuse or a proximity fuse. Diving was the initial mode of attack. Approaching the target at extreme low level with a speed of Mach 0.9, the pilot then climbed to an altitude of 300 m. The pilot then made a Split-S so that he could aim against the target, with the *CK 37* calculating when the bombs would be released automatically.

Level bombing (in poor weather) could also be performed. The bombs were then fitted with brake parachutes so that they would not go off until the aircraft had escaped.

Another method was bomb tossing. The pilot had to programe the *CK 37* prior to take-off where the bombs were to be released. The approach was the same as during diving attacks. When pulling up before reaching the target the pilot pressed the release button, with the *CK 37* releasing the bombs at the correct moment. During exercises, the 15 kg *m/71* practice bomb was often used in place of the 120 kg bomb.

Lepus m/71 was an 80 kg flash bomb indended for night time operations. To increase the accuracy, radar measurement was employed in hitting the target. When the bomb was released, it burned for 190 sec, descending by parachute at four m/sec. Its use gave the attacking aircraft the possibility of observing their target(s) in "daylight".

ARAK m/70 from Bofors was a lesser capacity demanding weapon against ground and naval targets. Carrying six 135 mm attack rockets (*ARAK*) each pod weighed 375 kg. Four such pods could be carried by one aircraft. The warhead worked through fragmentation, penetration or pressure. The various rocket variants weighed about 20 kg each. The target was approached at low level at speeds of up to Mach 0.9. About six km away, the aircraft climbed to an altitude of about 300 m, performing a Split-S so that the pilot could aim at the target and the *CK 37* could calculate when the rockets were to be fired off against the target. The rockets were salvoed off at a distance of between 5,000 and 1,500 m. 24 rockets from each aircraft represented a huge firepower. Following this, the aircraft climbed away at at between five or six Gs as to avoid explosions and shrapnel. Then again a Split-S and down to low level. During this time, the aircraft was visible to the enemy for about 35 sec. As the approach was not straight and level, it was difficult for the enemy anti-aircraft artillery defences to keep up. This tactic was later changed to a scenario when the aircraft flew alongside the explosions and shrapnel, which reduced the time of exposure to the enemy to 20 sec.

Both the AJ 37 and AJS 37 could carry the *KB* chaff and flare pod, as well as the *KA* and *U 22* jamming transmitter pods. These jamming transmitter were intended for active jamming (please refer to other relevant chapters). A laser reflector rod, the *BT 53*, could also be carried.

AJ 37 Technical Data and Performance Characteristics

Crew:	1
Quantity built:	108 (s/ns 37001–37108)
Length:	16.30 m
Wingspan:	10.60 m
Height:	5.60 m (4.0 m with fin folded)
Wing area:	52.20 m² (main wing 46.00 m²)

An AJS 37 of F 15 Söderhamn during the Wing's 31 May 1997 air show. The armament include the 30/55 cannon pod, 13.5 cm air-to-ground rockets, rocket pod, RB 75, RB 15F and the BK 90 Mjölner bomb pod. (Mikael Forslund)

Wheel base:	5.54 m
Fuel load:	5,525 l + one external fuel tank containing an additional 1,400 l
Empty weight:	11,800 kg
Maximum take-off weight:	20,450 kg
Engine:	*RM 8A*, license-built Pratt & Whitney JT8D
Thrust:	6,690 kp without afterburner, 11,790 kp with afterburner
Maximum speed:	Mach 2
Take-off run:	400 m
Landing run:	500 m
Service ceiling:	18,300 m

AJS 37 s/n 37053, coded F 10-13, at the end of the 1990s. The No.1 Squadron badge appear on the fin. Two dummy RB 04Es, among other armament, hangs from the attachment points. (Leif Fredin, via Archives of Mikael Forslund)

Chapter 6
SK 37

Early on in the *Viggen* planning stage, it was decided to build a two-seat variant (SK 37) to fulfil the requirements for pilot training. After the AJ 37, the SK 37 was the second variant to fly. On 2 July 1970, the test pilot Per Pellebergs made the first SK 37 flight in s/n 37800. This particular aircraft remained a test vehicle during its entire active career, mostly at *FC* and marked as FC-22. Initially, the aircraft was based at Vidsel for continued trials. S/n 37800 became the sole armed SK 37.

The intention was that the 18 SK 37s (s/ns 37800–37817) could be operated as AJ 37s. This did not reach fruition, as there was no room for the required electronics. Much later, ten SK 37s were modified as SK 37Es (please refer to the relevant chapter). Additionally, no radar was fitted to the SK 37. Navigation was performed using the ABR-system. The processing of data regarding speed and flights over land were performed by the Central Calculator (*CK*). In addition, visual observation was made with regards to certain terrain landmarks. Distance Measuring Equipment (DME) was later introduced. The DME broadcast radio signals from the aircraft to ground stations, which in turn reflected the signals. The computer calculated the distance to the ground station, based on how long the reflection lasted. Several stations could be included, meaning increased safety in navigation.

S/n 37800 was initially fitted with a fin identical to that of the AJ 37. However, following two months of modification work, the aircraft re-emerged with a larger fin, similar to that intended for the JA 37. The other 17 SK 37s all received the larger fin. The rear fuselage lower fin was somewhat increased compared to other *Viggen* variants. Including a second cockpit meant a reduced fuel capacity (4,275 l) compared to the AJ 37 (5,525 l). Due to this, the SK 37 almost always carried an external fuel tank (1,400 l). Similar to the Saab Sk 35C *Draken*, periscopes were fitted in the rear cockpit (one on each side of the fuselage), as the instructor's forward view otherwise would have been very restricted. Work on the periscopes began by testing different ideas. A wooden mock-up of the forward fuselage that could be raised or lowered was built, and mounted on a vehicle. With a test pilot perched in the mock-up, different positions for the periscopes were tested. The first flight from the rear cockpit in s/n 37800 took place on 28 January 1971, with Per Pellebergs at the helm. Everything worked according to plan. S/n 37800 remained active as a test vehicle until its final flight

SK 37 s/n 37808, coded F 7-62, taxiing out for take-off at F 7 on 12 May 1974. (Leif Fredin, via Archives of Mikael Forslund)

SK 37 s/n 37808, coded F 7-62, taxiing from its revetment at F 7 Såtenäs on 12 May 1974. In the background, a few AJ 37s, TP 84 Hercules s/n 84002, coded F 7-72, and SK 37 s/n 37803, coded F 7-67, can be seen. (Leif Fredin, via Archives of Mikael Forslund)

SK 37 s/n 37806, coded F 7-64, at F 7 Såtenäs on 12 May 1974. Almost without exception, the SK 37 carried an external fuel tank. (Leif Fredin, via Archives of Mikael Forslund)

SK 37 s/n 37803, coded F 7-67, at F 7 on 12 May 1974, along with TP 84 Hercules s/n 84002, coded F 7-72 and an Sk 50B (Saab Safir), s/n 50019, coded F 7-84. (Leif Fredin, via Archives of Mikael Forslund)

A Volvo tow truck with a conscript driver with SK 37 s/n 37805, coded F 7-03, under tow at F 7 on 24 May 1975. (Leif Fredin, via Archives of Mikael Forslund)

SK 37 Viggen s/n 37808, coded F 7-11, photographed on 3 September 1974. AJ 37 s/n 37053, coded F 7-53, can be seen in the background. Armament on the ground beside the aircraft include rocket pods, RB 04E and RB 05A anti-shipping missiles. When in active service, the SK 37 never carried any armament. (Benny Karlsson, via Archives of Mikael Forslund)

SK 37 Viggen s/n 37802, coded F 15-68, sometime in the mid-1970s. Note the Wing numeral 15 in Yellow, on the nose. (Leif Fredin, via Archives of Mikael Forslund)

A lovely piture of SK 37 s/n 37809, coded F 15-61, prior to landing at F 15 Söderhamn in the spring of 1981. (Pelle Lindqvist)

on 22 October 1992. Subsequently transferred to *Flygvapenmuseum*, Linköping, Sweden the aircraft is today (2022) preserved with *Stenbäcks Flygmuseum*, Skurup, Sweden.

The first production SK 37s delivered to F 7 began in June 1972. Initially, the *TIS:Ä* instructors converted to the SK 37. Formal training of *Viggen* pilots started in January 1973. On 11 June 1974, King Carl XVI Gustaf flew in the rear seat of s/n 37805, with Captain Bo Hellström at the controls.

When all three of F 7's squadrons had converted to the AJ 37, the *TIS:37* was transferred to F 15 at Söderhamn. All SK 37s were eventually transferred to F 15, remaining there until the summer of 1997, when they were transferred to F 4 at Östersund. The SK 37 was used as a conversion trainer for all *Viggen* variants. A few SK 37s were loaned to different Wings for flight training during certain periods.

SK 37 s/n 37804, coded F 15-66, seen taking off from F 4 Östersund during a 15 June 1996 air show. Note the two pilots and the badge of F 15 on the fin. (Mikael Forslund)

A pair of SK 37 Viggens of F 15 Söderhamn at high altitude, both with two pilots each, sometime during the early 1980s. Closest to the camera is s/n 37807, coded F 15-63, with s/n 37814, coded F 15-55, turning away. (Owe Fredin)

Chuck Yeager, the world famous American pilot, on 14 October 1947 had become the first pilot to break the sound barrier in the Bell X-1. Yeager had other things on his CV, including being a WW II fighter pilot, as well as flying operations during the Vietnam War. Brigadier General Chuck Yeager visited Sweden in 1986 to market his memoirs. During his visit, Yeager was offered a flight in the rear seat of an SK 37 (s/n 37809, code F 15-61) at F 15 Söderhamn, with Captain Ulf Gabrielsson in the front seat. Yeager considered the offer to fly in the SK 37's rear seat as an insult. Following the flight, Yeager did not have many positive things to say about the *Viggen*, considering it old fashioned as well as having one too many safety features. Nevertheless, Yeager had the good taste to sign the nose of s/n 37809. At the time of writing (2022), his signature remains on the aircraft.

The new trainee pilots had previously flown the SK 60 (Saab 105) jet trainer at F 5 Ljungbyhed. The *TIS-37* was divided into three phases during the five months of training:

Phase 1 consisted of five weeks of theoretical studies where the trainees learned the 37-system by heart. Twenty simulator flights were made before the trainee flew a first sortie in the SK 37. After about two more weeks, it was time to go solo on the SK 37.

Phase 2 consisted of instrument training flights, navigation and more advanced flying. Occasionally unaccompanied by an instructor.

Phase 3 consisted of further advanced training, and increased knowledge of the capabilities of the *Viggen*. Formation flying in pairs was also performed.

The *TIS-37* included some 45 hours in the SK 37 and AJ 37, as well as 25 hours in simulators. From 1990, the *TIS-JA 37* at F 16 was conducted by using loaned SK 37s from F 15. On 1 June 1998, the *TIS-JA 37* was transferred to F 4.

During the late 1990s, ten SK 37s were modified as SK 37Es, the so-called "*Störviggen*" (Counter-measures *Viggen*). (See below.)

SK 37 s/n 37802, coded F 15-68, ready for take-off at F 15 Söderhamn on 8 June 1996. (Mikael Forslund)

SK 37 Viggen s/n 37807, coded F 15-63 and s/n 37814, coded F 15-55, taking off from F 15 Söderhamn on full afterburner sometime in the early 1980s. (Owe Fredin)

SK 37 s/n 37804, coded F 15-66, taking off on full afterburner during a 15 June 1996 air show at F 4 Östersund. (Mikael Forslund)

Saab SK 37

1/72

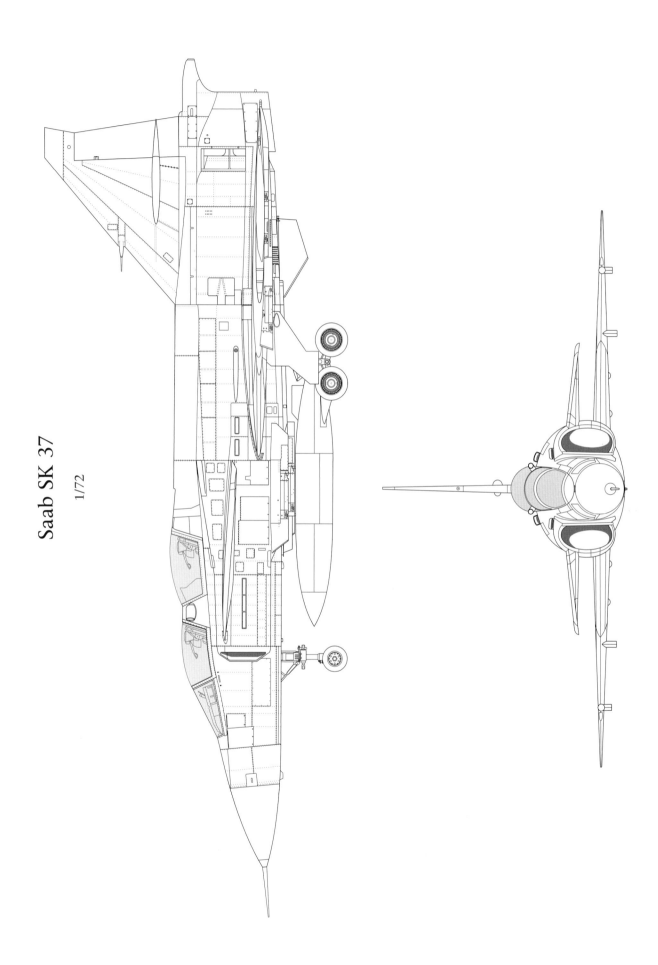

Saab SK 37

1/72

Saab SK 37 Viggen s/n 37806, coded Black 64, seen at F 7 Såtenäs on 12 May 1974.
The aircraft is overall Natural Metal.

a.m.olejniczak '22

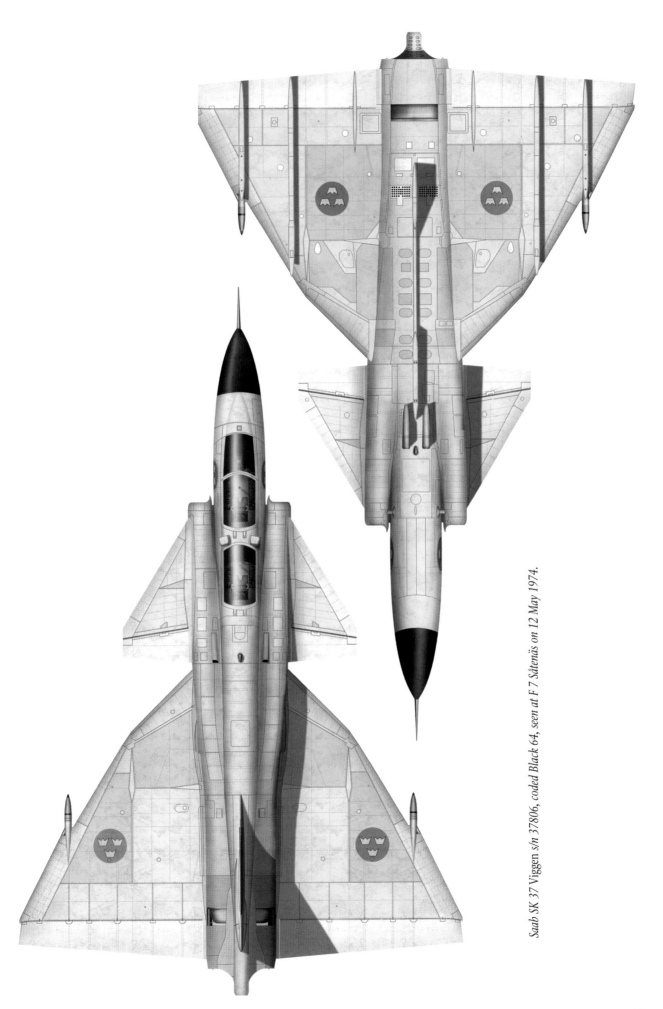

Saab SK 37 Viggen s/n 37806, coded Black 64, seen at F 7 Såtenäs on 12 May 1974.

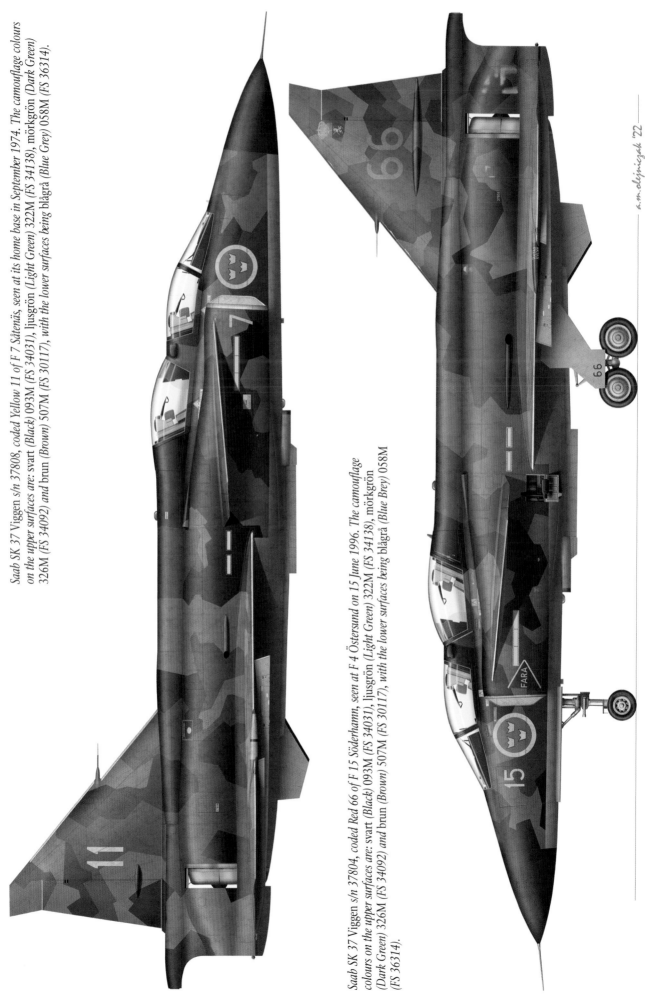

Saab SK 37 Viggen s/n 37808, coded Yellow 11 of F 7 Såtenäs, seen at its home base in September 1974. The camouflage colours on the upper surfaces are: svart (Black) 093M (FS 34031), ljusgrön (Light Green) 322M (FS 34138), mörkgrön (Dark Green) 326M (FS 34092) and brun (Brown) 507M (FS 30117), with the lower surfaces being blågrå (Blue Grey) 058M (FS 36314).

Saab SK 37 Viggen s/n 37804, coded Red 66 of F 15 Söderhamn, seen at F 4 Östersund on 15 June 1996. The camouflage colours on the upper surfaces are: svart (Black) 093M (FS 34031), ljusgrön (Light Green) 322M (FS 34138), mörkgrön (Dark Green) 326M (FS 34092) and brun (Brown) 507M (FS 30117), with the lower surfaces being blågrå (Blue Brey) 058M (FS 36314).

a.m. olijniczak '22

Type	S/n	Code/s	Taken on charge (ToC)	Struck off charge (SoC)	Remarks	Hrs flown
SK 37	37800	58, FC-22			Last flight 22 Oct 1992. To Flygvapenmuseum, Linköping, Sweden. Currently (2022) preserved at Stenbäcks Flygmuseum, Skurup, Sweden	
SK 37	37801	F 7-69 F 15-69 F 4-80	11 Oct 1972	12 Feb 2003	Last flight 29 Aug 2002. Scrapped	1,779 h 59 min
SK 37	37802	F 7-68 F 15-68 F 4-81	19 Jan 1973		Last flight 12 Mar 2003. Scrapped	
SK 37	37803	F 7-67 F 15-67 F 4-82, -67	25 Apr 1973	8 Nov 2002	Last flight 21 Jun 2000. Currently (2022) preserved at Teknikland, Optand, Sweden	1,728 h 47 min
SK 37	37804	F 7-66 F 15-66 F 4-83	8 May 1973		Last flight 24 Apr 2003. Scrapped	
SK 37	37805	F 7-65, -03 F 15-65	25 May 1973	6 Mar 1998	Last flight 23 Apr 1992. To Flygvapnets Tekniska skolor at Halmstad, Sweden, as ground instructional airframe. Currently (2022) preserved at Söderhamn/F 15 Flygmuseum, Söderhamn, Sweden	1,712 h 58 min
SK 37	37806	F 7-64, -15 F 15-64	2 Aug 1973	5 Aug 1981	W/o 26 Jun 1980, 14 km NW Wing F 15, Sweden. Pilot and technichian ejected	601 h 53 min
SK 37 SK 37E	37807	F 7-63, -33 F 15-63 F 4-70 F 21-70	18 Oct 1973		Modified 1 Dec 1999 as SK 37E. Last flight 2 Nov 2005. Scrapped	
SK 37 SK 37E	37808	F 7-62, -41, -11 F 15-62, -67 F 4-71 F 21-71	3 Oct 1974		Modified 20 Dec 1999 as SK 37E. Last flight 17 Oct 2005. Currently (2022) preserved at Musée de l'Air et de l'Espace, Paris, France	
SK 37 SK 37E	37809	F 7-61, -42 F 15-61 F 4-72 F 21-72 FC-09	4 Feb 1974		Modified 28 Jun 2000 as SK 37E. Currently (2022) airworthy with SwAFHF	
SK 37 SK 37E	37810	F 15-59 F 4-73	14 Apr 1975	5 Mar 2001	Modified 23 Jun 1999 as SK 37E. Last flight 13 Dec 2000. 2,899 flights. Scrapped	1,992 h 40 min
SK 37 SK 37E	37811	F 15-58 F 4-74, -73 F 21-73	6 Jun 1975		Modified 6 Oct 1999 as SK 37E. Last flight 12 Sep 2005. Currently (2022) preserved at Musée Européen de l'aviation de Chasse, Montelimar, France	
SK 37E	37812	F 15-57	22 Jul 1975	17 Nov 1977	W/o 15 Nov 1976 40 km W Edsbyn, Sweden. Pilot ejected	103 h 51 min
SK 37 SK 37E	37813	F 7-56 F 15-56 F 4-75, -74 F 21-74 FC-13	11 May 1976		Modified 8 Nov 2000 as SK 37E. Last flight 26 Jun 2007. Scrapped	
SK 37 SK 37E	37814	F 15-55 F 4-76	11 May 1976	7 Oct 2003	Modified 13 Jan 2000 as SK 37E. Last flight 25 Jun 2003. Scrapped	1,838 h 54 min
SK 37 SK 37E	37815	F 15-54 F 4-77	18 May 1976	27 Mar 2003	Modified 9 Mar 2000 as SK 37E. Last flight 6 Nov 2002. Scrapped	1,975 h 53 min
SK 37 SK 37E	37816	F 15-53 F 4-78	23 Jul 1976		Modified 31 May 2000 as SK 37E. Last flight 14 Aug 2003. Scrapped	
SK 37 SK 37E	37817	F 15-52 F 4-79 F 21-75	9 Sep 1976		Modified 10 Sep 2000 as SK 37E. Last flight 12 Oct 2005. Currently (2022) preserved at Flygmuseet F 21, Luleå, Sweden	

SK 37 Viggen s/n 37811, coded F 15-58, seen with the fin turned sideways at F 15 during the late 1970s. This feature made it possible to use older, relatively low, hangars to house the Viggen fleet. At the time of writing (2022), this particular aircraft is on display at the Musée Européen de l'aviation de Chasse, Montélimar, France. (Leif Fredin, via Archives of Mikael Forslund)

Chapter 7
SK 37E

When F 15 disbanded in the summer of 1997, the *TIS-37* was transferred to F 4 along with the 14 remaining SK 37s (s/ns 37801–37804, 37807–37811, 37813–37817 (s/ns 37800, 37805, 37806 and 37812 had been struck off charge). In 1997, s/n 37811 (code F 15-58/F 4-74) had been finished in a Grey, *mörkgrå 033M* (FS 36251) (upper) and *grå 032M* (FS 36463) (under), camouflage pattern, similar to that of the JA 37s and some AJSF 37s (the other SK 37/SK 37Es retained their splinter camouflage until struck off charge).

With the decreasing requirement for *Viggen* conversion training, ten SK 37s, s/ns 37807–37811 and 37813–37817, were modified as SK 37Es (E being short for Electronic). The SK 37Es replaced the Saab J 32E *Lansen* (based with the *Målflygdivisionen* at Malmen) as electronic counter measures aircraft. With the double set of controls being retained, the SK 37Es could be returned to conversion training status if required (which did not occur). However, a new instrument panel was installed in the rear cockpit.

In 1997, s/n 37814 was selected to become the SK 37E prototype. Modification work was undertaken by Saab at Linköping. The first check flight took place in the summer of 1998. The remaining nine SK 37s were modified at the F 21 workshops. Sixteen technicians were assigned to this work, with actual modification lasting 16 weeks. (The SK 37E was continuously upgraded in service).

The big news in the SK 37E was the *G 24* counter measures radar (taken from Saab J 32E *Lansens*), the counter measure *U 95 Axel* pod, and various training functions also from the J 32E *Lansen* (not the radio jamming functions, though). The original SK 37 counter measures gear was retained in the SK 37E.

The SK 37Es were never all operational at one time, with some aircraft being withdrawn from use and scrapped before the final ones had been modified and entered service!

SK 37E s/n 37814, coded F 4-76, at Malmen airfield outside Linköping on 19 May 2001. A KB flare and chaff dispenser can be seen beneath the right wing. The SK 37E was fitted with a different type of radome, with a G 24 ECM radar being fitted. A thin Yellow demarcation band and the text (in Yellow) "Tryck ej här" was painted on the upper section of the nose. This line masked the "window" for the G 24 radar. A new GPS and radio antenna for the FR 31 radio was fitted to the fuselage dorsal spine. Beginning on 13 January 2000, s/n 37814 was modified from SK 37 to SK 37E status. (Mikael Forslund)

Newly modified SK 37E Viggen s/n 37815, coded F 4-77, seen at F 7 Såtenäs on 18 June 2000. Beginning on 9 March 2000, s/n 37815 was modified from SK 37 to SK 37E status. An U 95 ECM pod can be seen below the left wing. An S 100B (Saab 340), s/n 100006 can be seen in the background. (Mikael Forslund)

SK 37E Viggen s/n 37815, coded F 4-77, at the F 16 Uppsala 26 August 2001 air show. A BT 53 laser reflector and an U 22/A ECM pod can be seen below the right wing. (Mikael Forslund)

SK 37E Viggen s/n 37815, coded F 4-77, seen at the F 16 Uppsala 26 August 2001 air show. An U 95 ECM pod can be seen beneath the left wing. (Mikael Forslund)

The rear seat systems operator used the *Generell Manöverapparat (GMA)* (General Maneouvering Device) to work the *U 95*. The pod carried *VMS*-gear (*Varnings- och Motmedelssystem* = Warning and Counter Measures System), which was identical to that carried by the JA 37D. The *KA (U 22)* electronics pod was carried on the right wing pylon, with the *KB* flare and chaff dispenser being carried underneath the left wing. The *U 95* jamming pod could be carried under the left wing. In such cases, the *KB* pod was moved to the right wing. For anti-aircraft artillery exercises, the SK 37E could use the *BT 53* laser reflector rod, which was mounted on one of the wing pylons. The White (FS 17886) rod was fitted with reflectors that were aimed in various directions.

G 24-gear was fitted in the nose section. This was a jamming transmitter against the *STRIL*-stations (*STRIL, or Stril,* being short for *Stridsledning,* i.e. Combat Operations Centre). The radome was exchanged for a thicker and lighter one. So that the Frequency S and C bands would not be dampened too much, a window of a different material was fitted in the upper section of the radome. The antenna radiation belt passed through this window. The window was outlined with a thin Yellow (FS 13655) stripe on the upper section of the radome.

The *FR 31* (*Flygradio* = Flight Radio) was installed in the rear seat, for radio communication on the VHF/UHF-band with other aircraft or with ground stations. An antenna for the *FR 31* and GPS was mounted on the dorsal spine.

An 8 Mb computer rod could also be used in the SK 37E.

Following the conclusion of initial trials with the SK 37E at *FC*, the aircraft were assigned to the Telecommunications Warfare Group at No.2 Sqn/F 4. Many exercises were conducted, with the aircraft being deployed to different air bases around the country. In 2003, *TIS-37* training ended at F 4 and with *Flygvapnet.* In the spring of 2003, six SK 37Es (s/ns 37807–37809, 37811, 37813 and 37817) were transferred from F 4 to No.1 Sqn/F 21 for *TK*-flight operations (*TK = Telekommunikation* = Telecommunications). Only one jamming systems operator was initially assigned to F 21.

In the electronic warfare (EW-*Viggen*) role, the SK 37E was used for training other air crews and radar personnel. It was also used for testing and evaluation purposes. Development of EW-libraries together with SWEWOSE (Swedish Electronic Warfare Operations Support Establishment) was another important task.

In 2004, two SK 37Es participated in the Nordic Air Meet (NOAM) exercise. The exercise was successful, including the SK 37E sorties. International exercises, including the ELITE 2003 to 2005, also included the participation of SK 37Es. The aircraft were held in high regard by foreign observers, with the jamming sorties being successful. On one occasion, 134 surface to air missiles were launched in one afternoon. However, no surface to air missiles managed to get off the ground when the SK 37Es were airborne! Sorties involving SK 37Es and RAF EF-3B Tornados armed with ASRAAM missiles were also conducted. This included functioning as a jamming escort for four

SK 37E s/n 37811, coded F 4-74, caught on camera soon after take-off. This particular SK 37E was the only SK 37/SK 37E which was painted in the Grey camouflage scheme: mörkgrå 033M (Dark Grey) (FS 36251), with the lower surfaces being grå 032M (Grey) (FS 36463). The panel below the national insignia appears to have been painted before being fastened to the aircraft. The front section of a KB flare and chaff dispenser can be seen below the left wing. (Lars-Åke Siggelin)

IDS Tornados, four ECT Tornados and two *Mirage* 2000s. Due to the jamming performed by the SK 37Es, the four attacking fighters failed in their mission.

The electronic warfare suit for the SK 37E *Viggen*, the Swedish supersonic EW aircraft
U 95 Axel: Consisted of the Saab Avionics (former Ericsson Saab Avionics) built *U 95* X-band (NATO I and lower J) jamming pod and onboard control and display units (CU/DU) for manual inputs by the EWO.

U 22/A: A self protection jammer pod, produced by Saab Avionics primarily for the AJS/AJSF 37.

G 24: Internal jammer mounted in the nose designed to jam surveillance radars covering S- and C-bands (NATO E-F and G-H).

KB: Chaff/flare dispenser pod produced by Saab Avionics (former SaabTech Electronics).

Other features: Integrated GPS, laser-reflectionpods, separate VHF/UHF-radio for EWO in rear seat and mission planning system.

When the SK 37E was phased out in 2005, they were replaced by JAS 39s. Two SK 37Es (s/ns 37809, code FC-09 and 37813, FC-13) remained in service with *FC* until 2007. S/n 37813 was then scrapped. S/n 37809 is currently (2022) airworthy, coded as F 15-61, with the SwAFHF at Såtenäs.

SK 37E s/n 37809, coded F 21-72, at the F 16 Uppsala 26 August 2001 air show. An U 95 ECM pod can be seen below the left wing. Beginning on 28 June 2000, the aircraft was modified from SK 37 to SK 37E status. At the time of writing (2022), the aircraft is airworthy with the Swedish Air Force Historic Flight (SwAFHF) at F 7 Såtenäs. The original code, F 15-61, has been reapplied. (Mikael Forslund)

SK 37 Technical Data and Performance Characteristics

Crew:	2
Quantity built:	18 (s/ns 37800–37817)
Length:	16.30 m
Wingspan:	10.60 m
Height:	5.60 m (4.0 m with fin folded)
Wing area:	52.20 m² (main wing 46.00 m²)
Wheel base:	5.54 m
Fuel load:	4,275 l + one external fuel tank containing an additional 1,400 l
Empty weight:	11,800 kg
Maximum take-off weight:	20,450 kg
Engine:	*RM 8A*, license built Pratt & Whitney JT8D
Thrust:	6,690 kp without afterburner, 11,790 kp with afterburner
Take-off run:	400 m
Landing run:	500 m
Max speed:	Mach 2
Service ceiling:	18,300 m
Armament:	(37800 used for various weapons trials at *FC*)

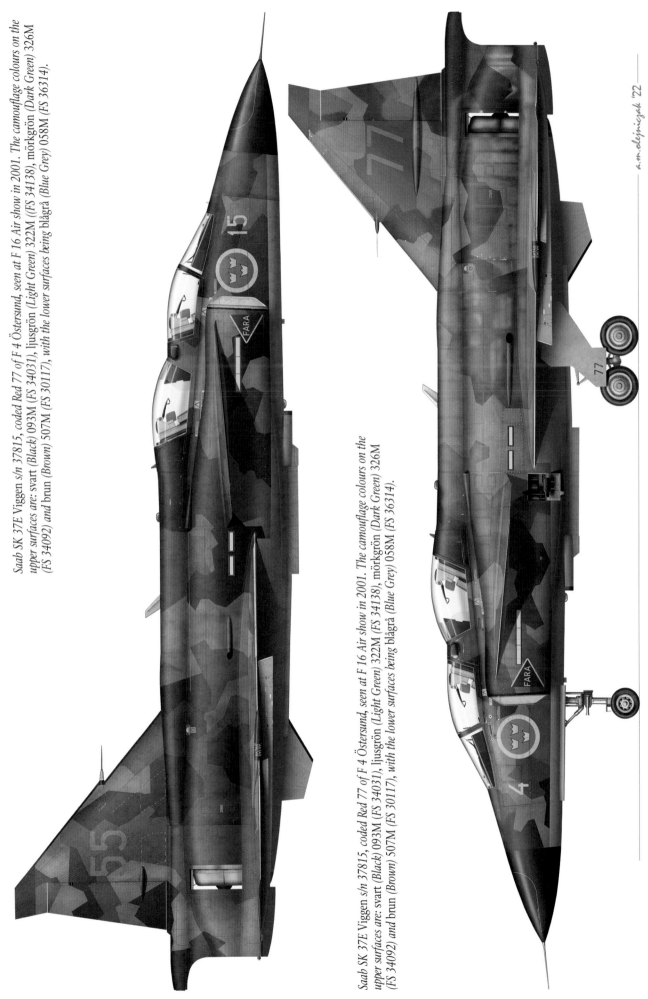

Saab SK 37E Viggen s/n 37815, coded Red 77 of F 4 Östersund, seen at F 16 Air show in 2001. The camouflage colours on the upper surfaces are: svart (Black) 093M (FS 34031), ljusgrön (Light Green) 322M (FS 34138), mörkgrön (Dark Green) 326M (FS 34092) and brun (Brown) 507M (FS 30117), with the lower surfaces being blågrå (Blue Grey) 058M (FS 36314).

Saab SK 37E Viggen s/n 37815, coded Red 77 of F 4 Östersund, seen at F 16 Air show in 2001. The camouflage colours on the upper surfaces are: svart (Black) 093M (FS 34031), ljusgrön (Light Green) 322M (FS 34138), mörkgrön (Dark Green) 326M (FS 34092) and brun (Brown) 507M (FS 30117), with the lower surfaces being blågrå (Blue Grey) 058M (FS 36314).

a.m.olejniczak '22

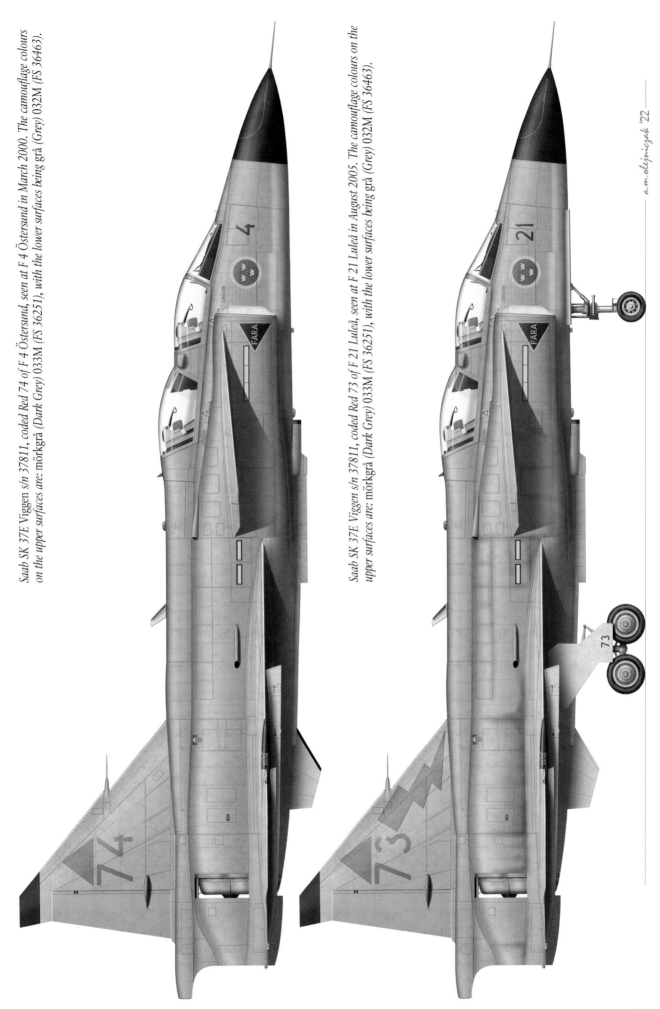

Saab SK 37E Viggen s/n 37811, coded Red 74 of F 4 Östersund, seen at F 4 Östersund in March 2000. The camouflage colours on the upper surfaces are: mörkgrå (Dark Grey) 033M (FS 36251), with the lower surfaces being grå (Grey) 032M (FS 36463).

Saab SK 37E Viggen s/n 37811, coded Red 73 of F 21 Luleå, seen at F 21 Luleå in August 2005. The camouflage colours on the upper surfaces are: mörkgrå (Dark Grey) 033M (FS 36251), with the lower surfaces being grå (Grey) 032M (FS 36463).

a.m. olejniczak '22

Chapter 8
SH 37 and AJSH 37

On 5 April 1968, a decision to order a dedicated reconnaissance variant of the *Viggen* (S 37) was made, to replace the Saab S 32C *Lansen* and Saab S 35E *Draken* in *Flygvapnet* service.

At the time it was thought that the dedicated reconnaissance Wing F 11 at Nyköping would be disbanded (this happened on 20 June 1979). Instead, F 13 at Norrköping, F 17 at Ronneby/Kallinge and F 21 at Luleå were to have one reconnaissance squadron each. However, it proved impossible to combine maritime reconnaissance and photographic reconnaissance into one S 37 *Viggen* variant. As a result, the SF 37 (*Spaning Foto* = Reconnaissance Photo) and the SH 37 (*Spaning Hav* = Reconnaissance Sea) were developed. It was intended that the two variants would operate in conjunction, complementing each other.

SH 37 development proceeded at a quicker pace than that of the SF 37. This was due to the similarity of the SH 37 and the AJ 37. One AJ 37, s/n 37003, was modified as the SH 37 prototype, receiving a new serial number, 37900. The initial SH 37 test flight took place in December 1973. S/n 37900 was subsequently used for various trials by *FC/FMV:Prov*.

A total of 28 SH 37s were built (s/ns 37900–37927). A similar quantity of SF 37s were built (see below). Both variants served side by side at the respective Wings.

The Flygvapnet *50th Anniversary air show at F 4 Östersund on 6 June 1976. Closest to the camera is SH 37 s/n 37904, coded F 7-08, in the then recently-applied splinter camouflage. A few AJ 37s of F 7 Såtenäs in overall Natural Metal and J 35D Drakens of F 4 Östersund can be seen in the background. Beginning on 10 January 1996, s/n 37904 was modified from SH 37 to AJSH 37 status. (Mikael Forslund)*

A large-scale exercise at Rommehed outside Borlänge on 18 August 1992. SH 37 s/n 37914, coded F 13-27, is being readied for take-off in front of three JA 37s of F 16 Uppsala. (Mikael Forslund)

The intention was that the first SH 37s would be delivered to No.1 Sqn/F 13. However, as that Wing's reorganisation from the fighter role, using the Saab J 35F *Draken*, to reconnaissance using the SH 37 and SF 37 (from October 1977) had not yet been completed, initial SH 37 deliveries were made to F 7 in June 1975. Aircraft transferred to F 7 included s/ns 37902 (coded F 7-06), 37903 (F 7-07), 37904 (F 7-08), 37900 (F 7-09), 37905 (F 7-15) and 37907 (F 7-45). One SH 37, s/n 37902, was fitted with an SF 37 nose section in August 1975, this being retained for about one year, before the aircraft was returned to SH 37 configuration, including nose and radar. This was done in order to provide the pilots with experience on the flight characteristics of the SF 37. Additionally, s/n 37900 (marked as 343) was briefly fitted with an SF 37 nose section for the 1976 Le Bourget, Paris, France, Air Show. (SF 37 deliveries commenced in early 1977). In October 1976, No.1 Sqn/F 13 was ready to receive its first SH 37s. Personnel had been transferred from F 11 at Nyköping.

Additional F 11 personnel were transferred to No. 2 Sqn/F 17, which initiated conversion training from the J 35F to the SH 37 and SF 37 in January 1979.

In March 1979, the first SH 37s and SF 37s arrived for ground training with No.1 Sqn/F 21. Reconnaissance sorties began in July 1979.

The SH 37 was intended for all-weather radar reconnaissance over the sea and along coasts. A monopulse radar, the PS 371/A, was fitted in the nose. This was a similar radar to that fitted to the AJ 37, with the difference being that the PS 371/A carried an *RKa 40* radar camera, which recorded radar images (time, target position, the aircraft's position, course, altitude, roll angle, pitch, with the radar warning system also being able to identify which kind of radar had struck the aircraft). Post-sortie, the radar images were evaluated by radar interpreters. During field exercises, the photo interpreting personnel had a truck with a trailer with a load of containers. The first container included film developing/interpretation/analysis gear, and the second container space for staff and reconnaissance squadron personnel, as well as an operational unit with water supply and electrical power.

The SH 37 was equipped with an *App 27* radar warning device, which indicated when the aircraft was hit by "enemy radar".

The SH 37 was equipped with a distance camera pod (AKK = *Avståndskamerakapsel* = long-range photo pod), including an Omera Type 31-1 *SKa 24D* (SKa = *Spaningskamera* = reconnaissance camera) camera, fitted with a curtain shutter and *BIRK = Bildrörelsekompensation* = Photo Motion Compensation). This meant that the film moved in the direction of flight during exposure. This helped to avoid movement fuzziness. So that the speed of the film would be correct, the altitude

The SH 37s almost always carried this AKK (avståndskamerakapsel, distance camera pod), which had an Omera Type 31-1 camera (SKa 24D, 600 mm lens focal length), on the right fuselage attachment point. This particular SH 37, coded F 15-77, was photographed on 28 May 1994. (Mikael Forslund)

SH 37 s/n 37907, coded F 13-13, seen sometime in the mid-1970s. A KB flare and chaff dispenser can be seen below the left wing. The aircraft was written off in a crash on 11 March 1977. (Leif Fredin, via Archives of Mikael Forslund)

An SH 37 Viggen showing off its different types of equipment: a KA ECM pod, "flash light pod", an MSK H (H meaning Höger, ie right) night reconnaissance pod containing four BXE 103 flashes (no cameras), an AKK camera pod (on the ground), an Omera Type 31-1 camera (SKa 24D, 600 mm lens focal length), a 1,400 litre external fuel tank, RB 24B Sidewinder (on the ground), computerised camera for registering naval vessels, MSK V (V being short for Vänster, i.e. left), three SKa 34 cameras, 75 mm focal length, for the MSK V pod, and a KB flare and chaff dispenser. (Rune Rydh, F 13)

must be known. This was handled by the aircraft radar altimeter, and calculated by the *CK 37*. The camera body had earlier been used on the Saab S 35E *Draken*. The new lens had a focal width of 600 mm, with the film format being 5.7 x 11.4 cm.

The camera had automatic exposure control. On the SH 37, the pod/camera was almost always mounted on the right pylon.

The camera took photographs straight ahead. During the 1980s, four SH 37s were modified to use the *CA 200* LOROP (Long Range Oblique Photography) camera system. This was housed in a pod carried on the external fuel tank pylon. The lens had a focal length of 1,676 mm. This camera system was gyro-stabilized, taking oblique photographs by means of a mirror. The camera was programmed and controlled through the *CK 37* central calculator. The *CA 200* could perform either route photography or target tracking. Such sorties were flown in pairs at high altitude. More often than not, "enemy territory" was photographed from international airspace.

A night reconnaissance pod (*MSK = Mörkerspaningskapsel*), could be carried on the left pylon (*MSK V*) (V = *vänster* = left. This had been used earlier on the Saab S 35E *Draken*. The pod contained three Vinten *SKa 34* cameras, with a 75 mm focus lens (Leitz lenses). The shutter time was 1/500 sec. The cameras (equipped with *BIRK*), were mounted obliquely to the right, to the left and vertically. As a result, the cameras covered a 120 degree view angle. The *MSK V* also contained flash gear (four flashes *BXE 103*) for the infrared spectrum. An infrared film, 5.6 x 5.7 cm, was used. A flash lightning pod (*MSK H*) (H = *höger* = right) could be necessary for certain sorties. This was carried on the right-hand fuselage pylon. Night photography up to altitudes of 300 m was possible.

The SH 37 could also make use of counter measures. Beneath the right wing, the electronic *KA* pod, later designated *U 22*, could be carried. The pod was intended to prevent the enemy from locating the aircraft. The *KB* pod was usually carried beneath the left wing. The pod contained flares and chaff. These could be released to counter heat-seeking missiles (flares) and radar-guided missiles (chaff) that had been fired against the aircraft. The SH 37 could also carry the heat-seeking *RB 24J* Sidewinder for protection against enemy aircraft. For attacks against naval targets, the *RB 04E* anti-ship missile was used.

The primary task for the SH 37 was maritime surveillance. Foreign military vessels were to be identified and photographed for intelligence purposes. The Swedish armed forces were interested in what was happening around the country's borders. As a result, ships were photographed (with the *SKa 24D*) as a matter of routine.

The approach was made at low altitude along the side of the ship. This was to obtain good-quality photographs, as well as not to provoke.

SH 37 s/n 37903, coded F 13-05, seen at F 6 Karlsborg on 4 June 1989. An MSK V night reconnaissance pod containing three SKa 34 75 mm focal length cameras and four BXE 103 flashes can be seen on the fuselage attachment point. Beginning on 25 February 1996, the aircraft was modified from SH 37 to AJSH 37 status. (Mikael Forslund)

SH 37 Viggen s/n 37917, coded F 17-33. An AKK camera pod, containing one Omera Type 31-1 camera hangs from the right fuselage attachment point. A 1,400 litre external fuel tank is fitted to the centre fuselage attachment point. From the left fuselage attachment point, an MSK V night reconnaissance pod, containing three SKa 34 cameras, 75 mm focal length, as well as four BXE 103 flashes. Beginning on 3 June 1996, the aircraft was modified from SH 37 to AJSH 37 status. (Via Archives of Peter Kempe/Mikael Forslund)

SH 37 s/n 37918, coded F 17-31. The aircraft is fitted with a 1,400 litre external fuel tank, and a KB flare and chaff dispenser. Beginning on 9 February 1995, the aircraft was modified from SH 37 to AJSH 37 status. (Leif Fredin, via Archives of Mikael Forslund)

Saab SH 37

1/72

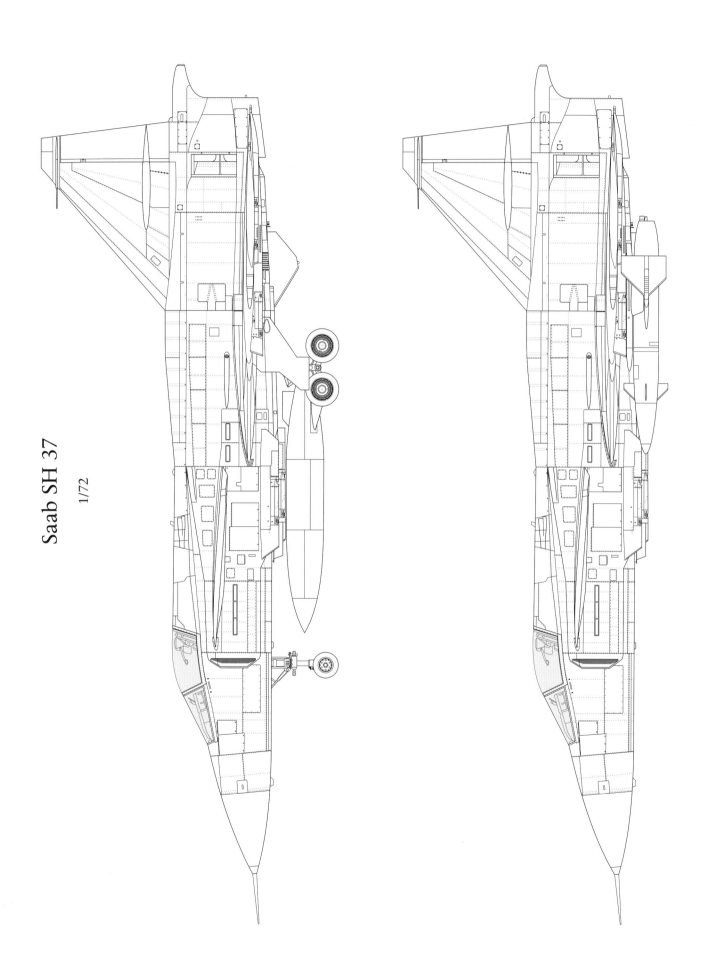

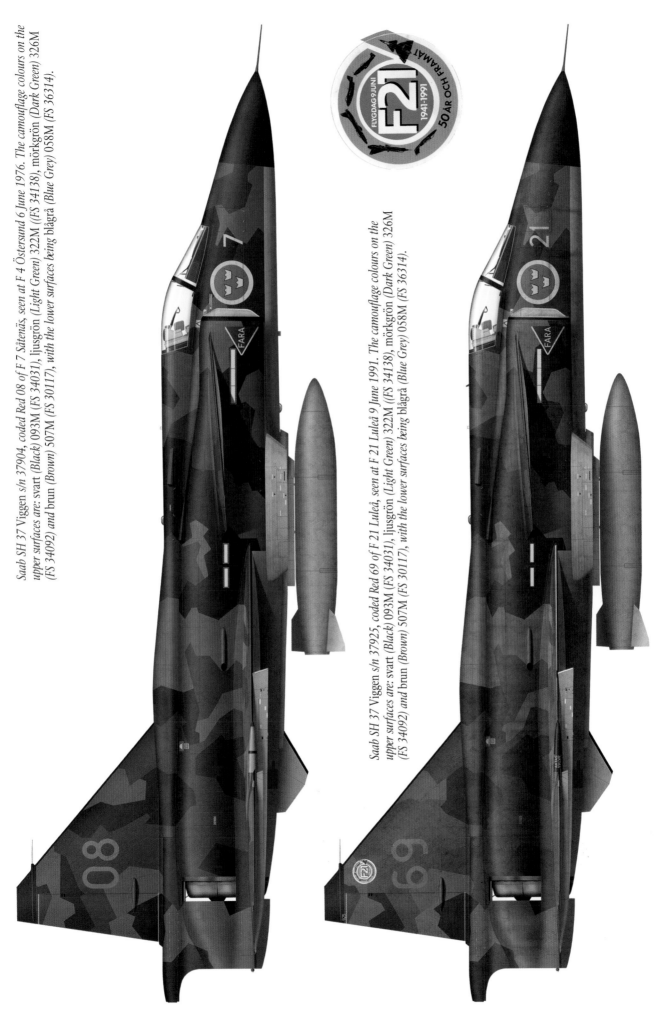

Saab SH 37 Viggen s/n 37904, coded Red 08 of F 7 Såtenäs, seen at F 4 Östersund 6 June 1976. The camouflage colours on the upper surfaces are: svart (Black) 093M (FS 34031), ljusgrön (Light Green) 322M ((FS 34138), mörkgrön (Dark Green) 326M (FS 34092) and brun (Brown) 507M (FS 30117), with the lower surfaces being blågrå (Blue Grey) 058M (FS 36314).

Saab SH 37 Viggen s/n 37925, coded Red 69 of F 21 Luleå, seen at F 21 Luleå 9 June 1991. The camouflage colours on the upper surfaces are: svart (Black) 093M (FS 34031), ljusgrön (Light Green) 322M ((FS 34138), mörkgrön (Dark Green) 326M (FS 34092) and brun (Brown) 507M (FS 30117), with the lower surfaces being blågrå (Blue Grey) 058M (FS 36314).

The SH 37s were part of the *"Incidentberedskap Spaning"* (Quick Reaction Alert Reconnaissance) during all hours of the day and throughout the year. The Quick Reaction Alert readiness was one hour, and for other sorties two hours. During the Cold War, the Quick Reaction Alert Reconnaissance was often required by the respective military commanders for identifying naval vessels and to keep track of maritime movements. It was initially discovered that the SH 37 capabilities when carrying the *SKa 24D* was inferior to that of its immediate predecessor, the Saab S 32C *Lansen*. An higher level of photographic detail was required. As a result, the SF 37 began to operate in conjunction with the SH 37. One example of this is the U-137 submarine incident, which took place in the Karlskrona archipelago beginning on 27 October 1981 (also see the AJ 37 chapter). Initially a group of four AJ 37s of F 6 and one SH 37 and one SF 37 of No.1Sqn/F 13, then serving with the Quick Reaction Alert Reconnaissance, took part. The aircraft photographed the submarine within Swedish territorial waters. Later on, F 17 SF/SH 37s replaced those of F 13.

During the 1980s, the Quick Reaction Reconnaissance was of course active during the Warsaw Pact exercises (the 1983 exercise was named *ZAPAD*). NATO exercises were also checked.

On Sunday 7 July 1985 an SH 37 (s/n 37902, code F 13-03), flown by Captain Göran Larsson, was confronted by two Soviet Su-15s (Flagon-F) from the 54th Fighter Regiment, while flying two naval identifying sorties off the Latvian coast. A large number of Warsaw Pact vessels were engaged in exercises in the area. During Larsson's first sortie, flying the unarmed s/n 37902, a Su-15 ("Yellow 36") joined formation with the SH 37, with the second Su-15 keeping some distance. The intention was to distract Larsson, which during some manoeuvres, was successful. Using his handheld camera, Larsson took some photos of "Yellow 36". Nevertheless, the mission was accomplished, with Larsson heading back to F 13 for refuelling before returning to the area for a second time. Taking off and flying towards the area, Larsson made a radar scan of the naval base at Liepaja shortly before 18.00 hours. He then turned northwards towards the naval exercise area. (A radar scan involved making a low level approach, then climb to an altitude between 500 and 1,000 m, turn on the radar, make some sweeps, select memory mode, turn 180 degrees and descend to the extreme low level allowed by the auto pilot in maintain altitude mode, followed by measuring the echoes. If this task involved simultaneous reporting, the pilot was forced to use the voice radio to transfer the information).

As Larsson was flying at low level, he could not establish direct radio contact with the base. Because of this, a pair of JA 37s over Gotland functioned as a relay station for s/n 37902. Larsson received a warning from the fighters that Soviet fighters had been scrambled from Vainode. As it turned out, it was the same pair of Su-15s as before.

One of the aircraft formated with the *Viggen* at a distance of about 50 m, resulting in yet another Swedish/Soviet manoeuver involving loops and tight turns. Larsson eventually tired of this, performing a high G-load Split-S at an altitude of 500 m and a speed of 700 km/h. The Su-15 pilot did not want to loose his grip, following his prey down to an altitude of about 100 m.

SH 37 s/n 37921, coded F 21-59, seen above F 21 Luleå during the 9 June 1991 air show. The special air show badge (F 21 1941–1991) appears on both sides of the fin. An AKK camera pod, containing one Omera Type 31-1 camera, hangs from the right fuselage attachment point. A 1,400 litre external fuel tank is fitted to the centre fuselage attachment point. On the left fuselage attachment point, an MSK V night reconnaissance pod, containing three SKa 34 cameras, 75 mm focal length, and four BXE 103 flashes, can be seen. Beginning on 27 October 1995, the aircraft was modified from SH 37 to AJSH 37 status. (Mikael Forslund)

The Soviet pilot did not realize the limitations of his aircraft at low level. Larsson noted in his rearview mirror the Su-15 making a nose-high stall and exploding on impact with the water surface. Larsson turned back to F 13, discovering the second Su-15 ("Yellow 36") following him. At a speed of Mach 1.1, Larsson received an indication that "Yellow 36" had locked his radar missiles on s/n 37902. The pair of JA 37s over Gotland turned to assist Larsson. After about one minute, "Yellow 36" broke off his pursuit.

The fatal crash affected the 54th Fighter Regiment at Vainode badly. Regular flight operations stopped for four days.

Eleven years later, a similar loss occurred with an AJSH 37 *Viggen* (see below).

During the 1980s, the USSR carried out several large-scale amphibious landing exercises in the Baltic Sea area. The SH/SF 37s were used to keep a close watch over these exercises, thus obtaining great training experience on how such sorties could be fulfilled during an armed conflict.

SH 37 s/n 37900 was for extended periods used for trials by *FC/FMV:Prov.* Another SH 37, s/n 37902, was also used by *FC* at different times.

AJSH 37

Between 1993 and 1996, the 25 remaining SH 37s (s/ns 37907, 37919 and 37926 had been written off) were modified at F 21 as AJSH 37s. S/n 37900 underwent modification work at *FC*. The AJSH 37 could carry the same amount of weaponry as the earlier SH 37, as well as the *RB 15F* and *Bombkapsel m/90 "Mjölner"*. The outer wing pylons were activated, being able to carry various Sidewinder variants - the *RB 24B, RB 24J* and *RB 74*.

On 16 October 1996, Captain Göran Carlsson of F 15 was flying a reconnaissance sortie over the Baltic Sea in s/n 37908 against the Russian nuclear cruiser *Pjotr Velikij*. Carlsson was killed when his *Viggen* hit the water surface. It appears likely that Carlsson had been distracted by a Beriev Be-12 flying boat close to the *Pjotr Velikij*.

The AJSH 37 was used by F 7, F 10, F 15, F 17 and F 21.

SH 37 Technical Data and Performance Characteristics

Crew:	One
Quantity built:	28 (s/ns 37900–37927)
Length:	16.30 m
Wingspan:	10.60 m
Height:	5.60 m (4.0 m with fin folded)
Wing area:	52.20 m² (main wing 46.00 m²)
Wheel base:	5.54 m
Fuel load:	5,525 l + one external fuel tank containing an additional 1,400 l
Empty weight:	11,800 kg

SH 37 s/n 37925, coded F 21-69, seen above F 21 Luleå during the 9 June 1991 air show. The special air show badge (F 21 1941–1991) appears on both sides of the fin. An AKK camera pod, containin one Omera Type 31-1 camera, hangs from the right fuselage attachment point. A 1,400 litre external fuel tank is fitted to the centre fuselage attachment point. Beginning on 18 April 1996, the aircraft was modified from SH 37 to AJSH 37 status. (Mikael Forslund)

SH 37 s/n 37912, coded F 21-55, at the F 21 Luleå 9 June 1991 air show. A KA (U 22) ECM pod can be seen on the right wing attachment point. An AKK camera pod, containing one Omera Type 31-1 camera, hangs from the right fuselage attachment point. A 1,400 litre external fuel tank is fitted to the centre fuselage attachment point. An MSK V pod can be seen on the left fuselage attachment point. Beginning on 22 February 1995, the aircraft was modified from SH 37 to AJSH 37 status. (Mikael Forslund)

Maximum take-off weight:	20,450 kg
Engine:	*RM 8A*, license built Pratt & Whitney JT8D
Thrust:	6,690 kp without afterburner, 11,790 kp with afterburner
Take-off run:	400 m
Landing run:	500 m
Max speed:	Mach 2
Service ceiling:	18,300 m
Armament:	*RB 04E, RB 24B, RB 24J*

Type	S/n	Code/s	Taken on charge (ToC)	Struck off charge (SoC)	Remarks	Hrs flown
SH 37 AJSH 37	37900	F 7-09 F 13-09, -01 FC-09, -39 F 10-01 F 21-51		17 Feb 1998	*Rebuilt from AJ 37 s/n 37003. Fitted with SF 37 nose for 1976 Paris (Le Bourget) Air Show, France. Marked as 343 on fin. Modified 2 Apr 1993 as AJSH 37. Last flight 15 Oct 1997. Scrapped*	1,656 h 02 min
SH 37 AJSH 37	37901	F 13-01 F 10-01 F 21-51	18 Aug 1975		*Modified 14 Nov 1995 as AJSH 37. Last flight 13 Jan 2006. Currently (2022) preserved at Aviodrome, Lelystad, the Netherlands*	
SH 37 AJSH 37	37902	F 7-06 F 13-06, -03 FC-06 F 17-39 F 10-03	18 Sep 1975	24 Oct 1997	*Aug 1975-July 1976 fitted with SF 37 nose (F 7-06). Modified 14 Nov 1995 as AJSH 37. Last flight 22 Apr 1997. Scrapped*	2,456 h 43 min
SH 37 AJSH 37	37903	F 7-07 F 13-05 F 10-05 F 21-53	11 May 1976		*Modified 27 Feb 1996 as AJSH 37. Last flight 6 Apr 2005. Scrapped*	
SH 37 AJSH 37	37904	F 7-08, -31 F 13-07	9 Jun 1976	17 Mar 2000	*Modified 10 Jan 1996 as AJSH 37. Last flight 11 Nov 1999. To Wing F 16 for fire and rescue exercises*	2,474 h 38 min
SH 37 AJSH 37	37905	F 7-15 F 13-15, -09 F 15-09, -75 F 10-75 F 21-53	9 Jun 1976	30 Jun 2000	*Modified 29 Mar 1995 as AJSH 37. Last flight 23 Sep 1999. To Wing F 21 for ground exercises. Scrapped*	2,271 h 53 min

Type	S/n	Code/s	Taken on charge (ToC)	Struck off charge (SoC)	Remarks	Hrs flown
SH 37 AJSH 37	37906	F 7- F 13-11 F 10-11 F 21-51, -53, -56	20 Sep 1976	30 Jun 2000	Modified 12 Feb 1996 as AJSH 37. Last flight 10 Mar 2000. Scrapped	2,666 h 45 min
SH 37 AJSH 37	37907	F 7-45 F 13-45, -13	23 Jul 1976	18 Nov 1977	W/o 11 Mar 1977 NW Öland, Sweden. Pilot ejected	108 h 07 min
SH 37 AJSH 37	37908	F 7-08, -52 F 13-15 F 17-69 F 15-33, -81, -89	20 Sep 1976		Modified 4 Sep 1995 as AJSH 37. W/o 16 Oct 1996 120 km SE Gotland, Sweden. Pilot killed	2,187 h 50 min
SH 37 AJSH 37	37909	F 13-17 F 17-67 F 15-67, -73 F 10-73	14 Oct 1976	12 May 1999	Modified 28 Mar 1995 as AJSH 37. Last flight 1 Oct 1998. Scrapped	2,257 h 12 min
SH 37 AJSH 37	37810	F 13-19 F 17-65 F 7-35 F 21-57	18 Jan 1977	14 Jun 2001	Modified 1 Dec 1995 as AJSH 37. Last flight 29 Mar 2001. Cockpit currently (2022) at Arboga Robotmuseum, Arboga, Sweden	2,345 h 16 min
SH 37 AJSH 37	37911	F 13-21 F 21-53, -33 F 7-33	18 Jan 1977		Modified 25 Nov 1996 as AJSH 37. Last flight 8 Dec 2005. Currently (2022) preserved, Aeroseum, Säve, Sweden	
SH 37 AJSH 37	37912	F 13-23 F 21-55	4 Apr 1977	8 Feb 1999	Modified 22 Feb 1995 as AJSH 37. Last flight 2 Oct 1998. Scrapped	2,149 h 27 min
SH 37 AJSH 37	37913	F 13-25 F 17-59 F 15-59, -79, -77 F 7-67 F 10-67 F 21-67	1 Sep 1977	22 May 2001	Modified 5 Sep 1995 as AJSH 37. Last flight 16 Feb 2001. Scrapped	2,525 h 24 min
SH 37 AJSH 37	37914	F 13-27 F 15-27, -77, -69 F 21-69, 67, -61	1 Sep 1977		Modified 4 Sep 1995 as AJSH 37. Last flight 27 May 2003. Scrapped	
SH 37 AJSH 37	37915	F 13-29 F 15-69 F 21-69	17 Oct 1977	13 Feb 2002	Modified 10 Apr 1995 as AJSH 37. Last flight 9 Aug 2001. Scrapped	2,493 h 36 min
SH 37 AJSH 37	37916	F 13-13, -29 F 10-13, -37 F 21-	17 Oct 1977	29 Jan 2003	Modified 24 May 1996 as AJSH 37. Last flight 2 Oct 2002. Scrapped	2,772 h 29 min
SH 37 AJSH 37	37917	F 17-33, -63, -37 F 15-37, -83 F 10-83		30 Jun 2000	Modified 3 Jun 1996 as AJSH 37. Last flight 25 Nov 1999. Scrapped	2,304 h 02 min
SH 37 AJSH 37	37918	F 13- F 17-61, -31 F 10-61, -71 F 21-57	23 May 1978		Modified 9 Feb 1995 as AJSH 37. Last flight 7 Feb 2006. Currently (2022) preserved at Newark Air Museum, Newark, UK	
SH 37	37919	F 17-39, -59 F 13-19			W/o 8 Nov 1984 30 km SE Öland, Sweden. Pilot killed	769 h 31 min
SH 37 AJSH 37	37920	F 21-57 F 7-39 F 10-39		21 Jun 2000	Modified 22 Aug 1995 as AJSH 37. Last flight 11 Nov 1999. Scrapped	2,235 h 45 min
SH 37 AJSH 37	37921	F 21-59		11 Nov 1998	Modified 27 Oct 1995 as AJSH 37. Last flight 21 Aug 1998. Scrapped	2,265 h 19 min
SH 37 AJSH 37	37922	F 21-61, -52, -67 F 17-61 F 13-21 F 10-61, -21			Modified 20 Sep 1996 as AJSH 37. Last flight 10 Nov 2005. Scrapped	
SH 37 AJSH 37	37923	F 17-57 F 15-57, -87		12 May 1999	Modified 7 Mar 1996 as AJSH 37. Last flight 21 Sep 1998. Scrapped	2,044 h 56 min
SH 37 AJSH 37	37924	F 17-55 F 15-55, -85 F 21-61		11 Nov 1998	Modified 13 May 1996 as AJSH 37. Last flight 24 Jun 1998. Currently (2022) preserved at Gotland, Sweden	1,980 h 01 min
SH 37 AJSH 37	37925	F 17-53 F 7-75 F 10-53 F 21-69		26 Aug 2002	Modified 18 Apr 1996 as AJSH 37. Last flight 26 Feb 2002. Scrapped	2,601 h 29 min
SH 37	37926	F 17-51			W/o 5 Sep 1981 Nogersund, Sweden. Pilot killed	418 h 07 min
SH 37 AJSH 37	37927	F 13- F 21-63		14 Nov 1997	Modified 24 Aug 1995 as AJSH 37. Last flight 21 Nov 1996. Currently (2022) preserved at Flygmuseet F 21, Luleå, Sweden	1,978 h 11 min

Chapter 9
SF 37

As described in the SH 37 chapter, a decision was taken on 5 April 1968 to order a reconnaissance variant of the *Viggen* (S 37) to replace the Saab S 32C *Lansen* and Saab S 35E *Draken* in *Flygvapnet* service, equipping one squadron each at F 13 Norrköping, F 17 Kallinge and F 21 Luleå. However, it was discovered that the twin duties of maritime reconnaissance and photographic reconnaissance could not be performed by a single *Viggen* variant. As a result, the SF 37 (*Spaning Foto* = Reconnaissance Photo) and SH 37 (*Spaning Hav* = Reconnaissance Sea) variants were developed. The intention was that the two reconnaissance *Viggen* variants were to operate in pairs, complementing each other. The SH 37 was ready for service a couple of years (1975) sooner than the SF 37 (1977). A total of 28 SF 37s were completed, s/ns 37950–37977. S/n 37033 was modified from AJ 37 status as an SF 37, receiving the new *Flygvapnet* s/n 37950.

In 1971, 37-1 was fitted with a sheet metal nose, externally similar to the planned SF-nose. Aerodynamic trials follwed. The SF 37 was a dedicated photographic reconnaissance variant, lacking radar, but having the ability to carry countermeasures gear, as well as IR missiles. The first SF 37, s/n 37950, took to the air for the first time on 21 May 1973. Many different camera trials were undertaken. The camera sight opening was located on the right-hand lower section of the nose. The cockpit sight was located at same place as the radar screen on the SH 37. The cameras were carried in pods attached to pylons beneath the aircraft, and in the nose section. There were seven cameras, all having automatic exposure control.

Nose:

In the nose section, directed obliquely, vertically, forward: One *SKa 24C* (a modified *SKa 24B* from the Saab S 35E *Draken*-era). This was an OMERA Type 31-1 low altitude and outline camera. Lenses by Matra (SFOM): *24C/120 MT* = 120 mm 1:2.8

BIRK (*Bildrörelsekompensation* = Photo Motion Compensation) and curtain shutter.

Negative format 5.7 x 11.4 cm.

SF 37 s/n 37952, coded F 13-04, seen at a remote revetment at Rommehed on 17 October 1992. The aircraft is ready to take-off, with a BRAGG operational readiness gear for electircal power support being plugged into the Viggen. A technician stands nearby. In front of the aircraft, a conscript motorcycle orderly can be seen. To the right is a Volvo lorry and a tractor tug. Beginning on 15 August 1996, the aircraft was modified from SF 37 to AJSH 37 status. (Mikael Forslund)

SF 37 Viggen s/n 37960 or 37962, coded F 13-14, on display at the F 15 Söderhamn 31 August 1980 air show. A U 22 ECM pod (earlier known as KA) hangs beneath the right wing. An RB 24B Sidewinder is fitted to the right fuselage attachment point, with the 1,400 litre external fuel tank occupying the centre fuselage attachment point. (Mikael Forslund)

SF 37 s/n 37961, coded F 13-12, lands at F 4 Östersund on 1 June 1986. The aircraft is fitted with the external fuel tank, with the MSK V night reconnaissance pod being fitted to the left fuselage attachment point. Beginning on 15 October 1996, this SF 37 was modified to AJSF 37 status. Note the F 13 badge on top of the fin. (Mikael Forslund)

Saab SF 37

1/72

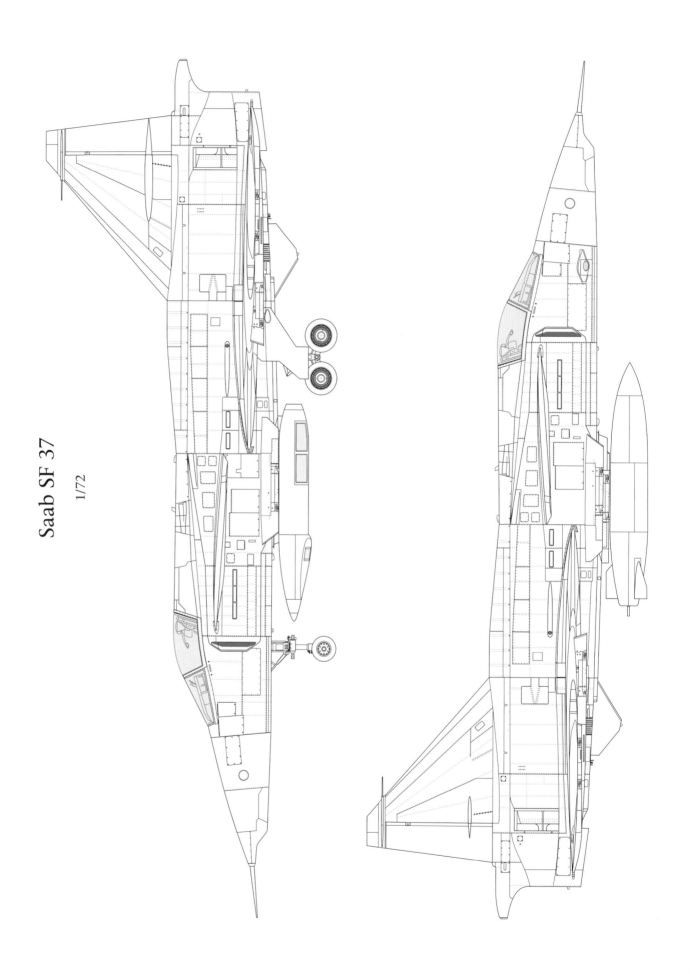

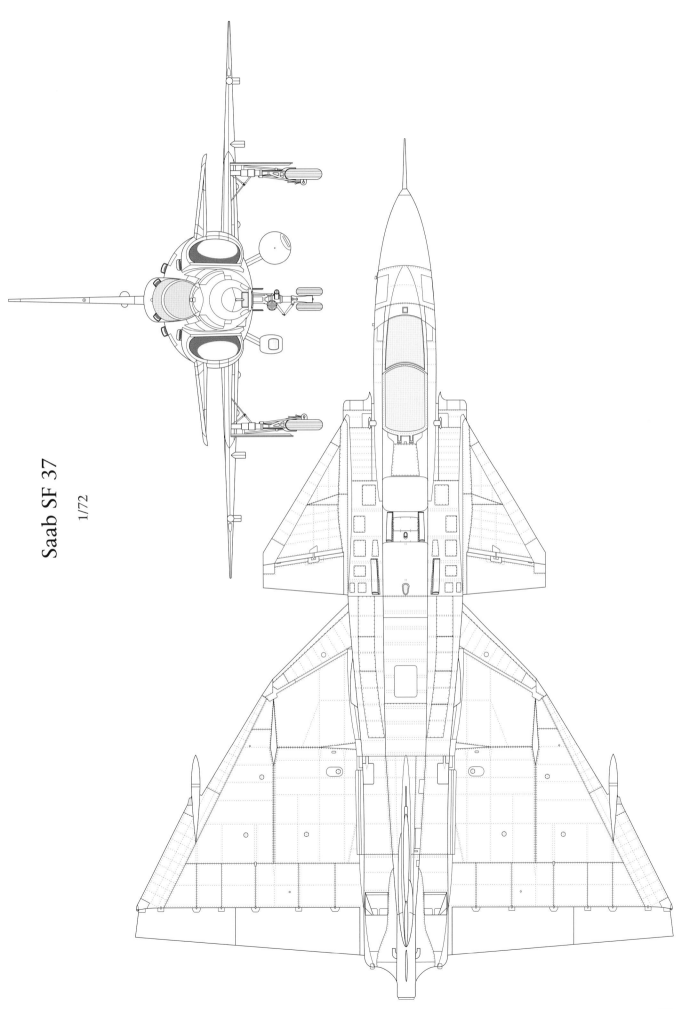

Saab SF 37

1/72

Saab SF 37

1/72

Saab SH 37 Viggen s/n 37902, coded Red 06 of F 7 Sätenäs, photographed at F 7 on 31 August 1975. The upper surfaces are camouflaged in svart (Black) 093M (FS 37038), ljusgrön (Light Green) 322M (FS 34082), mörkgrön (Dark Green) 326M (FS 34079) and brun (Brown) 507M (FS 30051), with the lower surfaces being blågrå (Blue Grey) 058M (FS 35237).

Saab SH 37 Viggen s/n 37902, coded F 7-06. This was not an SF 37, but rather an SH 37 used to test the SF 37 camera nose section. On the right hand fuselage attachment point, an MSK H (four BXE 103 flashes) can be seen, with an MSK V (containing three SKa 34 cameras and four BXE 103 flashes) on the left hand fuselage attachment point. As usual, a 1,400 l external fuel tank is fitted to the centre attachment point. The photo was taken on 31 August 1975. (Leif Fredin, via Archives of Mikael Forslund)

An MSK H (flash light pod) hung beneath an SF 37 during the F 15 Söderhamn 15 May 1993 air show. (Mikael Forslund)

An SKa 24C (OMERA Type 31-1) camera with a 120 mm 1:2,8 Matra lens as fitted to the front end of SF 37 s/n 37958, coded F 21-48. The photograph was taken during the F 21 Luleå 9 June 1991 air show. (Mikael Forslund)

SF 37 s/n 37958, coded F 21-48, with the nose camera hatches open during the F 21 Luleå 9 June 1991 air show. (Mikael Forslund)

A close-up of the nose of SF 37 s/n 37965, coded F 21-54, during the F 21 9 June 1991 air show. Note the air show badge on the nose. (Mikael Forslund)

Behind this camera a vertical camera was located, an *SKa 24C: 24C/57 MT* = 57 mm 1:2.8. (Other characteristics similar to the above).

Behind the vertical camera, two *SKa 24C (24C/120 MT)* were located, obliquely to the right and to the left respectively.

Behind the oblique cameras, two OMERA *SKa 31* high altitude/distance cameras were located. 600 mm lens, with a large diaphragm of 1:5.6. Shutter times 1/200–1/600 seconds. Negative format 23 x 23 cm. The photos from the "wide angle" *SKa 24C*, with a 57 mm focal distance, was used together with the *SKa 31* photos for photographic target orientation.

SF 37 Viggen s/n 37951, coded F 13-02, taking off sometime in the early 1980s. An MSK H (containing four BXE 103 flashes) is fitted to the right fuselage attachment point, with an MSK V (containing three SKa 34 cameras and four BXE 103 flashes) occupying the left fuselage attachment point. As was normal, the 1,400 litre external fuel tank is fitted to the centre fuselage attachment point. (Via Archives of Peter Kempe/ Mikael Forslund)

A vertical IR-camera, *VKa 702* (*Värmekamera 702* = Heat Camera 702), was located in the nose section. The camera had a 800–1,400 nanometer measuring range.

Similar to the SH 37, a night reconnaissance pod (*MSK*), previously used on the Saab S 35E *Draken*, could be carried on the left pylon. The pod contained three Vinten *SKa 34* cameras, with a 75 mm focus lens (Leitz lenses). The shutter time was 1/500 sec. The cameras (equipped with *BIRK*), were mounted obliquely to the right, to the left and vertically. As a result, the cameras covered a 120 degree view angle. The *MSK* also contained flash gear for the infrared spectrum. An infrared film, 5.6 x 5.7 cm, was used. A flash lightning pod could be necessary for certain sorties. This was carried on the right-hand fuselage pylon. Night photography up to altitudes of 300 m was possible.

The SF 37 could carry two *RB 24B* or *RB 24J* (Sidewinder) missiles. As the SF 37 lacked radar, the missiles could only be fired following visual contact with the "enemy aircraft".

The SF 37 was used to obtain photographic documentation of the enemy's activities. This involved long approaches at low altitude, often while maintaining radio silence. Flying at tree-top height was necessary to avoid enemy radar. During the photo run, slightly below supersonic speed (the fuel consumption was 900 l/min), the pilot used a tape recorder to record information.

The SF 37s flew numerous sorties, the most famous being the U-137 submarine (please refer to the SH 37 chapter).

Wings operating the SF 37 included F 13, F 15, F 17 and F 21.

SF 37 Technical Data and Performance Characteristics

Crew:	One
Quantity built:	28 (s/ns 37950–37977)
Length:	16.30 m
Wingspan:	10.60 m
Height:	5.60 m (4.0 m with fin folded)
Wing area:	52.20 m² (main wing 46.00 m²)
Wheel base:	5.54 m
Fuel load:	5,525 l + one external fuel tank containing an additional 1,400 l
Empty weight:	11,800 kg
Maximum take-off weight:	20,450 kg
Engine:	*RM 8A*, license built Pratt & Whitney JT8D
Thrust.	6,690 kp without afterburner, 11,790 kp with afterburner
Take-off run:	400 m
Landing run:	500 m
Max speed:	Mach 2
Service ceiling:	18,300 m
Armament:	*RB 24B*, *RB 24J* (Sidewinder)

SF 37 s/n 37952, coded F 13-04 performing a low altitude sortie sometime during the early 1980s. Beginning on 15 August 1996, this SF 37 was modified to AJSF 37 status. (Owe Fredin)

Type	S/n	Code/s	Taken on charge (ToC)	Struck off charge (SoC)	Remarks	Hrs flown
SF 37 AJSF 37	37950	-95, -37 F 13-55, -10 F 10-10 F 21-48			Rebuilt from 37033. Modified 11 Feb 1997 as AJSF 37. Last flight 8 Dec 2005. Scrapped. Front fuselage currently (2022) preserved at Teknikland, Optand, Sweden	
SF 37 AJSF 37	37951	F 13-02 F 15-82 F 21-50	17 Aug 1977		Modified 9 Jun 1995 as AJSF 37. Last flight 7 Sep 2004. Currently (2022) preserved at Kosice, Slovakia	
SF 37 AJSF 37	37952	F 13-04 F 15-84 F 21-56, -52	17 Aug 1977		Modified 15 Aug 1996 as AJSF 37. Last flight 4 Nov 2003. Scrapped	
SF 37	37953	F 13-06 F 15-86	17 Aug 1977	11 Nov 1997	Last flight 29 Apr 1997. Scrapped	2,008 h 26 min
SF 37 AJSF 37	37954	F 13-08 F 17-68 F 7-30 F 10-70 F 21-30, -52, -54	17 Oct 1977		Modified 18 Oct 1996 as AJSF 37. Last flight 29 Nov 2005. Currently (2022) preserved at Cracow, Poland	
SF 37 AJSF 37	37955	F 13-10 F 17-66 F 10-66		12 May 1999	Modified 4 Jun 1997 as AJSF 37. Last flight 13 Oct 1998. Scrapped	1,998 h 44 min
SF 37	37956	F 17-64 F 15-74 F 7-	12 May 1978	12 May 1999	Last flight 17 Apr 1997. Scrapped	1,915 h 35 min
SF 37 AJSF 37	37957	F 17-52 F 21-20, -46, -58, -56 F 7-	6 Jun 1978		Modified 24 Oct 1996 as AJSF 37. Last flight 25 Apr 2005. Currently (2022) preserved at VHU, Kbely, Czech Republic	
SF 37 AJSF 37	37958	F 21-18, -48, -58 F 7-34 F 17- F 10-34	22 Sep 1978		Modified 5 Sep 1996 as AJSF 37. Last flight 24 Nov 2004. Scrapped	
SF 37	37959	F 21-50	23 Nov 1978		W/o 29 Aug 1981 40 km SSE Luleå, Sweden. Pilot ejected	322 h 20 min
SF 37 AJSF 37	37960	F 13-14 F 21-52, -60 F 10-52	27 Apr 1979		Modified 12 Sep 1996 as AJSF 37. Last flight 22 Apr 2004. Scrapped	
SF 37 AJSF 37	37961	F 13-12 F 21-53, -50	30 Jan 1979	30 Jun 1998	Modified 15 Oct 1996 as AJSF 37. Last flight 6 Mar 1998. Cockpit currently (2022) preserved at F 11 Museum, Skavsta, Sweden.	1,761 h 43 min
SF 37	37962	F 13-14, F 7-36	1 Mar 1979	12 May 1999	Last flight 17 Apr 1997. Scrapped	2,028 h 06 min
SF 37	37963	F 17-62 F 10-62 F 15-72	6 Mar 1979	17 Feb 1998	Last flight 10 Jun 1997. Scrapped	1,919 h 35 min

SF 37 s/n 37960 or 37962, coded F 13-14, in the F 15 Söderhamn workshop during the 15 June 1993 air show. An SK 37 sits in the background.
(Mikael Forslund)

Type	S/n	Code/s	Taken on charge (ToC)	Struck off charge (SoC)	Remarks	Hrs flown
SF 37	37964	F 17-60 F 15-70 F 10-70	20 Feb 1979	6 Mar 1998	Last flight 7 Aug 1997. Scrapped	1,963 h 11 min
SF 37 AJSF 37	37965	F 21-54	28 Mar 1979	8 Feb 1999	Modified 15 Dec 1995 as AJSF 37. Last flight 5 Nov 1998. Scrapped	2,038 h 28 min
SF 37	37966	F 21-56	25 Apr 1979	12 May 1999	Last flight 22 May 1997. Scrapped	1,771 h 53 min
SF 37	37967	F 21-58	22 May 1979	12 May 1999	Last flight 22 May 1997. Scrapped	2,082 h 15 min
SF 37	37968	F 13-16 F 21-67, -60 F 15-76	8 Jun 1979	12 May 1999	Last flight 14 May 1997. Scrapped	2,156 h 24 min
SF 37	37969	F 13-18	20 Aug 1979		W/o 29 Aug 1985 at Vingåker, Sweden. Pilot ejected	797 h 40 min
SF 37	37970	F 13-20	27 Jun 1979		W/o 29 Aug 1985 at Vingåker, Sweden. Pilot ejected	652 h 38 min
SF 37 AJSF 37	37971	F 17-58 F 15-78 F 21-62	8 Sep 1979		Modified 10 Apr 1997 as AJSF 37. Last flight 23 Nov 2005. Currently (2022) preserved at Zoppola, Italy	
SF 37	37972	F 17-56 F 10-56	26 Oct 1979	11 Nov 1997	Last flight 4 Sep 1997. Currently (2022) preserved at Gotlands Försvarsmuseum, Tingstäde, Sweden	1,969 h 01 min
SF 37	37973	F 17-54, F 7- F 15-54, 72, -74	23 Oct 1979	12 May 1999	Last flight 30 Jun 1997. Scrapped	1,748 h 20 min
SF 37 AJSF 37	37974	F 21-62, -64 F 7-66	1 Feb 1980		Modified 11 Dec 1996 as AJSF 37. Last flight 16 Jan 2006. Currently (2022) preserved at Hermeskeil, Germany	
SF 37	37975	F 21-64	16 Jan 1980	12 May 1999	Last flight 2 Jul 1997. Scrapped	1,964 h 17 min
SF 37 AJSF 37	37976	F 21-66 F 7-38 F 10-38	1 Feb 1980		Modified 12 May 1997 as AJSF 37. Last flight 6 Apr 2005. Currently (2022) preserved at Ängelholms Flygmuseum, Ängelholm, Sweden	
SF 37	37977	F 21-68 F 15-	8 Feb 1980	24 Feb 2000	Last flight 17 Mar 1999. Currently (2022) preserved at Flygmuseet F 21, Luleå, Sweden	2,082 h 01 min

SF 37 s/n 37969, coded F 13-18, seen during a photo reconnaissance sortie during the early 1980s. The F 13 Wing badge appears on both sides of the fin. The aircraft was lost on 29 August 1985. (Owe Fredin)

Saab SF 37 Viggen s/n 37950, coded Red 10 of F 13 Norrköping, seen at F 17 11 June 1994. The upper surfaces are camouflaged in svart (Black) 093M (FS 37038), ljusgrön (Light Green) 322M (FS 34082), mörkgrön (Dark Green) 326M (FS 34079) and brun (Brown) 507M (FS 30117), with the lower surfaces being blågrå (Blue Grey) 058M (FS 35237).

Saab SF 37 s/n 37950, coded F 13-10, photographed at F 17 11 June 1994 during an Air Show. Note the F 13 badge on the fin. RB 24B Sidewinder on fuselage attachment point. An MSK V (containing three SKa 34 cameras and four BXE 103 flashes) on the left hand wing attachment point. (Mikael Forslund)

Saab SF 37 Viggen s/n 37969, coded Red 18 of F 13 Norrköping, seen at its home base sometime in the early 1980s. The upper surfaces are camouflaged in svart (Black) 093M (FS 34031), ljusgrön (Light Green) 322M (FS 34138), mörkgrön (Dark Green) 326M (FS 34092) and brun (Brown) 507M (FS 30117), with the lower surfaces being blågrå (Blue Grey) 058M (FS 36314).

Saab SF 37 s/n 37969, coded F 13-18, photographed during an operation sortie during the early 1980s. Note the F 13 badge on the fin. (Owe Fredin)

Saab SF 37 Viggen s/n 37964, coded Red 60 of F 17 Kallinge, seen at its home base during the early 1980s. The upper surfaces are camouflaged in svart (Black) 093M (FS 34031), ljusgrön (Light Green) 322M (FS 34138), mörkgrön (Dark Green) 326M (FS 34092) and brun (Brown) 507M (FS 30117), with the lower surfaces being blågrå (Blue Grey) 058M (FS 36314).

Preparing SF 37 s/n 37964, coded F 17-60, for another sortie during the early 1980s. (Sven Stridsberg, via Archives of Peter Kempe/Mikael Forslund)

Saab SF 37 Viggen s/n 37974, coded Red 62 of F 21, photographed at its home base in the mid-1980s. The upper surfaces are camouflaged in svart (Black) 093M (FS 34031), ljusgrön (Light Green) 322M (FS 34138), mörkgrön (Dark Green) 326M (FS 34092) and brun (Brown) 507M (FS 30117), with the lower surfaces being blågrå (Blue Grey) 058M (FS 36314).

SF 37 s/n 37974, coded F 21-62, photographed at F 21 in the mid-1980s. Unusually, the external fuel tank is not fitted. The tail section of SF 37 s/n 37958, code F 21-48, can be seen in the background. (Via Archives of Peter Kempe/Mikael Forslund).

Saab SF 37 Viggen s/n 37965, coded Red 54 of F 21 Luleå, seen in 1987. The upper surfaces are camouflaged in svart (Black) 093M (FS 34031), ljusgrön (Light Green) 322M (FS 34138), mörkgrön (Dark Green) 326M (FS 34092) and brun (Brown) 507M (FS 30117), with the lower surfaces being blågrå (Blue Grey) 058M (FS 36314).

Saab SF 37 s/n 37965, coded F 21-54, photographed autumn 1987 (Christmas card). Note the 1st Squadron F 21 badge on the fin, the Bright Red (FS 28905) Wing nr 21 (instead of Yellow) and the Wolf's head (Grey FS 36463, Black FS 37038, Bright Red FS 28905 and White (FS 37925), emblem on the nose. (Via Archives of Swedish Aviation Historical Society)

Saab SF 37 Viggen s/n 37967, coded Red 58 of F 21 Luleå, seen 24 September 1996. The upper surfaces are camouflaged in svart (Black) 093M (FS 34031), ljusgrön (Light Green) 322M (FS 34138), mörkgrön (Dark Green) 326M (FS 34092) and brun (Brown) 507M (FS 30117), with the lower surfaces being blågrå (Blue Grey) 058M (FS 36314).

Saab SF 37 Viggen s/n 37967, coded F 21-58, photographed 24 September 1996 at F 21 Luleå. 1st Squadron F 21 badge on fuselage behind the canopy, and the 9 June 1991 Air Show F 21 badge (F 21 50 years 1941–1991) still on top of the fin. (Leif Fredin, via Archives of Mikael Forslund)

Chapter 10
AJSF 37

Thirteen SF 37s (37950–37952, 37954, 37955, 37957, 37958, 37960, 37961, 37965, 37971, 37974 och 37976) were modified as AJSF 37s, being able to carry *RB 24B*, *RB 24J* and *RB 74* Sidewinder missiles. Lacking radar, the pilot would have to establish visual contact with the target before firing the missiles. Despite having the A (Attack) type designator, no air-to-ground or anti-shipping weaponry was carried by the AJSF 37s.

SWAFRAP

Saab AJSF 37 Viggen *s/n 37952, coded F 21-52, in the workshop of F 21 in 2000. The aircraft was part of SWAFRAP, hence the English language texts. Previously, it had been finished in the classic splinter camouflage before being repainted in Light Ghost Grey (FS 36375) and Light Grey (FS 36495). (Rune Lundberg, via Archives of Mikael Forslund)*

Following a request from the United Nations and NATO, *Flygvapnet* formed a special unit, designated SWAFRAP (Swedish Air Force Rapid Reaction Unit), on 1 January 2001. AJSF 37 *Viggens* of Wing F 21 formed the photo reconnaissance establishment of SWAFRAP. In case of an emergency on the European continent, SWAFRAP would be ready for action within 30 days. The unit would be self-sufficient, having six AJSF 37 *Viggens*, 250 personnel and the support equipment necessary. Handling the film would be performed in three specially-built containers flown to the area by TP 84 (Lockheed Hercules) transports. The Swedish photo interpreters were trained in Great Britain, being introduced to NATO's working methods. In Sweden, photos taken from extreme low altitude were interpreted, but the training here involved interpreting photos taken from high altitude. The pilots had to wear metric vs feet and km/h vs knot conversion tables in their knee pad pockets. This was due to the fact that the AJSF 37s were fitted with metric-scale instruments, with NATO using feet and knots as standard in their aircraft.

High-altitude photography over the conflict area was to be made from an altitude of 3,000 m in order to avoid anti-aircraft fire. All sorties were to be performed using two aircraft. One aircraft was to descend to 1,500 m while the second aircraft maintained an altitude of 3,000 m, checking and defending the area. Realistic exercises using the AJSF 37s were flown in the confined airspace over Germany and Hungary. Differences in training methods between Sweden and NATO became apparent. The pilots underwent, for instance, escape and evasion training in order to avoid being caught after ejecting over enemy territory.

In 2000, SWAFRAP trained for 17 days in Sweden.

AJSF 37 Viggen s/n 37957, coded F 21-56, was statically displayed at the F 16 Uppsala 26 August 2001 air show. All of the camera hatches in the nose are open. The bump with the "window" beneath the 21 Wing numeral contain the camera sight. S/n 37957 was part of SWAFRAP, which meant that some of the texts on the aircraft appeared in English. Beginning on 24 October 1996, this SF 37 was modified to AJSF 37 status. At the time of writing (2022), the aircraft is on display with the Letecké Muzeum, Praha-Kbely, Czech Republic. (Mikael Forslund)

SWAFRAP also participated in the huge Strong Resolve exercise, held in Poland in March 2002. Six AJSF 37s deployed to Powidz, supported by 116 ground personnel. The Swedish organisation was extensive. Equipment, including 34 vehicles and 28 containers, were sent by railway in 25 freight carriages. Three lorries, three TP 84 Hercules and an S 100B (Saab 340) was used for cargo and personnel transports. A total of 20,000 personnel from 23 nations participated in Strong Resolve.

The AJSF 37s of SWAFRAP were finished in a two-tone Grey camouflage scheme (same as the JA 37, Light Ghost Grey (FS 36375) and Light Grey (FS 36495), with the national insignia, numerals and the text DANGER in Low-Viz Dark Grey (FS 36176). The text DANGER appeared in front of the air intakes.

During 2004, JAS 39 *Gripens* replaced the SWAF-RAP *Viggens*.

The Wings using the AJSF 37 were F 7, F 10, F 15, F 17 and F 21.

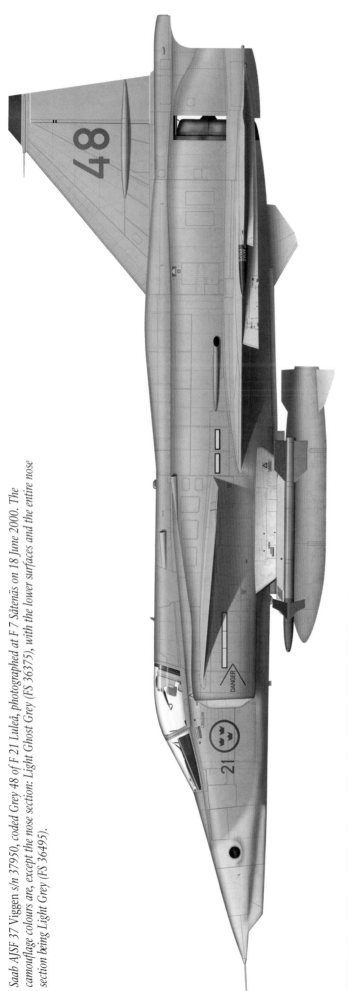

Saab AJSF 37 Viggen s/n 37950, coded Grey 48 of F 21 Luleå, photographed at F 7 Såtenäs on 18 June 2000. The camouflage colours are, except the nose section: Light Ghost Grey (FS 36375), with the lower surfaces and the entire nose section being Light Grey (FS 36495).

AJSF 37 s/n 37950, coded F 21-48, on display at the F 7 Såtenäs 18 June 2000 air show. Two RB 74 Sidewinders are mounted on the fuselage attachment points. On the left wing attachment point, a KB flare and chaff dispenser can be seen. The aircraft was part of SWAFRAP, thus having some texts in English. (Mikael Forslund)

Saab AJSF 37 Viggen s/n 37957, coded Grey 56 of F 21 Luleå, photographed at the F 16 Uppsala 26 August 2001 air show. The camouflage colours are, except the nose section: Light Ghost Grey (FS 36375), with the lower surfaces and the entire nose section being Light Grey (FS 36495).

AJSF 37 s/n 37957, coded F 21-56, on display at the F 16 Uppsala 26 August 2001 air show. An U 22 ECM pod (previously designated KA) can be seen below the right wing. (Mikael Forslund)

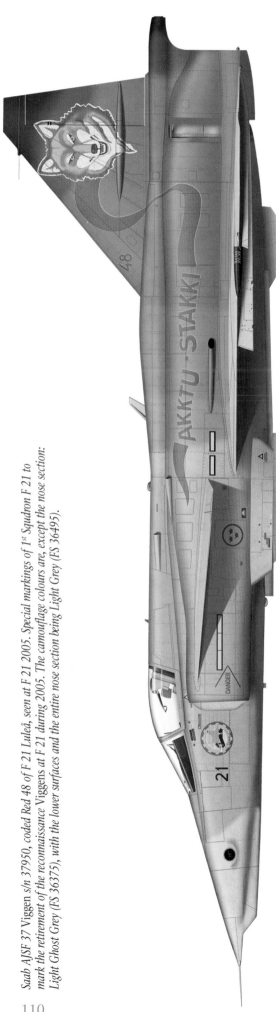

Saab AJSF 37 Viggen s/n 37950, coded Red 48 of F 21 Luleå, seen at F 21 2005. Special markings of 1ˢᵗ Squdron F 21 to mark the retirement of the reconnaissance Viggens at F 21 during 2005. The camouflage colours are, except the nose section: Light Ghost Grey (FS 36375), with the lower surfaces and the entire nose section being Light Grey (FS 36495).

AJSF 37 s/n 37950, coded F 21-48, photographed at F 21 Luleå 2005. Special markings of 1ˢᵗ Squdron F 21 to mark the retirement of the reconnaissance Viggens at F 21 during 2005. The 37950 was earlier part of SWAFRAP, thus having some texts in English. Akktu Stakki (Lappish) means Lonesome Wolf. Text and 48 Bright Red FS 28905. 1ˢᵗ Squadron badge (Wolf) on both sides of the fin/rudder. On the nose (both sides) are the badge of 1ˢᵗ FU-kompani/F 21 (technical) and the Wing nr 21 in Black FS 37038. Observe the Crown Mark under the canard wing. At least four shades of Blue on the tail and upper side of the wing: FS 35550, FS 35526, FS 35250 and FS 35183. (Jan Jørgensen)

Saab AJSF 37 Viggen s/n 37950, coded Red 48 of F 21 Luleå, seen at F 21 2005. Special markings of 1st Squadron F 21 to mark the retirement of the reconnaissance Viggens at F 21 during 2005.

Chapter 11
JA 37

The AJ 37 was developed into the SF 37 (photographic reconnaissance) and SH 37 (maritime reconnaissance) variants. The JA 37 dedicated fighter variant had the more powerful *RM 8B* engine, stronger wing, new electronics systems and a fixed 30 mm Oerlikon cannon. The cannon had such powerful recoil that a pressure wave indicator was introduced. The cannon's impact ratio was so precise that after a while its suspension was changed somewhat, so that when firing the projectiles (22 per second) struck a larger area. The 30 mm grenades/projectiles were loaded in a magazine behind the cannon. When reloading on the ground, the rear section of the magazine could be folded downwards via a simple procedure.

A Head-up Display (HUD) was fitted, rendering it unnecessary for the pilot to look down to the instrument panel, as important data was presented at eye level on a transparent display.

Due to the location of the Oerlikon, the fin (similar to that on the SK 37) was enlarged. To obtain experience with the manufacture of fins built from composite materials intended for the future Saab JAS 39 *Gripen*, twenty JA 37 composite fins were manufactured. The first such fin was fitted to s/n 37301. The fin weighed more than its metal counterpart, but during the subsequent series production, the composite fin's weight was reduced by 15 percent when compared to the metal fin. The first JA 37 to have a series-production composite fin was s/n 37412, with all such fins being fitted to *Viggens*.

With the *RM 8B* engine being seven cm longer than its predecessor, the fuselage was lengthened. The front fuselage was also tilted one degree downwards, which enhanced the flight characteristics at high speeds. The flap of the canard wing had one flight mode instead of two for the earlier variants. Another maneuvering cylinder (three against the earlier two) was fitted for elevator control. The overall length of the JA 37 was 13 cm longer than that of the AJ 37. Additionally, the air intakes were reshaped. A small VHF-antenna was fitted behind the fin.

A total of 149 JA 37 *Viggens* were ordered in three batches (30, 60, 59) between 1975 and 1980. As mentioned previously, the JA 37 prototype first flew on 15 December 1975. Several aircraft were used as trials aircraft for the JA 37 series (please refer to earlier chapters). Following the loss on 22 August 1978 of the first production JA 37, it was replaced by s/n 37301.

JA 37 Viggen *coded F 13-39 (s/n unknown). As usual, the external 1,400 l capacity fuel tank occupies the centre fuselage attachment point. Two RB 71* Sky Flash *missiles are mounted on the wing's inner attachment points, with a pair of RB 74* Sidewinders *occupying the outer wing attachment points. (Via* Flygvapnet)

The first JA 37 had made its first flight on 4 November 1977 with test pilot Gösta Sjöström at the controls. Marked as 301-50, s/n 37301 was retained by Saab as a test aircraft, later also being used by *FMV: Prov* (as *Försökscentralen*, *FC*, had been renamed). The second production JA 37, s/n 37302, was also utilized as a trials aircraft.

JA 37 Viggen *s/n 37343, coded F 4-43, landing back at F 4 Östersund on 15 June 1996. The aircraft is armed with RB 74* Sidewinders, RB 71 *Sky Flash and RB 24J* Sidewinders. Note the F 4 badge on the fin. (Mikael Forslund)

The JA 37 *Viggen* was fitted with a PS-46/A Pulse doppler radar developed by Ericsson. This radar had excellent capacity. One huge advantage was that it was insensitive to flare jamming. Through the doppler effect, the radar could discern a moving object from the static ground reflection. Radar lighting on an enemy target was low, meaning that the enemy did not react to the radar lightning, not activating its counter-measures.

The JA 37 radar warning device indicated radar signals through one or several of the four lamps on the instrument panel being turned on, with a sound signal simultaneously being heard in the pilot's headphones.

Compared with the earlier *Viggen* variants, the JA 37 featured a completely new computer which had five times higher capacity. The so-called fighter link made it possible for different JA 37s, in the air or on the ground, to obtain use of each other's radar information. This made it possible to approach a target with the radar turned off, being led through the radar emissions from another aeroplane. The radar was then turned on when within shooting range, which reduced the defensive abilities of the enemy aircraft. All flight and firing data was presented on two screens, *TI (Taktisk Indikator* = Tactical Indicator) or *MI (Målindikator* = Target Indicator). Additionally, the JA 37 pilot could obtain flight data through the sight indicator at eye level on the front screen.

The *MI* was located at the centre of the instrument panel. The indicator showed one's own radar image along with the enemy's echo, and the position of one's own aircraft.

Slightly above and to the right of the *MI*, the *TI* was located. The position of one's aircraft as well as other aircraft were presented on an electical chart. Other Swedish military aircraft appeared with an *IK (Igenkänningssignal* = Identification Signal) to prevent being shot down by one's own air and ground forces (this system was used by all military units).

The *SI (Siktlinjesindikator* = Sight Line indicator) was located at the top of the instrument panel. The Oerlikon cannon featured a radar sight.

Via a special radar panel, the pilot could place the target marker over a radar echo, and then by means of a control stick and by pushing a button lock the radar onto the echo, which was then tracked automatically.

The JA 37 also had a *UTB (databandspelare*, computer tape recorder). This registered all flight data, time, position and the radar images that had been built up in the computer. This meant that the flight could be reprised for analysis during the post-sortie briefing.

The fighter link was developed for the *Viggen*. The link was a system of communication between different aircraft, independent of weather and position. The aircraft could operate independently

JA 37 Viggen s/n 37387, coded F 4-57, under tow at F 15 Söderhamn on 2 June 1985. The aircraft has been painted in the two-tone Grey camouflage, which largely replaced the splinter camouflage for the JA 37 fleet: mörkgrå (Dark Grey) 033M (FS 36251), and grå (Grey) 032M (FS 36463) for the lower surfaces and the entire nose section. The aircraft was written off in a crash on 21 March 1986. (Mikael Forslund)

JA 37 s/n 37350, coded F 13-40, photographed prior to landing in the early 1980s. Note the F 13 badge on the fin. The aircraft is finished overall mörkgrå (Dark Grey) 033M (FS 36251). This particular colour scheme only appeared on two JA 37s for test purposes. (Leif Fredin, via Archives of Mikael Forslund)

of information provided by ground stations. Thanks to the fighter link, operational readiness could be maintained using only a few aircraft.

To assist the ground staff, the JA 37 had a tape recorder, known as *RUF* (Registration, Maintenance and Aviation Safety) fitted. The tape recorder registered some 200 parameters, including the condition of the aircraft, functionality of systems as well as some 450 logistic signals. The tape recorder was a great help during maintenance.

The fixed 30 mm Oerlikon cannon was mounted underneath the fuselage. Weighing 136 kg, it had a load capacity of 150 rounds, being able to fire 22 rounds per second. Various air-to-air missiles, including the *RB 24J* and *RB 74* Sidewinder, and *RB 71* Sky Flash, could be carried. For the secondary ground attack role, four rocket pods containing 24 135 mm rockets were carried. Later on, the *RB 99* (AMRAAM) was added to the already extensive armament options.

Various pods containing *ECM* and other counter measures were normally carried, including flares. The *U 95 ECM* pod was added later. There were nine under wing hardpoints on the JA 37.

The first JA 37 Wing was F 13 at Norrköping, with No.2 Sqn (known as *Martin Blå*, ie Martin Blue) being the first to relinquish its Saab J 35F *Drakens* for *Viggens*. The first *Viggen* (37309, F 13-49)

arrived on 24 June 1980. With the JA 37, the ability to intercept and turn away foreign aircraft violating Swedish airspace increased. The JA 37 had excellent supersonic characteristics with a much better range and weapons load than the earlier Saab J 35F *Draken*.

To build up experience in service and expose technical flaws, two different test series were initiated. Intensified service trials were undertaken at Saab, using s/n 37302, involving 401 flights (301 hrs) between 8 January 1979 to 20 December 1979. The second test series involved Pre-service flights, using JA 37s of F 13, s/ns 37309, 37310, 37316 and 37317, with s/ns 37306 and 37307 functioning as reserve aircraft. The Pre-service flights lasted from 11 August 1980 to 4 October 1983, which included accumulating more hours than usual with these aircraft in order to obtain information on fatigue issues. A total of 4,104 flights were made, accumulating 3,013 hours.

During these flights an engine problem was found in the third fan stage. In 1981, all *Viggens* were grounded between week 13 and week 44. The problem was solved by slightly cutting off the outer corners of the fan blades.

Between 26 October 1982 and 28 July 1988, there were 52 "QRA contacts" (Quick Reaction Alert) over the Baltic Sea between *Flygvapnet* fighters, J 35F (eight occasions), AJ 37 (one occasion) and JA 37 (43 occasions), and the USAF's Mach 3 SR-71 Blackbird. The first time was at 14.26 hrs on 26 October 1982, when a pair of JA 37s of No.2 Sqn/F 13 flown by Flight Master Technician Jan Angner (s/n 37309, code F 13-49) and Captain Ulf Johansson (s/n unknown). The target was flying at an altitude of 20,000 m with a speed of Mach 2.

JA 37 s/n 37365, coded F 16-12, taxiing at F 16 Uppsala 2002. (Tor Karlsson)

JA 37s at F 21 Luleå 9 June 1991. (Mikael Forslund)

The rear sections of JA 37s of F 17. The photo was taken on 11 June 1994. The JA 37 fleet was painted in Grey as well as the splinter camouflage. The Green cisterns contain aviation fuel. (Mikael Forslund)

Numerous JA 37s of F 16. Note the different fin colours, the Dark Grey (FS 36173) external fuel tank on code F 16-28, and the pair of splinter camouflaged JA 37s. (Tor Karlsson)

Despite radar jamming, the *Viggens* managed to achieve a radar lock-on. As a result, the *RB 71s* could have been fired (they weren't, though), resulting in the target being hit.

In most instances, a radar lock-on with the *RB 71* Sky Flash was achieved. Apart from the aforementioned SR-71 intercepts between 1982 and 1988, a large number of SR-71 contacts has occurred through the years!

The SR-71 usually entered the Baltic Sea at an altitude of 21,500 m some 80 km south of Copenhagen in Denmark. Following this, the speed rose to Mach 3. The flight plan called for flying between the Swedish island of Gotland and the Soviet-controlled Baltic states, up towards the Aaland islands and then turning south, flying over international waters between mainland Sweden and Gotland. Between 1977 and 1988, no fewer than 322 SR-71 flights were made over the Baltic Sea. In Sweden, this route was named "Baltic Express".

The ability to take-off quickly was made possible through the highly skilled JA 37 ground crews. Preparing a JA 37 for its next sortie lasted about ten minutes, being performed by a team of five conscript mechanics and a Chief Technician. Replenishing ammunition, including missiles, fuel, oxygen and oil, were made quickly and efficiently. Changing a wheel took six minutes, the radio five minutes, and the central computer seven minutes. Replacing the canopy could be made in 25 minutes. The Quick Reaction Alertness was often trained on road bases around Sweden. Apart from regular flight training, the JA 37 pilots would also hone their skills in *Viggen* simulators.

In 1994, F 13 disbanded, with their *Viggens* being transferred to No.2 Sqn/F 17 at Kallinge/ Ronneby, which operated a mix of SF 37 and SH 37s. These were subsequently handed over to No.1 Sqn/F 10 at Ängelholm. In the event, Wing F 17 continued to operate its JA 37s until the summer of 2002, when the first Saab JAS 39 *Gripens* began to arrive.

In 1985, F 21 at Luleå became an all-*Viggen* unit. No.1 Squadron had been operating SF 37 and SH 37s for some years, but in 1985 Nos.2 and 3 Squadrons re-equipped with JA 37s. In January 1999, the latter units were merged into one squadron. However, No.3 Squadron became a conversion training squadron, with a number of Austrian pilots learning to handle the *Viggen*. At the time, both Saab and *Flygvapnet* expected Austria to select the JA 37 *Viggen* as replacement for the ageing Saab 35OE *Drakens*. However, Austria chose to buy the Eurofighter Typhoon instead...

In August 1983, the Saab J 35Ds of F 4 at Östersund began to be replaced by JA 37 *Viggens*. In the event, both squadrons of F 4 received JA 37s. In July 1997, the *Viggen* conversion unit with their SK 37s was transferred from F 15 at Söderhamn to F 4. By the early 2000s, ten of the surviving two-seat *Viggens* had been modified as SK 37E ECM aircraft.

F 16 at Uppsala also had two JA 37 squadrons, with deliveries commencing in early 1986. The first two aircraft were transferred from F 13, with the others being delivered directly from Saab. In 1990, the last of 149 JA 37 *Viggens* were delivered, with the last one, s/n 37449, arriving at No.3 Sqn/F 16 on 29 June 1990.

The JA 37 was naturally a part of the QRA Operations. During the *Viggen* era, the QRA Operations continued every hour, year-round. A pair of *Viggens* (or J 35 *Drakens*) was part of the QRA Operations, also known as "*fisk*" (Fish). Armed with live ammunition, the aircraft were usually parked at the end of a runway at an air base in the south of Sweden. The AJ 37 was armed with cannon pods, while the other variants carried air-to-air missiles. The pilots remained close to their aircraft, or sat in the cockpit awaiting orders to scramble, something which happened up to 500 occasions each year! More often than not, the scramble involved identification. It never became necessary to fire during border violations, with the foreign intruder being turned away.

On 19 April 1988, the *Falu-Kuriren* newspaper published a story in its supplement *Kurren* about the Falun-born pilot, Captain Ulf Johansson, at the time a JA 37 pilot with F 13 at Norrköping:

"*With 2,500 hours at the helm, the 38-year old Captain Ulf Johansson from Falun, is safe behind the controls of his* Viggen. *By this time, his flying is so well practised that he by a wide margin can count himself among the cream of the crop of Swedish pilots. When Sweden invites a State visit, it is Ulf who will show King Hussein, Kaspar (sic) Weinberger and all the others what* Flygvapnet *is capable of. With a safe hand, Ulf takes his JA 37* Viggen *into an advanced looping at extreme low level, and the next second drills himself toward the ground.*

Everyday life is of course different. At Bråvalla Wing (F 13), a few km west of Norrköping, working as a pilot in a fighter squadron also becomes routine. The paper work must continue even where the flying duties are planned in detail and new pilots trained. Work-related injuries exist, as they do for

JA 37 s/n 37333, coded F 17-33. The photo was taken at F 17 in May 1983. The aircraft is largely unpainted, apart from the nose section, which was originally fitted to a splinter camouflaged AJ 37. The external fuel tank is Dark Grey (FS 36173). (Sven Stridsberg, via Archives of Swedish Aviaytion Historical Society)

clerks or the assembly line worker. Here, gravity is the scourge. The neck, spine and bottom withstand much strain during each sortie, about two every day. When the aircraft is airborne, the body is pressed down in the seat with a weight of about 500 kg for a man who weighs 75 kg. Just the load on the neck can be up to 50 kg. In order to handle the strain in the air, the pilot has an overall (G-Suit) which is filled with air to dampen the pressure against the body so that the blood will continue to circulate.

The pilot, Captain Ulf Johansson, in front of an JA 37 of F 13 at Norrköping on 19 April 1988. (Mikael Forslund)

The pilot, Captain Ulf Johansson, on an JA 37 of F 13 at Norrköping on 19 April 1988. (Mikael Forslund)

It is vital that the blood supply to the head works, as every moment of the flight must be as precise as possible, demanding a skilled pilot.

The physical demands are the main reason why women are still banned from working as *Flyg-vapnet* pilots. At least according to the male pilots at F 13.

"*It is also for economic reasons*", says Ulf.

"*If a woman chooses to become a pilot, it will cost nearly ten million kronor to train her. If she then chooses to have kids, it means that she can not fly during the entire pregnancy, as we today do not know if the foetus can withstand the strain. Her active flying career does not correspond to the cost that* Flygvapnet *has paid for her training. It's not about gender discrimination or narrow-minded officers who thinks that women should stay at home. Of course, women are welcome everywhere else in the armed forces! Paternity leave for the pilots is not a problem in* Flygvapnet. *So far, the pilots have elected to remain at home for short spells only.*"

For the *Flygvapnet* pilot, there is military everyday life. This can include slightly less-than pleasant experiences, such as mysterious visits by Polish painting salesmen, as well as others who for different reasons are interested in getting to know where and how the pilots live.

"*We are, of course, of great interest to a foreign power which has an interest in Sweden.*

In case of war, pilots are important, which is why we are under surveillance", says Ulf as if it is the most natural thing in the world to look over one's shoulder all of the time to see if someone is following you or is showing an excessive interest. To cure this inquisitiveness the pilots avoid being photographed where their name is noted. They are not listed in the phone directory, also being careful against home visits by unknown people.*"

The pilot must know his AJ 37 *Viggen* work tool inside and out. The more than 16 m long, 10 m wide and almost 20 ton aircraft carries a fair amount of advanced technology. The cockpit is cluttered to the brim with all imaginable kinds of button designs, gauges and clocks which all fill important functions. The pilot has to handle all of these instruments perfectly, even in his sleep.

The possibilities to move in the cockpit are limited, and the maximum height of the pilot is about 190 cm. During the summer, the cockpit can be compared to a pressure cooker, according to Ulf. Carrying a summer overall, which is sufficient for staying alive in zero-degree water for a couple of hours, knee-high military boots as well as helmet and face mask, things can easily become unbearable. Exaggerating slightly, Ulf claims that a *Viggen* pilot knows every nut and bolt of his aircraft. Although not entirely true, the pilot must nevertheless be knowledgeable of the aircraft's construction. Before take-off, a technician checks that everything is ok. but the pilot as well makes a pre-flight check to ensure that everything is as it should be. An open hatch or poor wheel can mean that life hangs in the balance.

Security is of immense importance, and each year the pilots fly at least 20 hours in simulators. Each year, about two percent of the *Viggen* pilots are killed in accidents. Good physical health and

JA 37 s/n 37433, coded F 16-33, photographed at Västerås (Hässlö) on 17 June 1990. Note that the nose section has been exchanged (the camouflage colours). The aircraft is armed with RB 74 Sidewinders, RB 71 Sky Flash and RB 24J Sidewinders. (Mikael Forslund)

ability to react is of the utmost importance to handle the work. The age of retirement is low, and most quit when they have reached the age of 40.

"*It is important that the pilot sees the danger before it has arrived*", says Ulf.

"*We are trained to have a cool reaction in emergencies, but the thing is to react in the correct manner as well.*"

For many years, Ulf retained the title of Swedish model helicopter Champion. This year, however, he has lost this title. Flying model helicopters takes up all the spare time available after work and display flying. Within the next couple of years, it seems likely that Ulf will fly helicopters for a living. As the age of retirement is so low, it is time to find an alternative.

"*I will not settle down behind a desk after I've retired as a pilot. Hopefully, I will secure an assignment as a* Flygvapnet *helicopter pilot, as I'll have difficulty considering anything else*", says Ulf.

The JA 37 sorties at No.2 Sqn/F 13, which was the first unit to receive the JA 37, began in the early 1980s. On average, there were three daily sorties flown by every pilot. Ulf Johansson's fellow flight training school cadet, Thorbjörn Engback (b. 1951) was one of the other JA 37 pilots:

"*My pilot training began in 1970 at F 5 Ljungbyhed, where I flew the Sk 50 and SK 60. We were later to select to proceed either to flying the* Draken *or the Lansen. I began flying* Draken *at F 16 Uppsala's TIS-35 using the Sk 35C. In 1972, I was transferred to F 13, flying the J 35F until the first JA 37 Viggens arrived in 1980. Four SK 37s from F 15 were seconded to F 13 for conversion training. I managed to fly two sorties before the JA 37s were grounded. This lasted between the weeks 13 to 44 in 1981. The problem was the source of the problem. When the aircraft remained on the ground, much simulator flying ensued. When the grounding order was rescinded, there was one further SK 37 flight before it was time to go solo on the JA 37. Compared with the J 35F, it was a fantastic aircraft. The cockpit was very well thought-out. Roomy, light with the instruments being fitted in a logical manner.* With the J 35F Draken, Saab had not devoted the same amount of thought. A dark cockpit with some of the instruments located in a haphazard way. The thrust reverse when landing the JA 37 was a fantastic experience, what a braking effect! Landing at 800 m runways was no problem.*

With the introduction of the JA 37, we got longer endurance. Almost twice as long as with the J 35F. During the Quick Reaction Alert sorties using the J 35F, we could have 30 min at our disposal, and with the JA 37 about 50 min. There were numerous sorties, as were the intercepts of aircraft from NATO and the Warsaw Pact. West German F-4 Phantom IIs and Soviet MiG-29s were common. I did not encounter any serious incidents. We always flew with our radar turned on so that the 'adversary' wouldn't be surprised. If we had our radar turned on, we were 'visible'. During eye contact with NATO aircraft we looked at each other from a very close distance, making a few light turns. Our eastern

A pair of JA 37s, coded F 21-13 and F 21-09, tumbling around in the skies. Note the White (FS 27925) surfaces on the rear part the wings. This was a temporary exercise marking. (Via Archives of Mikael Forslund)

counterparts were more strict. They often disappeared from view when we got closer. I remember once when a Flygvapnet *TP 85 Caravelle was close to being courted by Soviet MiG-29s. The radar control officer had noted the MiG-29s heading towards the TP 85 at high altitude. Me and my fellow pilot received orders to scramble, taking off from F 13 at full throttle. We almost reached the* Caravelle *at the same time as the MiG-29s. I had a speed of Mach 1.78. As we got closer, the MiG-29s turned away.*

Encountering the USAF's SR-71 Blackbird over the Baltic Sea at heights over 20,000 m was exciting. We could not reach that high with the JA 37. The service ceiling is 16,000 m, but I have once reached 17,800 m. On about ten occasions, I've been ordered to intercept the SR-71. For a few minutes, things went at a fast pace to achieve a lock-on using the JA 37 radar onto the high-flying SR-71. If it had been serious, which it never was, I'd just have had to fire off an RB 71 Sky Flash *towards the target. The missile was then guided semi-actively by the aircraft's radar, being able to find the target. These proved to be interesting exercises for us. During the 1980s and 1990s, many* Flygvapnet *fighter pilots (more than has previously been revealed in printed sources, prior to 2020), had radar and visual contact with SR-71s while flying J 35Fs, AJ 37s and JA 37s.*

I flew the JA 37 until 1992, when I had accumulated 1,007 hours on the Viggen. *I then began flying TP 84 Hercules transports at F 7. I've written about this in two previously released books. At the time of writing (2020), my autobiography* 'Mitt flygande liv' *(My Flying Life) is almost ready for publication."*

Through the years, the JA 37 underwent a large number of modifications. Among these was a ground collision warning system *(MKV = Markvarning)*, introduced in 1986. The *MKV* warned the pilot if there was a risk of a ground collision. The *MKV* evoked mixed feelings... However, through the years, some five pilots have with the help of *MKV* survived potential accidents!

In 1991, some of the hardware was modified as "*Modpaket C*" (Modification package C). This included the *ED 30*, which contained additional target presentation information from ground control. The radar control commander was now able to point out five different targets. Chaff and flare dispensers were introduced, which was a standard feature on earlier *Viggen* variants.

As the air brakes were ineffectual, they were removed. It was more effective to reduce engine rpm and increase the angle of attack.

The aiming calculation for long range firing using attack rockets similar to the AJ 37 was introduced.

JA 37 Viggen s/n 37357, coded F 4-57, landing with the thrust reverse activated at Værnes/ Trondheim, Norway, on 16 May 1996. (Mikael Forslund)

Type	S/n	Code/s	Taken on charge (ToC)	Struck off charge (SoC)	Remarks	Hrs flown
JA 37	37301	-50, 301 FC-01	25 Oct 1977	30 Jun 2000	Trials. Last flight 6 Apr 2000. To Flygvapenmuseum, Linköping, Sweden, in 2000. Currently (2022) preserved at Flygvapenmuseum, Linköping, Sweden	1,166 h 58 min
JA 37	37302	F 13-39, -42, 02 F 21- F 17-02	8 Jan 1978	3 Jun 1999	Last flight 18 Feb 1999. Scrapped	1,748 h 20 min
JA 37	37303	-03, FC-03 F 17-03	16 Mar 1979	24 Jan 2000	Last flight 1 Jun 1999. Scrapped	1,738 h 46 min
JA 37	37304	F 13-34, -44 F 17-04, -01 F 21-04, -01	26 Oct 1979	15 Mar 2001	Last flight 9 Aug 2000. To Wing F 17 for fire and rescue exercises	1,632 h 57 min
JA 37	37305	F 13-45 F 17-05 F 4-	28 Nov 1979	31 Jul 2003	Last flight 27 Jun 2002. Cockpit to Volvo Museum, Gothenburg, Sweden	1,725 h 44 min
JA 37	37306	F 13-46, -39 F 21-02	11 Feb 1980	24 Jan 2000	Last flight 21 Jun 1999. Scrapped	1,702 h 17 min
JA 37	37307	F 13-47 F 17-07 F 4-07	10 Mar 1980	5 Jun 2000	Last flight 16 Dec 1999. To Wing F 4 for fire and rescue exercises. Front fuselage preserved (2022) at Teknikland, Optand, Sweden	1,618 h 37 min
JA 37	37308	F 13-48 FC-48, -38 F 21-48	30 Aug 1979	24 Jan 2000	Last flight 11 Aug 1999. Scrapped	1,731 h 41 min
JA 37	37309	F 13-49 F 17-09	24 Apr 1980		Last flight 2 Oct 1992. To FFV Arboga, Sweden, for aerials trials	1,686 h 02 min
JA 37	37310	F 13-50 F 4-10	12 Jun 1980	1 Jul 1996	Last flight 5 Sep 1995. Cockpit to Saab, with remainder to Flygvapnets Halmstadsskolor, Halmstad, Sweden, as ground instructional airframe	1,748 h 31 min
JA 37	37311	F 13-51 F 21-51, -03	19 May 1980	30 Jun 2000	Last flight 9 Mar 2000. Scrapped	1,596 h 25 min
JA 37	37312	F 13-52 F 17-12	26 Jun 1980		W/o 15 Jan 1985 six km NW Wing F 17, Sweden. Pilot ejected	403 h 43 min

JA 37 Viggen s/n 37432, coded F 16-32, taxiing out for take-off from Highway 70 at Rommehed on 18 August 1992. The aircraft is armed with one RB 71 Sky Flash and three RB 74 Sidewinders (dummy missiles are painted Green). (Mikael Forslund)

Type	S/n	Code/s	Taken on charge (ToC)	Struck off charge (SoC)	Remarks	Hrs flown
JA 37	37313	F 13-53 F 16-53	27 Jun 1980	27 Nov 2001	Last flight 14 Jun 2000. Scrapped	1,688 h 34 min
JA 37	37314	F 13-54 F 16-54	29 Aug 1980		W/o 24 Jan 1991 S Fagersta, Sweden. Pilot ejected	784 h 22 min
JA 37	37315	F 13-55 F 21-15 F 4-15 F 16-55	27 Oct 1980	30 Jun 2000	Last flight 7 Apr 2000. To Flygvapnets Halmstadsskolor, Halmstad, Sweden, as ground instructional airframe	1,605 h 02 min
JA 37	37316	F 13-56 F 17-16, -56	2 Dec 1980	29 Jan 2003	Last flight 23 May 2002. Scrapped	2,673 h 56 min
JA 37	37317	F 13-57 F 21-06	12 Dec 1980	28 Nov 2001	Last flight 23 Aug 2000. Scrapped	2,163 h 29 min
JA 37	37318	F 13-58 F 16-58	16 Dec 1980	28 Feb 2002	Last flight 19 Oct 2001. Scrapped	2,152 h 58 min
JA 37	37319	F 13-59 F 16-59	21 Jan 1981	8 Nov 2002	Last flight 8 May 2002. To Fyrisskolan, Uppsala, Sweden, as ground instructional airframe	2,446 h 19 min
JA 37	37320	F 13-60- F 17-20 F 16-20, -60	27 Jan 1981	15 Oct 2001	Last flight 23 Aug 2001. Scrapped	2,384 h 20 min
JA 37	37321	F 13-61 F 16-61, -21 F 17-21	26 Jun 1981	24 Jan 2000	Last flight 26 Aug 1999. Scrapped	1,894 h 50 min
JA 37	37322	F 13-62 F 16-62	4 Mar 1981	8 Jun 2004	Last flight 25 Sep 2003. Scrapped	2,402 h 32 min
JA 37	37323	F 13-63 F 17-23 F 4-23 F 16-73	26 Oct 1980	9 Nov 2001	Last flight 25 Sep 2000. Scrapped	1,900 h 48 min
JA 37	37324	F 13-64 F 17-24 F 4-24	20 Aug 1981		W/o 10 Oct 1996 WSW Ramsele, Sweden. Pilot ejected	1,493 h 53 min
JA 37	37325	F 13-65 F 17-25 F 4-25	19 Apr 1982	13 Nov 2002	Last flight 22 May 2002. Scrapped	2,231 h 55 min
JA 37 JA 37D	37326	F 13-26, -66 F 17-26	17 Sep 1981		Modified 18 Apr 1996 as JA 37D. Last flight 24 Mar 2004. Currently (2022) preserved at Svedinos Bil- och Flygmuseum, Ugglarp, Sweden	
JA 37	37327	F 13-67 F 16-67, -08 F 21-14, -08 F 4-08	24 Aug 1982	8 Dec 2004	Last flight 13 Feb 2003. Scrapped	2,015 h 10 min
JA 37	37328	F 13-68 F 17-28 F 16-68	27 Aug 1982	15 Mar 2001	Last flight 28 Sep 2000. Scrapped	2,052 h 57 min
JA 37	37329	F 13-69 FC-29 F 4-29	21 Sep 1982	9 Nov 2001	Last flight 14 Jun 2000. Scrapped	2,085 h 24 min
JA 37	37330	F 13-30 F 16-30	24 Nov 1982	21 Feb 2005	Last flight 2 Dec 2003. Scrapped	1,944 h 21 min
JA 37	37331	F 13-31 F 17-31 F 4-31	31 Aug 1982	25 Oct 2001	Last flight 30 May 2001. Scrapped	2,009 h 29 min
JA 37	37332	F 13-32 F 16-32, -12, -73	18 Nov 1982	14 Jun 2001	Last flight 14 Mar 2001. Scrapped	1,974 h 51 min
JA 37	37333	F 17-33 F 4-33	20 Dec 1982	25 Oct 2000	Last flight 2 Mar 2000. Scrapped	1,885 h 44 min
JA 37	37334	F 17-34	29 Mar 1983		W/o 14 Mar 1988 at Fröseke, N Orrefors, Sweden. Pilot killed	621 h 59 min
JA 37	37335	F 17-35 F 16-75	18 Jan 1983	26 Mar 2001	Last flight 31 Aug 2000. Scrapped	1,910 h 40 min

A few JA 37s of F 4 in various styles of camouflage and markings lined up at F 4 Östersund on 1 June 1986. (Mikael Forslund)

Type	S/n	Code/s	Taken on charge (ToC)	Struck off charge (SoC)	Remarks	Hrs flown
JA 37	37336	F 21-04, -13 F 17-50 F 16-04	27 Jan 1983	23 Mar 2004	Last flight 28 May 2003. Scrapped	2,033 h 02 min
JA 37	37337	F 21-05 F 17-37, -15	3 Mar 1983	24 Mar 2003	Last flight 10 Sep 2002. Scrapped	1,749 h 54 min
JA 37	37338	F 21-06	6 May 1983		W/o 14 Jan 1985 Fällfors, Sweden. Pilot ejected	130 h 01 min
JA 37	37339	F 21-07 F 17-	7 Apr 1983	27 Feb 1983	Last flight 27 Jun 2002. Scrapped	1,885 h 43 min
JA 37	37340	F 21-08	22 Jun 1983		W/o 14 Jan 1985 Fällfors, Sweden. Pilot ejected	134 h 25 min
JA 37	37341	F 4-41 F 13-41	25 Oct 1983	28 Apr 2003	Last flight 13 May 2002. Scrapped	2,261 h 46 min
JA 37	37342	F 4-42	23 Aug 1983		W/o 1 Mar 1988 Anarisfjällen, Sweden. Pilot killed	513 h 53 min
JA 37	37343	F 4-43 F 17-43	16 Sep 1983	13 Nov 2002	Last flight 8 Mar 2002. Scrapped	1,987 h 16 min
JA 37	37344	F 4-44 F 21- F 13-44 F 17-32 F 16-32, -44	20 Dec 1982	25 Oct 2000	Last flight 25 Apr 2000. Scrapped	1,984 h 26 min
JA 37	37345	F 4-45 F 17-45 F 21-30	8 Nov 1983	19 Sep 2001	Last flight 30 May 2001. Scrapped	1,953 h 30 min
JA 37	37346	F 4-46	16 Nov 1983	15 Oct 1999	Last flight 29 Apr 1999. Scrapped	1,741 h 22 min
JA 37 JA 37D JA 37Di	37347	F 13-37 F 16-37, -47 F 17-47	19 Feb 1982	13 May 2005	Modified 14 Apr 1998 as JA 37D, later modified as JA 37Di. To Magyar Repüléstörténeti Múzeum at Szolnok, Hungary, 2 May 2005. Currently (2022) preserved	1,560 h 02 min
JA 37	37348	F 13-38 F 16- F 4-48	4 Jun 1982	19 Jan 1999	Last flight 8 Sep 1998. Scrapped	1,837 h 30 min
JA 37	37349	F 13-39, -49 F 17-49	12 Aug 1982	20 Mar 2000	Last flight 11 Nov 1999. Scrapped	1,944 h 18 min
JA 37	37350	F 13-40 F 4-40 F 17-50 F 21-	8 Oct 1982	28 Nov 2000	Last flight 6 Oct 2000. Scrapped	2,002 h 52 min
JA 37	37351	F 17-39, -51 F 21-31	5 Oct 1982	28 Nov 2000	Last flight 11 Sep 2000. Scrapped	2,099 h 19 min
JA 37	37352	F 17-40 F 16-40	10 Nov 1982	8 Sep 2000	Last flight 26 Apr 2000. Scrapped	1,874 h 48 min
JA 37	37353	F 17-41, -33, -13 F 13-33 F 21-33	18 Nov 1982	8 Sep 2000	Last flight 9 Mar 2000. Scrapped	1,693 h 19 min

Type	S/n	Code/s	Taken on charge (ToC)	Struck off charge (SoC)	Remarks	Hrs flown
JA 37	37354	F 17-42 F 21-34	17 Dec 1982	24 Jan 2001	Last flight 17 Nov 2000. Scrapped	1,861 h 23 min
JA 37	37355	F 17-43 F 21-36	21 Dec 1982	25 Apr 2002	Last flight 15 Jun 2000. Scrapped	2,009 h 07 min
JA 37	37356	F 17-44 F 16-76	17 Mar 1983	28 Nov 2001	Last flight 25 Sep 2000. Scrapped	1,942 h 58 min
JA 37	37357	F 17-45 F 4-57	8 Feb 1983	29 Apr 2003	Last flight 22 Apr 2002. Scrapped	2,016 h 51 min
JA 37	37358	F 17-46 F 16-46	2 Mar 1983	8 Nov 2001	Last flight 20 Sep 2001. Scrapped. Cockpit to Kreativum, *Karlshamn, Sweden*	1,937 h 43 min
JA 37	37359	F 17-47, -59, -29 F 13-59 F 21-08	3 Mar 1983	25 Apr 2002	Last flight 15 Jun 2000. Scrapped	1,776 h 02 min
JA 37	37360	F 17-48 F 4-06 F 16-60	14 Mar 1983		W/o 10 Oct 1996 WSW Ramsele, Sweden. Pilot ejected	1,421 h 56 min
JA 37	37361	F 17-49, -61, -51 F 13-61 F 16-71	20 Apr 1983	16 Jan 2001	Last flight 18 Oct 2000. 2,670 flights. Scrapped	1,962 h 33 min
JA 37	37362	F 21-09	21 Apr 1983	14 Jun 2001	Last flight 4 May 2000. Currently (2022) preserved at Flygmuseet F 21, *Luleå, Sweden*	1,760 h 53 min
JA 37	37363	F 21-10 F 13-	1 Jul 1983	17 May 2002	Last flight 19 Dec 2001. Scrapped	1,920 h 46 min
JA 37	37364	F 21-11 F 4-	30 Jun 1983	10 Oct 2002	Last flight 19 Dec 2001. Scrapped	1,844 h 54 min
JA 37	37365	F 21-12, -30 F 16-12	22 Jun 1983	23 Mar 2004	Last flight 1 Oct 2003. Scrapped	1,957 h 58 min
JA 37	37366	F 21-13, -30 F 16-13 F 13-36	22 Aug 1983	31 Mar 2004	Last flight 11 Nov 2003. To Saab for fire and rescue exercises. Currently (2022) preserved at F 13 Kamratförening *exhibition, Norrköping, Sweden*	2,025 h 23 min
JA 37	37367	F 4-26 F 21-14 F 16-37	11 Aug 1983	14 Feb 2003	Last flight 5 Dec 2002. Currently (2022) preserved on pole along E 4, north of Linköping, Sweden	1,988 h 52 min
JA 37	37368	F 21-15 F 16-15	1 Sep 1983	28 Nov 2000	Last flight 17 Apr 2000. Scrapped	1,771 h 23 min
JA 37	37369	F 21-16	12 Sep 1983	25 Oct 2000	Last flight 8 Jun 2000. Scrapped	1,682 h 59 min
JA 37	37370	F 21-17	14 Oct 1983	15 Mar 2001	Last flight 12 Dec 2000. Scrapped	1,699 h 52 min
JA 37	37371	F 21-18	29 Nov 1983	28 Feb 2002	Last flight 21 Jun 2000. Scrapped	1,758 h 36 min
JA 37	37372	F 4-32 F 13-62 F 17-22 F 16-22	1 Dec 1983	15 Mar 2001	Last flight 16 Dec 1999. To Flygvapnets Halmstadsskolor, *Halmstad, Sweden, for battle damage repair training*	1,958 h 49 min
JA 37	37373	F 4-33	30 Nov 1983		W/o 21 Mar 1986 Hallviken, Sweden. Pilot ejected	242 h 07 min
JA 37	37374	F 4-34 F 17-24 F 16-74	15 Dec 1983	18 Sep 2001	Last flight 19 Jun 2001. To Klippans gymnasium, *Klippan, Sweden, as ground instructional airframe*	1,983 h 14 min
JA 37	37375	F 4-35 F 13-35, -65 F 17-25	15 Dec 1983	31 Jul 2003	Last flight 27 Jun 2002. Scrapped	2,011 h 03 min
JA 37	37376	F 4-36 F 16-36	2 Mar 1984		Last flight 16 Sep 2003. Scrapped	
JA 37	37377	F 4-37	2 Mar 1984	8 Oct 2001	Last flight 19 Jun 2001. Scrapped	1,718 h 34 min
JA 37	37378	F 4-38	10 Feb 1984	29 Jan 2003	Last flight 4 Sep 2002. To FMV:Prov, *Vidsel, as gunnery range target. Currently (2022) preserved at* RFN Museum, *Vidsel, Sweden*	2,026 h 40 min
JA 37	37379	F 4-39 F 21-15	20 Mar 1984	25 Apr 2002	Last flight 7 Nov 2001. Scrapped	1,928 h 46 min
JA 37	37380	F 4-50	2 May 1984	26 Jul 2001	Last flight 6 Mar 2001. Scrapped	1,977 h 58 min
JA 37	37381	F 4-51	2 Aug 1984		W/o 8 Feb 1990 NE Ramsele, Sweden. Pilot ejected	556 h 02 min

JA 37 Viggen, *coded F 13-33, taxiing towards the tarmac at Visby airport, Gotland, Sweden. The aircraft is armed with RB 74 Sidewinders and RB 71 Sky Flash air-to-air missiles (dummy missiles are painted Green). (Tor Karlsson)*

Type	S/n	Code/s	Taken on charge (ToC)	Struck off charge (SoC)	Remarks	Hrs flown
JA 37	37382	F 4-52	8 Jun 1984	22 Mar 2002	Last flight 30 Nov 2001. Scrapped	1,979 h 06 min
JA 37	37383	F 4-53 F 21-	14 Aug 1984	16 Jan 2001	Last flight 25 Aug 2000. 2,312 flights. To Wing F 4 for fire and rescue exercises	1,637 h 53 min
JA 37	37384	F 4-54, F 16-54, -35	10 Aug 1984	20 Mar 2000	Last flight 18 Nov 1999. Scrapped	1,987 h 06 min
JA 37	37385	F 4-55	29 Aug 1984	8 Nov 2002	Last flight 22 Apr 2002. Scrapped	2,014 h 02 min
JA 37D	37386	F 4-56, -46 F 17-46	11 Sep 1984		Modified 23 Apr 2001 as JA 37D. Last flight 9 Dec 2004	
JA 37	37387	F 4-57	8 Oct 1984		W/o 21 Mar 1986 Hallviken, Sweden. Pilot ejected	193 h 25 min
JA 37	37388	F 4-58	3 Oct 1984	26 Aug 2002	Last flight 25 Mar 2002. Scrapped	1,487 h 33 min
JA 37 JA 37D JA 37Di	37389	F 4-59	24 Oct 1984	22 Jan 2004	Modified 13 Oct 1999 as JA 37D, 22 Feb 2001 modified as JA 37Di. Last flight 28 Feb 2003	
JA 37	37390	F 4-60	19 Nov 1984	15 Mar 2001	Last flight 21 Jan 2000. Scrapped	1,679 h 43 min
JA 37	37391	F 4-61	4 Dec 1984	2 Oct 2000	Last flight 15 Jun 2000. Scrapped	1,741 h 10 min
JA 37	37392	F 4-62	17 Dec 1984	27 Feb 2001	Last flight 23 Oct 2000. 2,399 flights. Currently (2022) preserved at Teknikland, Optand, Sweden	1,751 h 25 min
JA 37	37393	F 4-63	5 Feb 1985		Last flight 27 May 2002. Scrapped	
JA 37	37394	F 4-64, F 17-42, -47	19 Feb 1985	24 Mar 2003	Last flight 29 Aug 2002. Scrapped	1,813 h 23 min
JA 37	37395	F 4-65, F 17-65 F 13-65	11 Mar 1985	23 Jan 2003	Last flight 5 Sep 2002. Scrapped	2,013 h 12 min
JA 37	37396	F 4-66 F 16-66	9 Apr 1985		W/o 1 Dec 1989 of Gävle coast, Gulf of Bothnia, Sweden. Pilot ejected	535 h 35 min
JA 37 JA 37D	37397	F 4-67, -20 F 21-20 F 17-20	24 Apr 1985		Modified 22 Oct 1998 as JA 37Di. Last flight Jun 2004. Scrapped	
JA 37 JA 37D JA 37Di	37398	F 4-68, -08 F 13-68 F 17-28, -08	4 Jun 1985	24 Feb 2005	Modified 25 Nov 1998 as JA 37. 26 Oct 2000 modified as JA 37Di. Last flight Dec 2004. Scrapped	1,888 h 57 min
JA 37	37399	F 4-69 F 21-19 F 16-19	17 Jun 1985	16 Jan 2001	Last flight 5 Oct 2000. To Wing F 16 for fire and rescue exrecises	1,652 h 07 min
JA 37	37400	F 21-20 F 16-50	20 Aug 1985		Last flight 20 Aug 2003. Scrapped	

Type	S/n	Code/s	Taken on charge (ToC)	Struck off charge (SoC)	Remarks	Hrs flown
JA 37 JA 37D JA 37Di	37401	F 21-21 F 17-01 F 4-01	5 Sep 1985		Modified 20 Apr 1999 as JA 37D, 1 Dec 2000 modified as JA 37Di. Last flight 23 Nov 2004. Scrapped	
JA 37 JA 37D JA 37Di	37402	F 21-22, -02 F 17-02	23 Sep 1985	8 Dec 2004	Modified 25 Feb 1999 as JA 37D, later modified as JA 37Di. Last flight 17 Jun 2004. Scrapped	1,795 h 32 min
JA 37	37403	F 21-23 F 17-03	2 Oct 1995	23 Mar 2004	Last flight 16 Oct 2003. Scrapped	1,924 h 05 min
JA 37 JA 37D JA 37Di	37404	F 21-24 17-24, -37	11 Nov 1985	19 Feb 2007	Modified 3 Nov 1998 as JA 37D, 3 Oct 2001 modified as JA 37Di. Last flight 24 May 2004	
JA 37	37405	F 21-25 F 4-	18 Dec 1985	6 Jun 2002	Last flight 1 Feb 2002. Scrapped	1,681 h 34 min
JA 37	37406	F 21-26 F 4-26	20 Dec 1985	13 Nov 2002	Last flight 22 Apr 2002. Scrapped	1,521 h 40 min
JA 37	37407	F 21-27	7 Feb 1986	28 Apr 2003	Last flight 26 Mar 2003. Scrapped	1,444 h 08 min
JA 37	37408	F 21-28 F 13-48 F 16-28	24 Mar 1986	27 May 2004	Last flight 6 Mar 2003. Scrapped	1,826 h 19 min
JA 37	37409	F 21-29 F 17-29	26 Mar 1986	27 Mar 2003	Last flight 16 Aug 2002. Scrapped	1,570 h 14 min
JA 37	37410	F 21-30 F 16-30, -10	24 Apr 1986	31 Mar 2004	Last flight 8 Oct 2003 (Red fin). To Wing F 16 Förbandsmuseum. Currently (2022) preserved at Österlens Flygmuseum, Östra Vemmerlöv, Sweden	1,943 h 54 min
JA 37	37411	F 21-31 F 16-11	26 May 1986	28 Jan 2004	Special Dark Grey arrow colour scheme. Last flight 14 Oct 2003. Scrapped	1,839 h 28 min
JA 37 JA 37D JA 37Di	37412	F 21-32 F 13-32 F 17-12 F 4-12	19 Sep 1986		Modified 26 Jun 1998 as JA 37D, 6 Sep 2000 modified as JA 37Di. Last flight 24 Apr 2005. Currently (2022) preserved at Teknikland, Optand, Sweden	
JA 37 JA 37D JA 37Di	37413	F 21-33 F 13-33 F 17-13, -17 F 4-13	29 Sep 1986		Modified 1 Jun 1998 as JA 37D, 4 Apr 2001 modified as JA 37Di. Last flight 22 Oct 2004. Scrapped	
JA 37 JA 37D JA 37Di	37414	F 21-34 F 13-34 F 17-14 F 16- F 4-14	8 Oct 1986	7 Sep 2005	Modified 18 Feb 1998 as JA 37D, 17 Oct 2000 modified as JA 37Di. Last flight 14 Sep 2004. Scrapped	1,918 h 14 min
JA 37D JA 37Di	37415	F 21-35 F 17-15 F 4- F 16-15	28 Oct 1986		Modified 12 Sep 1997 as JA 37D, 2 Oct 2001 modified as JA 37Di. Last flight 18 Jun 2005. Scrapped	
JA 37 JA 37D	37416	F 21-36 F 17-36	13 Nov 1986	8 Dec 2004	Modfied 26 May 1998 as JA 37D. Last flight 17 Jun 2004. Scrapped	1,494 h 37 min
JA 37	37417	F 16-17 F 17-17	18 Dec 1986	28 Apr 2003	Last flight 23 May 2002. Scrapped	1,943 h 16 min
JA 37D	37418	F 13- F 16-18 F 17-18, -68 F 4-18	19 Dec 1986	8 Dec 2004	Modified 1 Mar 1999 as JA 37D. Last flight 16 Sep 2004. Scrapped	1,937 h 55 min
JA 37	37419	F 16-19	18 Mar 1987	25 Apr 2002	Last flight 5 Feb 2002. Scrapped. Parts to Saab	1,564 h 07 min
JA 37	37420	F 16-20	5 Mar 1987		Last flight 7 Oct 2003. Scrapped	
JA 37 JA 37D JA 37Di	37421	F 16-21 F 13-21, -41 F 17-21 F 4-21	24 Mar 1987		Modified 12 Oct 1999 as JA 37D, 12 Nov 2000 modified as JA 37Di. Last flight 11 Nov 2004. Scrapped	
JA 37 JA 37D	37422	F 16-22 F 17-22 F 4-22	25 May 1987		Modified 19 Aug 1999 as JA 37D. Last flight 19 Aug 2004. Scrapped	
JA 37	37423	F 16-23	26 Jun 1987		Last flight 26 Aug 2003. Scrapped	

JA 37 Viggen s/n 37316, coded F 13-56, being prepared for the next sortie at Dala Airport/ Rommehed sometime in the early 1980s. (Via Archive of Falu Kuriren)

Type	S/n	Code/s	Taken on charge (ToC)	Struck off charge (SoC)	Remarks	Hrs flown
JA 37 JA 37D JA 37Di	37424	F 16-24 F 17-24 F 4-24	14 Sep 1987		Modified 18 Feb 1999 as JA 37D, 5 Mar 2003 modified as JA 37Di. Last flight 6 Dec 2004. Scrapped	
JA 37	37425	F 16-25	5 Oct 1987	24 Jan 2001	Last flight 28 Apr 2000. Currently (2022) preserved on pole at Wing F 16, Uppsala, Sweden	1,526 h 34 min
JA 37	37426	F 16-26	13 Oct 1987	31 Jul 2003	Last flight 10 Sep 2002. Scrapped	1,536 h 53 min
JA 37 JA 37D JA 37Di	37427	F 16-27 F 17-27, -37 F 4-27	23 Nov 1987		Modified 24 Mar 1999 as JA 37D, 6 Dec 2000 modified as JA 37Di. Last flight 17 Sep 2003. Scrapped	
JA 37 JA 37D JA 37Di	37428	F 16-28 F 17-28 F 4-28	16 Dec 1987		Modified 11 May 1999 as JA 37D, 5 Mar 2001 modified as JA 37Di. Last flight 9 Dec 2004. Scrapped	
JA 37 JA 37D JA 37Di	37429	F 16-29 F 17-29 F 4-29	23 Dec 1987	15 Dec 2004	Modified 17 Sep 1998 as JA 37D, 5 Dec 2000 modified as JA 37Di. Last flight 28 Sep 2004. Currently (2022) preserved at Eesti Lennundusmuuseum (EAM), Tartu, Estonia	1,560 h 34 min
JA 37	37430	F 16-30	6 May 1988		W/o 5 Jul 1988 15 km NE Gotska Sandön Baltic Sea, Sweden. Pilot ejected	12 h 47 min
JA 37 JA 37D	37431	F 16-31 F 17-31 F 21-	7 Apr 1988		Modified 25 Aug 1998 as JA 37D. Last flight 11 Apr 2005. Currently (2022) preserved at Luftfahrtmuseum, Graz-Thalerhof, Austria	
JA 37	37432	F 16-32	16 Jun 1988	25 Jan 2002	Finished in Blue colour scheme. Last flight 10 Oct 2001. Currently (2022) preserved at Bunge Flygmuseum, Gotland, Sweden	1,286 h 19 min
JA 37	37433	F 16-33	21 Jun 1988		Last flight 19 Nov 2002. Scrapped	
JA 37	37434	F 16-34	14 Sep 1988	25 Jan 2002	Last flight 30 Oct 2001. Scrapped	1,570 h 13 min
JA 37 JA 37D JA 37Di	37435	F 16-35 F 17-35 F 4-35	3 Oct 1988	22 Apr 2004	Modified 23 Mar 1999 as JA 37D, 24 Jan 2001 modified as JA 37Di. Last flight 28 Oct 2003. Scrapped	1,565 h 10 min
JA 37 JA 37D JA 37Di	37436	F 21-36, -32 F 4-32	25 Nov 1988		Modified 22 Feb 2000 as JA 37D, 27 Apr 2001 modi-fied as JA 37Di. Last flight 9 Nov 2004. Scrapped	
JA 37 JA 37D	37437	F 17-37 F 16-47 F 4-37 F 21	9 Jan 1989		Modified 3 Mar 2000 as JA 37D. Last flight 4 Dec 2003. Scrapped	

Type	S/n	Code/s	Taken on charge (ToC)	Struck off charge (SoC)	Remarks	Hrs flown
JA 37 JA 37D JA 37Di	37438	F 13-48 F 17-38	9 Feb 1989		Modified 25 Mar 1999 as JA 37D, 26 Feb 2001 modified as JA 37Di. Last flight 4 Aug 2004. Scrapped	
JA 37	37439	F 4-01 F 16-39	13 Mar 1989	16 Jan 2001	Last flight 30 Oct 2000. Scrapped	1,437 h 48 min
JA 37 JA 37D JA 37Di	37440	F 21-33 F 16-40 F 17-40 F 4-40	21 Jun 1989		Modified 12 Oct 1999 as JA 37D, 12 Mar 2001 modified as JA 37Di. Last flight 9 Nov 2004. Scrapped	
JA 37 JA 37D JA 37Di	37441	F 17-41 F 21-	21 Jun 1989		Modified 5 Mar 1998 as JA 37D, 14 Dec 2000 modified as JA 37Di. Last flight 12 Jan 2005. Scrapped	
JA 37 JA 37D JA 37Di	37342	F 13-52 F 17-52 F 4-52	21 Jun 1989		Modified 23 Mar 1999 as JA 37D, 20 Nov 2000 modified as JA 37Di. Last flight 22 Oct 2004. Scrapped	
JA 37 JA 37D JA 37Di	37443	F 4-02, F 17-02, -43 F 4-43	13 Oct 1989		Modified 2 Mar 1998 as JA 37D, 6 Sep 2002 modified as JA 37Di. Last flight 17 Nov 2004. Scrapped	
JA 37 JA 37D JA 37Di	37444	F 21-34 F 17-04 F 4-04	19 Dec 1989	22 Dec 2004	Modified 8 Apr 1998 as JA 37D, 22 Nov 2000 modified as JA 37Di. Last flight 5 Nov 2003. Scrapped	1,120 h 14 min
JA 37 JA 37D JA 37Di	37445	F 16-45	8 Jan 1990	8 Dec 2004	Modified 25 Mar 1998 as JA 37D, 10 Apr 2001 modified as JA 37Di. Last flight 28 Aug 2004. Scrapped	1,497 h 56 min
JA 37 JA 37D JA 37Di	37446	F 4-03, -06 F 17-06	21 Mar 1990		Modified 13 Jan 1998 as JA 37D, 15 Aug 2000 modified as JA 37Di. Last flight 12 Jan 2005. Scrapped	
JA 37 JA 37D	37447	F 21-35 F 16-35	6 Apr 1990		Modified 28 Aug 1998 as JA 37D. Last flight 26 Aug 2003. Scrapped	
JA 37 JA 37D	37448	F 16- F 4-04	25 Jun 1990	19 Sep 2001	Modified 8 Mar 1999 as JA 37D. Last flight 23 Nov 2000. Currently (2022) preserved at Teknikland, Optand, Sweden	1,065 h 19 min
JA 37 JA 37D JA 37Di	37449	F 16-49 F 17-49 F 4-49	29 Jun 1990		Modified 11 Oct 1999 as JA 37D, 15 Mar 2001 modified as JA 37Di. Last flight 18 Jun 2005. Currently (2022) preserved at Flygvapenmuseum, Linköping, Sweden	

Three JA 37 Viggens lined up at the No.2 Sqn/F 13 Norrköping on 19 May 1990. (Tor Karlsson)

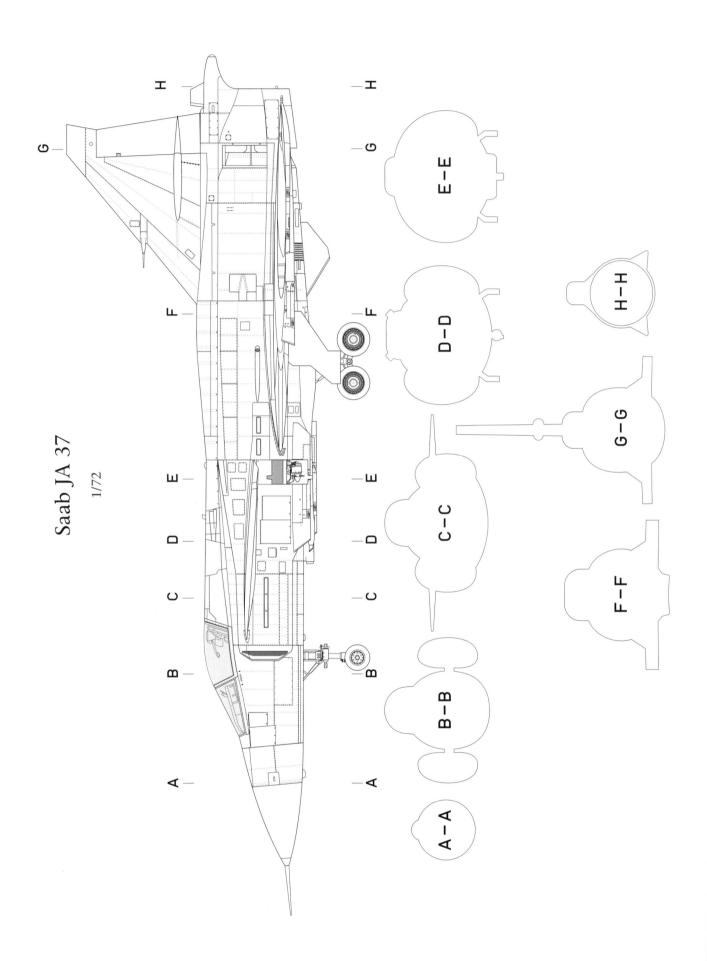

Saab JA 37

1/72

A–A B–B C–C D–D E–E

F–F G–G H–H

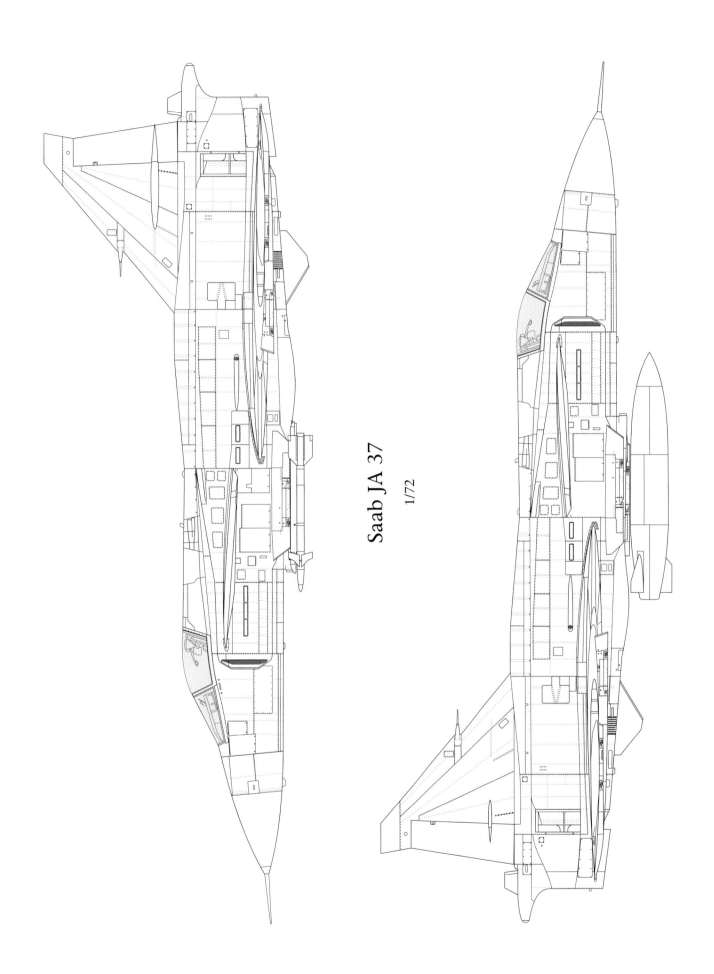

Saab JA 37
1/72

Saab JA 37

1/72

132

Saab JA 37

1/72

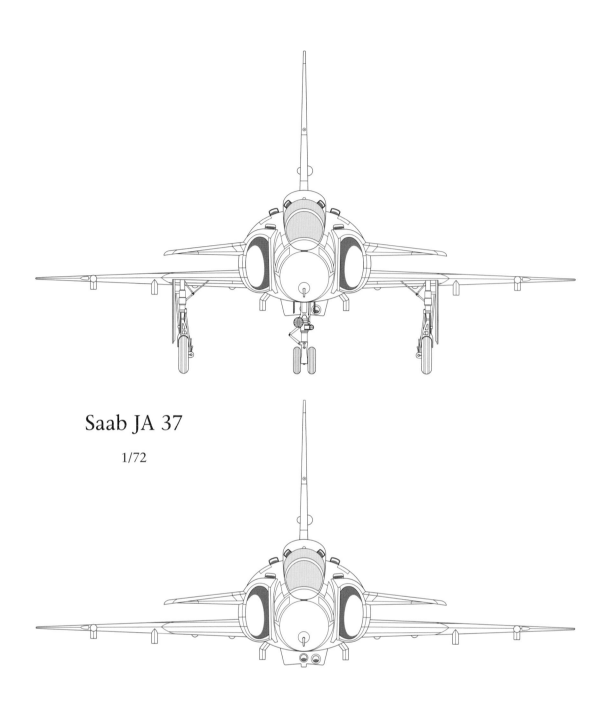

Saab JA 37

1/72

JA 37 s/n 37407, coded F 21-27, with White numerals on the wings. Such White numeral subsequently became standard on the Grey-camouflaged aircraft. (Via Archives of Mikael Forslund)

JA 37 s/n 37408, coded F 21-28, with Black numerals on the wings. The numerals was applied for trials purposes only, and did not become standard. (Via Archives of Mikael Forslund)

Saab JA 37 Viggen s/n 37304, coded Yellow 01 of F 21 Luleå, photographed in June 2000 at F 17 Ronneby. The upper surfaces are camouflaged in svart (Black) 093M (FS 34031), ljusgrön (Light Green) 322M (FS 34138), mörkgrön (Dark Green) 326M (FS 34092) and brun (Brown) 507M (FS 30117), with the lower surfaces being blågrå (Blue Grey) 058M (FS 36314). The fin is Purple (FS 37100), with the cartoon Hägar the Horrible superimposed on a Yellow (FS 33591) roundel.

a.m. olejniczak '22

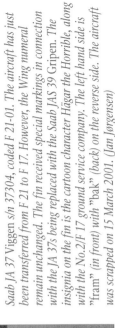

Saab JA 37 Viggen s/n 37304, coded F 21-01. The aircraft has just been transferred from F 21 to F 17. However, the Wing numeral remain unchanged. The fin received special markings in connection with the JA 37s being replaced with the Saab JAS 39 Gripen. The insignia on the fin is the cartoon character Hägar the Horrible, along with the No.2/F 17 ground service company. The left hand side is "fram" (in front) with "bak" (back on the reverse side. The aircraft was scrapped on 15 March 2001. (Jan Jørgensen)

135

Saab JA 37 Viggen s/n 37304, coded Yellow 01 of F 21 Luleå, photographed in June 2000 at F 17 Ronneby. The upper surfaces are camouflaged in svart (Black) 093M (FS 34031), ljusgrön (Light Green) 322M (FS 34138), mörkgrön (Dark Green) 326M (FS 34092) and brun (Brown) 507M (FS 30117), with the lower surfaces being blågrå (Blue Grey) 058M (FS 36314). The fin is Purple (FS 37100), with the cartoon Hägar the Horrible superimposed on a Yellow (FS 33591) roundel.

Saab JA 37 Viggen s/n 37304, coded F 21-01. The aircraft has just been transferred from F 21 to F 17. However, the Wing numeral remain unchanged. The fin received special markings in connection with the JA 37s being replaced with the Saab JAS 39 Gripen. The insignia on the fin is the cartoon character Hägar the Horrible, along with the No.2/F 17 ground service company. The left hand side is "fram" (in front) with "bak" (back) on the reverse side. The aircraft was scrapped on 15 March 2001. (Jan Jørgensen)

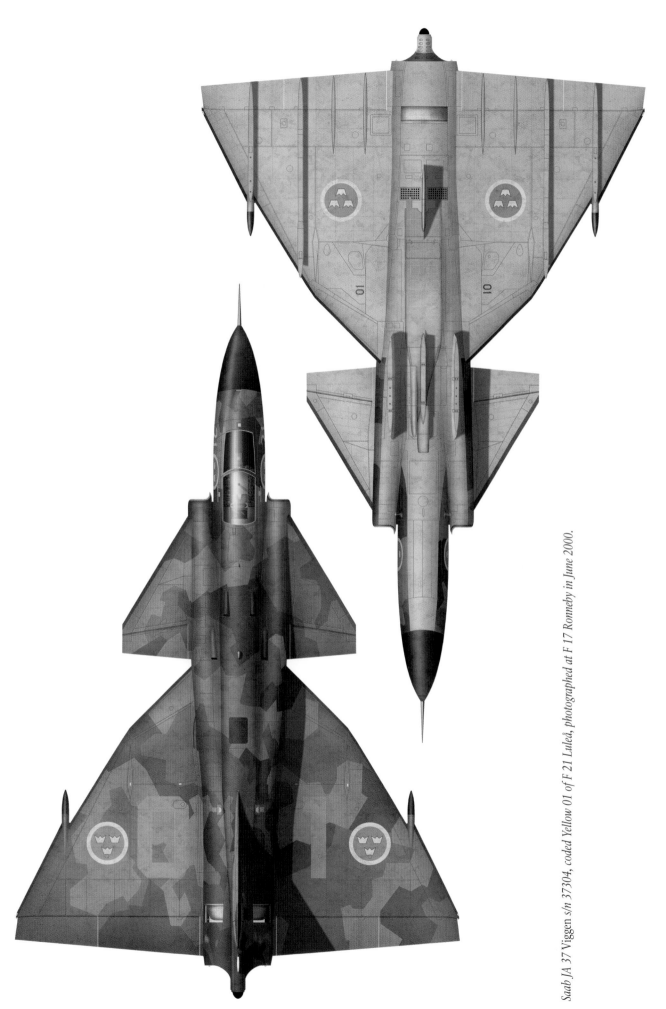

Saab JA 37 Viggen s/n 37304, coded Yellow 01 of F 21 Luleå, photographed at F 17 Ronneby in June 2000.

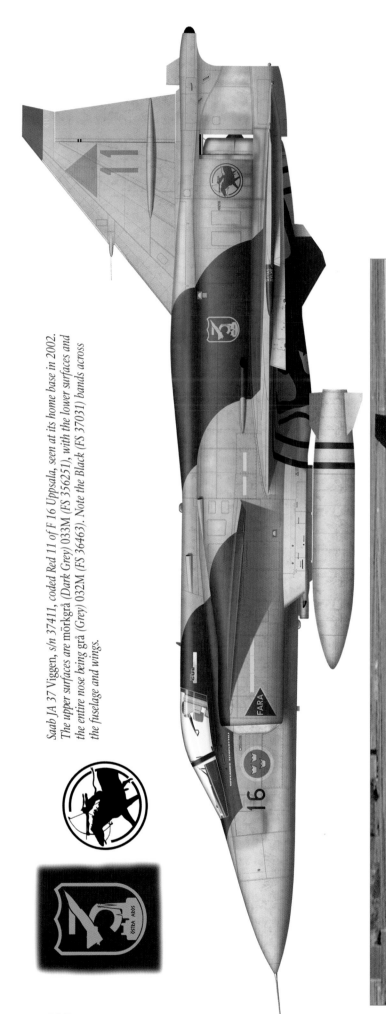

Saab JA 37 Viggen, s/n 37411, coded Red 11 of F 16 Uppsala, seen at its home base in 2002. The upper surfaces are mörkgrå (Dark Grey) 033M (FS 36251), with the lower surfaces and the entire nose being grå (Grey) 032M (FS 36463). Note the Black (FS 37031) bands across the fuselage and wings.

Saab JA 37 Viggen s/n 37411, coded F 16-11. The aircraft was part of No.3 Sqn/F 16, being painted in these special colours in June 2000 which signified its use as Flygvapnet's official Viggen air display aircraft. The Black bands symbolizes arrows. The F 16 Mustang insignia (an indian on a horse) appeared on the lower surfaces of the wings. A smaller variant appeared on both sides of the rear fuselage. Another, even smaller variant appeared on the main undercarriage doors, with the background being Red. The badge of No.3 Sqn/F 16 ground servicing company appeared in Grey on the left hand side of the fuselage. The badge of No.3 Sqn/F 16 appeared behind the canopy on the left hand side of the fuselage. The last flight took place on 14 October 2003, with the destination being Halmstad where it was scrapped. (Sven Stridsberg)

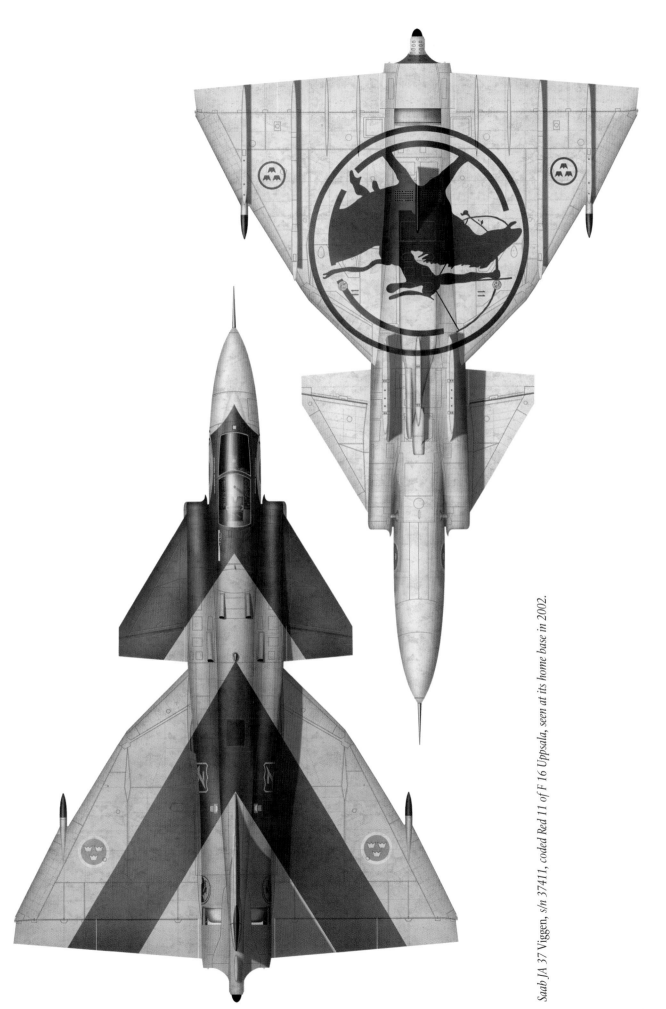

Saab JA 37 Viggen, s/n 37411, coded Red 11 of F 16 Uppsala, seen at its home base in 2002.

Saab JA 37 Viggen s/n 37432, coded Black P 32 of F 16 Uppsala, photographed at the 16 June 2001 air show at Dala Airport, Rommehed. The aircraft is overall Blue (FS 25095), with parts of the fin and wing leading edges being Yellow (FS 23655).

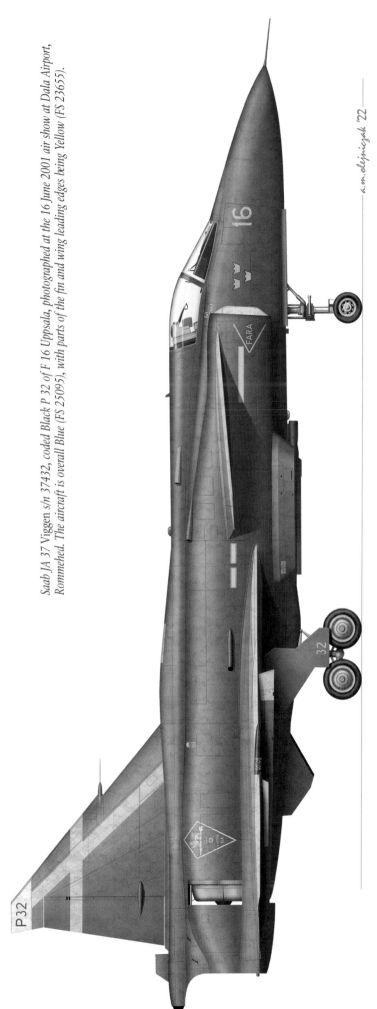

Saab JA 37 Viggen s/n 37432, coded Black P 32 of F 16 Uppsala. The photograph was taken on 16 June 2001 at Dala Airport, Rommehed. The aircraft is finished overall Blue (FS 25095), with some Yellow (FS 23655) on the fin and the wing leading edges. (Mikael Forslund)

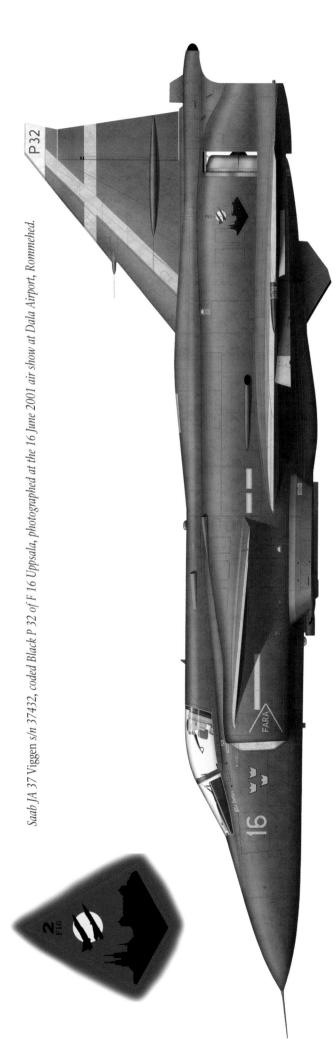

Saab JA 37 Viggen s/n 37432, coded Black P 32 of F 16 Uppsala, photographed at the 16 June 2001 air show at Dala Airport, Rommehed.

Saab JA 37 Viggen s/n 37432, coded F 16-32. In July 2000, the aircraft painted in the Blue colours of No.2 Sqn/F 16. The wing leading edges and fin were painted Yellow. The Yellow cross of the Swedish flag appeared on both sides of the fin. The national insignia (without the Yellow outer ring) appeared on both sides of the front fuselage only. The legend Blå Petter appeared in Yellow cursive style below the front screen on the left hand side of the fuselage. (Petter is the Call sign for F 16, being the designated Swedish alphabet, with blå (ie Blue) being the designated colour for No.2 Sqn). The two different badges of No.2 Sqn appeared separately on both sides of the rear fuselage as well as the upper and lower surfaces of the wings. On both sides of the upper section of the fin, the code P 32 (in Black) was superimposed on a White square. Among the various air show appearances, s/n 37432 took part in the 16 June 2001 air show at Dala Airport, Rommehed. The final flight took place on 10 October 2001. At the time of writing (2022), s/n 37432 is preserved at the Bunge Flygmuseum on the island of Gotland, Sweden. (Mikael Forslund)

Saab JA 37 Viggen s/n 37302, coded Red 02 of F 13 Norrköping, photographed at F 17 Kallinge on 11 June 1994. The camouflage colours are: fin: svart (Black) 093M (FS 34031), ljusgrön (Light Green) 322M (FS 34138), mörkgrön (Dark Green) 326M (FS 34092) and brun (Brown) 507M (FS 30117). The upper surfaces except the nose section is mörkgrå (Dark Grey) 033M (FS 36251), with the lower surfaces and entire nose section being grå (Grey) 032M (FS 36463).

Saab JA 37 Viggen s/n 37302, coded F 13-02. The aircraft was photographed in the F 17 workshop on 11 June 1994. A new fin of a former F 17 JA 37 (note the F 17 badge on the fin). Occasionally, spares from scrapped aircraft were reused. S/n 37302 was delivered to F 17 on 8 March 1994, being coded F 17-02 shortly afterwards. (Mikael Forslund)

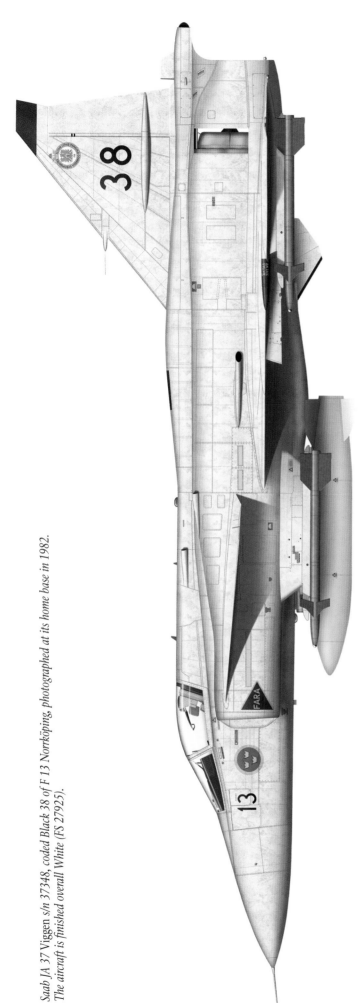

Saab JA 37 Viggen s/n 37348, coded Black 38 of F 13 Norrköping, photographed at its home base in 1982. The aircraft is finished overall White (FS 27925).

Saab JA 37 Viggen s/n 37348, coded F 13-38. Beginning in early 1982, different types of camouflage, apart from the splinter camouflage, was tested on six JA 37s of F 13: s/ns 37347 (coded F 13-37) and 37348 (F 13-38) were finished overall vit (White) (FS 37925), 37328 (F 13-68) and 37349 (F 13-39) overall mellangrå (Medium Grey) (FS 36314), and 37329 (F 13-69) and 37350 (F 13-69) overall mörkgrå (Dark Grey) 033M (FS 36251). It was discovered that White could not be used. In the event, a standard two-tone camouflage scheme, consisting of grå (Grey) 032M (FS 36463) for the lower surfaces and mörkgrå (Dark Grey) 033M (FS 36251) for the upper surfaces was adopted. The photo shows s/n 37348, armed with a pair of RB 24J Sidewinders on the fuselage attachment points, two RB 71 Sky Flashes on the inner wing attachment points and two RB 24J Sidewinders on the outer wing attachment points. All of the missiles are dummies. (Via Saab)

Chapter 12
JA 37D and JA 37Di

A total of 36 JA 37s (s/ns 37326, 37347, 37386, 37389, 37397, 37398, 37401, 37402, 37404, 37412–37416, 37418, 37421, 37422, 37424, 37427–37429, 37431, 37435–37438, 37440–37449) underwent a modification programme to make their computerized systems and weapons array compatible with those of the Saab JAS 39 *Gripen*. The modification programme involved four phases - A, B, C and D. The initial three involved upgrading the computers, fitting a GPS and making it possible to use the *RB 99* AMRAAM and the *störkapsel U 95 Axel ECM* pod. In addition, the instrument grading was changed from the metric system to feet.

The D phase involved fitting 9,500 m new wiring along with 2,200 new connections while removing 750 old ones and upgrading 400 existing ones. The JA 37D had a JAS 39-type radio, upgraded computer and radar as well as a computer stick, the latter being a small computer into which information about the sortie had been programmed. The modification work was performed at Wing level, lasting about four months for each aircraft. Externally, the JA 37 and JA 37D were identical.

The first JA 37D first flew on 4 June 1996. Initially, all JA 37Ds were transferred to Wing F 17, with the respective aircraft retaining the markings of the unit they had served with previously. With the arrival of the Saab JAS 39 *Gripens*, the JA 37Ds were gradually transferred to Wings F 16, F 4 and F 21.

JA 37Di Viggen s/n 37441, coded F 17-41. RB 24J Sidewinders hang from the fuselage attachment points, and RB 74 Sidewinders from the wing attachment points. Beginning on 5 March 1998, this JA 37 was modified as a JA 37D, being further upgraded on 14 December 2000 to JA 37Di status. On 14 February 2002, s/n 37441 was transferred from F 17 to F 21. (Lars-Åke Siggelin)

A total of 25 JA 37Ds (s/ns 37347, 37389, 37398, 37401, 37402, 37404, 37412–37415, 37421, 37424, 37427–37429, 37435, 37436, 37438, 37440–37446 and 37449) underwent further modification work, being redesignated as the JA 37Di. Late production aircraft with few flying hours were selected. Modification work involved refitting the instrument panel with colour LCD-screens similar to those of the Saab JAS 39 *Gripen*. When the JA 37Dis were withdrawn from use, these instrument panels were transferred to Saab JAS 39C/D *Gripens*.

JA 37, JA 37D and JA 37Di Armament

The JA 37 had nine external pylons:

The central fuselage pylon (1, maximum load of 2,250 kg) was often used to carry a 1,400 l external fuel tank.

The Nos.2 and 3 pylons beneath the fuselage could each carry a maximum load of 500 kg.

The Nos.4 and 5 (hydraulic) pylons, one beneath each wing, fitted on one of the elevator hinges, was used to carry chaff and flare dispensers.

The Nos.6 and 7 pylons could each carry a maximum load of 1,350 kg.

The outer missile pylons (Nos.8 and 9) were each able to carry a maximum load of 180 kg. The chaff dispenser *BOL 451* could be carried on these pylons simultaneously with a missile.

The JA 37 armament consisted of:

Akan m/75: Air and ground targets. Switzerland: One 30 mm fixed KCA Oerlikon (Swiss-made) cannon. 150 rounds

RB 24J: Air-to-Air Missile. US: AIM-9J Sidewinder, Infra Red

RB 71: Air-to-Air Missile. UK: Sky Flash, Radar (Mach 4)

RB 74: Air-to-Air Missile. US: AIM-9L Sidewinder, Infra Red (previous designation *RB 24L*)

RB 99: Air-to-Air Missile. US: AIM-120B AMRAAM, Radar. (Carried by JA 37D and Di) (Mach 4)

ARAK m/70: Multi-purpose rocket. Sweden: 6 x 135 mm pod-mounted rockets

Akan m/75 was a 136 kg and 2.69 m long gas-fed automatic revolving cannon, built by the Swiss company Oerlikon KCA. The magazine had four chambers of 150 rounds (30 x 173 mm). Each round weighed 360 gr. The muzzle velocity was 1,030 m/sec. Rate of fire was twenty-two rounds/sec. The firing distance was up to two km. For the most part, the radar, *CK 37* and the auto-pilot took care of aiming in all kinds of weather, day and night. In 1983, it became possible to by means of electronic guidance to fire straight at the enemy.

It was estimated that one hit was enough to take out an enemy aircraft. Compared with the pod-mounted 30 mm Aden of the AJ 37, it was estimated that the JA 37's Oerlikon cannon was six times as efficient.

RB 71 was a British (British Aerospace) semi-active radar missile developed from the American Sparrow. Compared with the US original, the Sky Flash featured increased electronics reliability, more up-to-date components, a proximity fuse with increased jamming consistency, as well as a radar target seeker with increased range and jamming consistency. When firing the 193 kg missile, the aircraft had to light up the target using a special transmitter in its radar. When the missile was within a range of up to 50 km, the target was then presented to the pilot on the target indicator *(MI)*. The missile then flew towards the lit-up target at a speed of Mach 4. This method meant that it was very difficult for the target to escape the missile. However, as long as the attacking aircraft had its radar locked onto the target, it was exposed to enemy aircraft. After firing off the missile, the aircraft could leave the area.

RB 99 was an American AMRAAM (Advanced Medium Range Air to Air Missile), designated AIM-120B, which began to be delivered by Hughes in 1991. *Flygvapnet* was looking for a replacement for the *RB 71* Sky Flash, eventually selecting the AMRAAM, which became the *RB 99*. The *RB 99* weighed 152 kg and was 3.8 m in length. It had a solid fuel rocket engine, which gave a maximum speed of Mach 4. The advantage of the *RB 99* when compared with the *RB 71* was that the former had its own target acquisition gear, not requiring the target to be illuminated from the aircraft. The *RB 99* equipped the JA 37D, JA 37Di and the Saab JAS 39 *Gripen*.

The JA 37 could also carry chaff and flare dispensers, initially from pod *KB*. This was replaced during the 1990s by the chaff dispenser *BOL 451*, and the chaff and flare dispenser *BOY 401*. The latter was fitted on the inner hinge of the elevator (pylon *H7*), thus not occupying a regular weapons pylon.

Initially jamming transmitters, pod *KA*, for active jamming were used. The pod *KA* was replaced during the 1990s with the jamming pod *U 95*.

JA 37 Technical Data and Performance Characteristics

Crew:	1
Quantity built:	149 (s/ns 37301–37449)
Length:	16.43 m
Wingspan:	10.60 m
Height:	5.90 m (4.0 m with fin folded)
Wing area:	52.20 m² (main wing 46.00 m²)
Wheel base:	5.54 m
Fuel load:	5,860 l + one external fuel tank containing an additional 1,400 l
Empty weight:	12,200 kg
Maximum take-off weight:	22,500 kg
Take-off run:	400 m
Landing run:	500 m
Time to 10,000 m (including start):	100 sec
Service ceiling:	18,300 m
Max speed:	Mach 2.1
Engine:	*RM 8B*
Thrust:	7,350 kp without afterburner, 12,750 kp with afterburner

Wings operating the different JA 37 variants were F 4, F 13, F 16, F 17 and F 21.

JA 37Di Viggen s/n 37441, coded Red 41 of F 17 Kallinge, photographed at Malmen outside Linköping on 19 May 2001. Apart from the rear fuselage, the camouflage colours are: upper surfaces and lower surfaces except the nose section: mörkgrå (Dark Grey) 033M (FS 36251), lower surfaces and the entire nose section grå (Grey) 032M (FS 36463). The rear fuselage colours are: svart (Black) 093M (FS 34031), ljusgrön (Light Green) 322M (FS 34138), mörkgrön (Dark Green) 326M (FS 34092) and brun (Brown) 507M (FS 30117).

JA 37Di Viggen s/n 37441, coded F 17-41, landing at Malmen airfield outside Linköping on 19 May 2001. As can be seen, the aircraft has received the tail section from a different JA 37. Note the pair of antennas (indicating JA 37D/Di) on the dorsal spine. Also of note is the F 17 badge on the fin, and the No.2 Sqn/F 17 (Quintus Blå) badge behind the canopy. Beginning on 5 March 1998, the aircraft was modified to JA 37D status, being further upgraded to JA 37Di status on 14 December 2000. On 14 February 2002, s/n 37441 was transferred from F 17 to F 21. (Sven Stridsberg, via Archives of Swedish Aviation Historical Society)

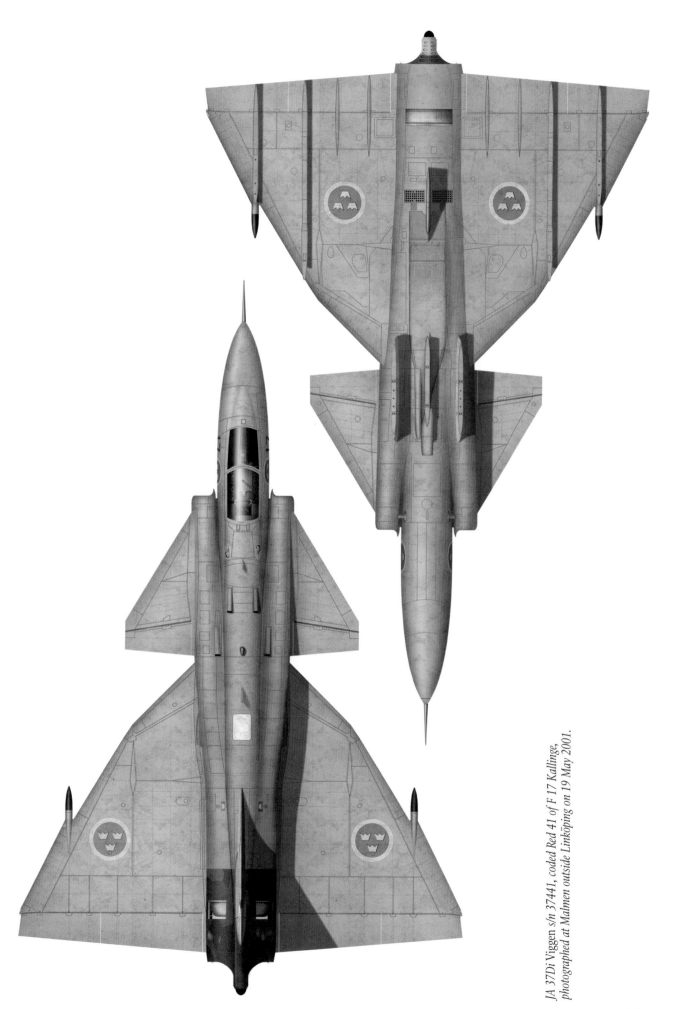

JA 37Di Viggen s/n 37441, coded Red 41 of F 17 Kallinge, photographed at Malmen outside Linköping on 19 May 2001.

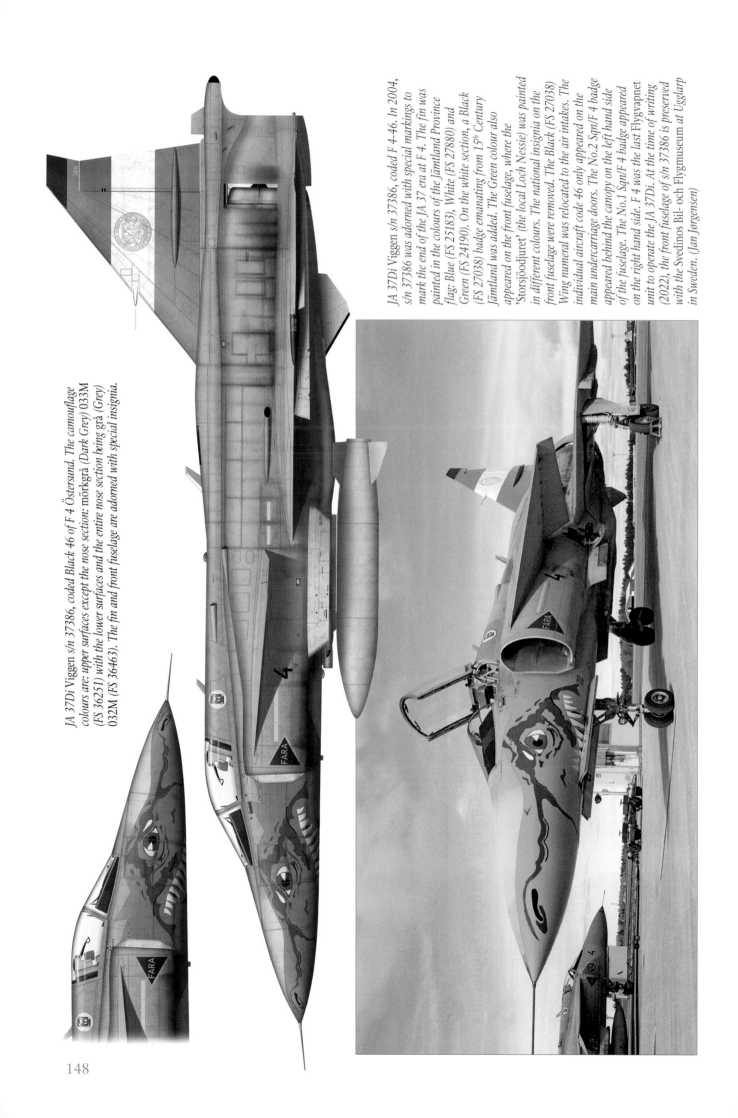

JA 37Di Viggen s/n 37386, coded Black 46 of F 4 Östersund. The camouflage colours are: upper surfaces except the nose section: mörkgrå (Dark Grey) 033M (FS 36251) with the lower surfaces and the entire nose section being grå (Grey) 032M (FS 36463). The fin and front fuselage are adorned with special insignia.

JA 37Di Viggen s/n 37386, coded F 4-46. In 2004, s/n 37386 was adorned with special markings to mark the end of the JA 37 era at F 4. The fin was painted in the colours of the Jämtland Province flag: Blue (FS 25183), White (FS 27880) and Green (FS 24190). On the white section, a Black (FS 27038) badge emanating from 15th Century Jämtland was added. The Green colour also appeared on the front fuselage, where the 'Storsjöodjuret' (the local Loch Nessie) was painted in different colours. The national insignia on the front fuselage were removed. The Black (FS 27038) Wing numeral was relocated to the air intakes. The individual aircraft code 46 only appeared on the main undercarriage doors. The No.2 Sqn/F 4 badge appeared behind the canopy on the left hand side of the fuselage. The No.1 Sqn/F 4 badge appeared on the right hand side. F 4 was the last Flygvapnet unit to operate the JA 37Di. At the time of writing (2022), the front fuselage of s/n 37386 is preserved with the Svedinos Bil- och Flygmuseum at Ugglarp in Sweden. (Jan Jørgensen)

148

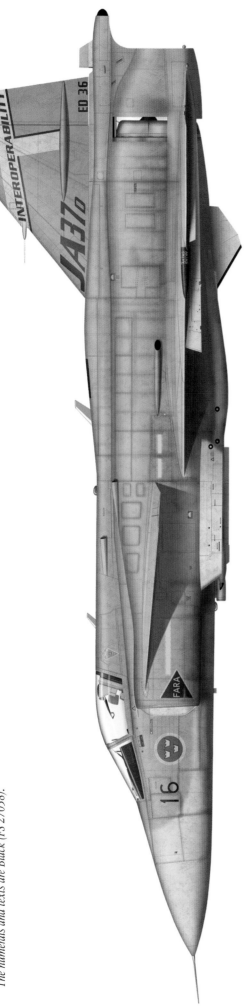

JA 37Di Viggen s/n 37347, coded Black 47 of F 16 Uppsala. Central Sweden in 2003. The camouflage colours are: upper surfaces except the nose section, mörkgrå (Dark Grey) 033M (FS 36251), lower surfaces and the entire nose section, grå (Grey) 032M (FS 36463). The left side of the fin is marked in the colours of the Swedish flag: gul (Yellow) (FS 23655) and blå (Blue) (FS 25183). The numerals and texts are Black (FS 27038).

JA 37Di s/n 37347, coded F 16-47. In 2002, the left side of the fin received special markings. ED 36 indicates Edition 36, ie JA 37Di. The right hand side of the aircraft remained as usual, apart from five White (FS 27880) measuring points painted on small, Black (FS 27038) square areas on the dorsal spine, wing and fuselage attachment points and nose. The point on the fin was located on a pentagon-shaped Black surface. The No.2 Sqn/F 16 badge appeared on behind the canopy on both sides of the fuselage. (Jan Jørgensen)

JA 37Di Viggen s/n 37412, coded Gold 12 of F 4 Östersund, photographed in 2004. The aircraft has been finished overall Black (FS 27038) with a smattering of Gold (FS 27043). There is no national insignia on the lower surfaces of the wings.

DAVID RÖD

n.m.olijniczek '22

JA 37Di Viggen s/n 37412, coded Gold 12 of F 4 Östersund, photographed in 2004.

Chapter 13
Viggen Trials

Viggen trials at *Försökscentralen FC* and *FMV: Prov*

At Malmen airfield in the district of Malmslätt in the city of Linköping, several military aviation units have been based since the early 1910s. During the time of the *Viggen's* introduction, and for many years afterwards, these units included *Försökscentralen (FC)* (the Test Centre), and Wing F 3 (as well as other *Flygvapnet* units later on). A great variety of Saab and *Flygvapnet* aircraft underwent tests at *FC*. All of the *Viggen* variants were tested at *FC*, which later became known as *FMV:Prov* (*Försvarets Materielverk:Prov* = The Defence Material Administration:Test). The aircraft were often marked *FC*, also having an Orange (FS 22510) band about 50 cm wide on the nose section. The most comprehensive *Viggen* trials undertaken were the different weapons tests. S/n 37800 was solely operated by *FC*. Another SK 37, s/n 37806 (coded F 7-64) was used to carry two pylon-mounted rocket pods. In *Flygvapnet* service, the SK 37s remained unarmed. Trials for the forthcoming JAS 39 *Gripen* were also undertaken using *Viggens*. The IR-OTIS sensor, intended for the JAS 39, was tested using s/n 37301, located at the foot of the windscreen. A second JA 37, s/n 37308 (coded FC-48), saw many years of service with *FC*. During firing tests *FUNK 10* and *FUNK 11* pods carrying cameras for the firing or separation of sharp weaponry were used. From 1981, a parachute pod (known as the *FC* Para drop pod) was used when releasing different kinds of gear.

The FC-logotype.

Four AJ 37 Viggens, *s/ns 37018, 37023, 37006 and 37007, all on charge with FC in 1972 for the training of the instructors who would become responsible for training* Viggen *pilots at F 7. All of the aircraft have an Orange band around the respective nose sections, indicating FC. (Ingemar Thuresson, Saab, via Archives of Swedish Aviation Historical Society)*

JA 37 s/n 37308, coded FC-48, photographed at F 15 Söderhamn on 2 June 1985. Note the FC badge on the fin. (Mikael Forslund)

SK 37E s/n 37813, coded FC-13, photographed at F 7 on 18 June 2006. Note the FC badge on the fin, and Yellow numeral (13) on the main undercarriage door. (Mikael Forslund)

153

Chapter 14
Viggen Crashes and Pilots

Write offs

As with most military aircraft, a number of *Viggens* were lost in crashes. Three of the prototypes were written off, as well as 48 production aircraft. A total of 20 pilots were killed, with 32 ejecting safely. Two pilots also managed to get out of burning aircraft on the ground (please refer to the tables).

AJ 37 s/n 37001 was written off on 14 September 1971 at F 3/FC outside Linköping. (Via Archives of Swedish Aviation Historical Society)

Viggen pilots with most flying hours

Tord Kvartsten	2,924.76 hrs	Sven Huldberg	2,267.94 hrs
Jan Setterberg	2,825.96 hrs	Bo Lönnblom	2,212.82 hrs
Bernt Andersson	2,651.22 hrs	Bertil Höglund	2,201.22 hrs
B-O Hagelin	2,438.42 hrs	Torbjörn Halling	2,193.07 hrs
Bo Hagertz	2,384.51 hrs	Lars Bengtsson	2,154.06 hrs

A JA 37 Viggen of F 17 at high altitude in a cloudless sky. Note the No.2 Sqn/F 17 badge behind the canopy. (Gösta Bolander, F 17)

Chapter 15

Viggen Simulators

Several flight simulators were used to train *Viggen* pilots. The first of these, an AJ 37 simulator, was built by the US company Singer-Link and delivered to F 7 in September 1972. The second AJ 37 simulator was delivered to F 15 in January 1973. The *Viggen* pilots of F 6 underwent simulator training at F 7. The third AJ 37 simulator arrived at F 13 in 1974. One year later, this simulator was modified to SH 37 status. Pilots from F 13, F 17 and F 21 all trained on the SH 37 simulator at F 13.

Beginning in 1980, Singer-Link supplied four JA 37 simulators, which were transferred to *FFC U/CVA* at Arboga, F 13, F 4 and F 17 respectively. The JA 37 simulator differed from the earlier AJ/SH 37 simulator in having a new computer system, a new computer-to-computer transfer system, a new instructor's panel, a new visual system from McDonnell Electronics which, among other things, included a 120-degree wide field of view and a G-seat. The seat had inflatable air cushions fitted, and individually monitored seat harnesses in order to give the pilot a realistic feel of flight.

In late 1982, the JA 37 simulator at *CVA* was transferred to F 21. In 1986, F 17's simulator was moved to F 16, where *Flygvapnet's TIS (Typinflygningsskede* = conversion training) for the JA 37 was centred from 1990 until June 1998, when it was transferred to F 4. In 1990, F 17 inherited F 13's simulator. From that point, the JA 37D was handled by F 4.

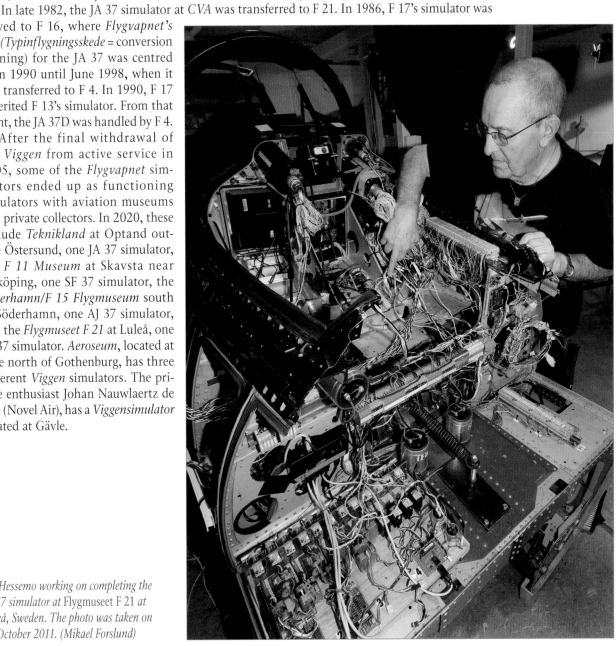

After the final withdrawal of the *Viggen* from active service in 2005, some of the *Flygvapnet* simulators ended up as functioning simulators with aviation museums and private collectors. In 2020, these include *Teknikland* at Optand outside Östersund, one JA 37 simulator, the *F 11 Museum* at Skavsta near Nyköping, one SF 37 simulator, the *Söderhamn/F 15 Flygmuseum* south of Söderhamn, one AJ 37 simulator, and the *Flygmuseet F 21* at Luleå, one JA 37 simulator. *Aeroseum*, located at Säve north of Gothenburg, has three different *Viggen* simulators. The private enthusiast Johan Nauwlaertz de Agé (Novel Air), has a *Viggensimulator* located at Gävle.

Per Hessemo working on completing the JA 37 simulator at Flygmuseet F 21 at Luleå, Sweden. The photo was taken on 25 October 2011. (Mikael Forslund)

Chapter 16
Viggen Export Attemps

Without a doubt, the *Viggen* was a world-class aircraft. Attempts to export the *Viggen* were made, but in the event, *Flygvapnet* remained the sole operator. The *Viggen* was designed for specific Swedish specifications, which may have influenced the failed foreign sale efforts. However, at that time as well as in the present day, it seems likely that "Friendship Politics" was and is a factor. The Swedish policy of neutrality only allowed for exports to politically stable countries that weren't expected to become embroiled in military conflicts. Additionally, the *Viggen* included components built in a variety of countries. For instance, 22 different components were manufactured in Denmark. This was due to the earlier sale of 51 Saab 35 *Drakens* to the Royal Danish Air Force (RDAF). In all likelihood, the foreign sub-contractors were not willing to sell their products to any third countries.

Following the first flight of the *Viggen* in 1967 and the presentation at Le Bourget, Paris, two years later, much interest was shown in the Swedish aircraft. A handful of countries, including Australia, Belgium, Denmark, France, Italy, Japan, Canada, the Netherlands, Norway, Switzerland, Great Britain, West Germany and Austria, asked for information on the *Viggen*. The *Viggen* was of course compared with other combat aircraft, such as the French *Mirage* F.1 and the Soviet MiG-23. Both the *Mirage* and the MiG-23 featured variable air intakes, which was an advantage during maximum speed at maximum altitude. However, the *Viggen* accelerated more quickly to the more realistic speeds used operationally. The *Viggen* required 5.5 minutes from take-off to reaching a speed of Mach 1.6 at an altitude of 11,000 m, with the *Mirage* F.1 requiring 18 min...

The maximum speed of the *Mirage* F.1 (Mach 1.86) at 11,000 m was principally theoretical. When carrying four air-to-air missiles, the fuel load of the F.1 was inadequate to reach maximum speed following a Quick Reaction Alert take-off! The various systems of the *Viggen* were superior. Despite the advantages of the *Viggen*, it was difficult to whip-up foreign interest. The "customers" were for the most part only interested in looking at "simple" numbers.

In 1967, Britain took an interest in the *Viggen*, but then only in much modified variants. The twin-engine and two-seat variants aroused the most interest. As a result, Saab quickly responded in August 1967, presenting three different variants:

The single-engine 37XE-1 (Rolls-Royce Spey RB 168-62R) with increased fuel load. Otherwise, relatively similar to the AJ 37. Maximum speed Mach 1.56.

The single-engine 37XE-2 (Bristol-Olympus B-Ol. 22R), lengthened fuselage and increased fuel load. Maximum speed Mach 2.08.

The twin-engine 37XE-3 (Rolls-Royce RB 193), lengthened fuselage and further increased fuel load. Maximum speed Mach 2.5+.

However, British interest soon waned though the British returned in 1968. Further drafts with the future JA 37 as foundation were made. Yet again, nothing came of this.

In 1970, Australia showed interest in a replacement for the *Mirage* III, known as 37AU. The new aircraft was intended to enter service in 1976. In December 1970, a Saab team presented the *Viggen* in the Australian capitol, Canberra. Disadvantages put forward by the Australians included the poor range and load factor spectrum. In March 1972, technical information and price for the 37AU was handed over. The data was later augmented with proposals for a cooperation with the Australian aviation industry. The net result was that the *Viggen*, *Mirage F.1* and Northrop Cobra became the subject for further studies. An offer for 27, alternatively 67 or as many as 127 Saab 37AUs was delivered on 11 May 1973. Consideration regarding cooperation between the two countries were included in the offer. Australia was offered to participate in the development of the *Viggen*, as well as producing the engine under licence and building certain electronics.

The 37AU was based on the JA 37, but had a different armament, additional airframe life, as well as a higher maximum speed. The latter necessitated a redesigned variable air intake in order for the aircraft to fly at speeds of over Mach 2. Due to a government crisis, no deal resulted, despite the fact that a full-scale mock-up of the new air intake had been constructed. Another request in 1976 included an estimate for 72 *Viggens*. Estimates for both the AJ 37 and the JA 37 were supplied. Once again, it was found that the high altitude performance and range did not fulfil the Australian

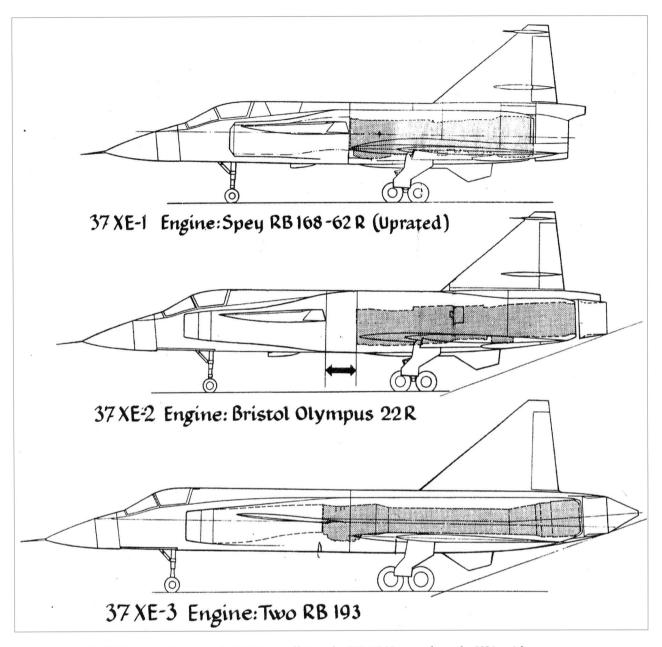

37 XE-1 Engine: Spey RB 168-62 R (Uprated)

37 XE-2 Engine: Bristol Olympus 22 R

37 XE-3 Engine: Two RB 193

requirements. In 1981, Australia ordered 75 McDonnell Douglas F/A-18 Hornets from the USA, with deliveries commencing in 1985.

In 1971, Saab was approached by India with regards to information on the *Viggen* in anticipation of a possible evaluation. Nothing came of this, but India returned in 1974. Several meetings were held, resulting in India asking for an offer for 40 somewhat modified AJ 37 *Viggens*. Deliveries were to commence within 24 months. It was intended that an unknown quantity of aircraft would be delivered from Sweden, followed by licence production. Nothing in particular happened, though. However, an Indian delegation arrived at F 7 Såtenäs in 1976 to test fly the AJ 37! The Indians required a number of modifications, including a built-in cannon. The basic idea was to graft the front fuselage of a JA 37 onto that of an AJ 37. The single-seater was known as 37V-A, and the two-seater as 37V-AT. The Indians wanted rapid delivery of 40 aircraft, with 130 to be produced under licence. Two different offers were delivered on 15 March 1978. The first offer stated that the initial 15 aircraft were to be picked from the Swedish orders, with delivery beginning within six months. Thereafter, the aircraft were to undergo modification work. The second offer stated that initial deliveries were to commence within 24 months, with regular production schedule being maintained.

Saab sent a request to the USA regarding permission for the export of American components, including the US-designed *Viggen* engine to India. The US authorities refused to grant permission, resulting in the end of the proposed deal. Instead, the Franco-British Jaguar was ordered by India.

During the so-called "Weapons deal of the Century" of the early 1970s, the *Viggen* was one of the competitors for an order for 348 (290 single-seat and 58 two-seat) aircraft for the NATO countries Belgium, Denmark, the Netherlands and Norway. Delivery was to take place between 1979 and 1984. These NATO countries were to replace their Lockheed F-104 Starfighters with something new.

Saab presented the 37E Eurofighter, to be pitted against rival aircraft. Following formal evaluation, four candidates remained in 1974: the Saab 37E *Viggen*, the French Dassault *Mirage* F-1E and the US General Dynamics YF-16 and Northrop YF-17. Indeed tough competition from aircraft intended for NATO countries...

As compensation in case of a deal, a 100 percent buy-back policy was promised. In this regard, Sweden was in a good position with companies including Saab-Scania, Volvo and Ericsson. However, the strict Swedish policy regarding weapons export did not seem to favour the sale of *Viggens*.

The Saab offer was delivered on 20 August 1974. Following a few different questionings from the Steering Committee counterpart, it was decreed that the reply would come on 15th May 1975. On 13 January 1975, it was announced that the General Dynamics YF-16 had been selected as the new USAF fighter. This meant an even lower chance for the *Viggen*. In early July 1975, it was announced that the four NATO countries had all selected the YF-16.

Austria also showed an interest, with their air arm having operated various Saab aircraft for many years: B 17A, J 29F *Tunnan*, 105OE, *Safir* and the 35OE *Draken*. In March 1975, an Austrian delegation arrived at F 7 to study and fly the *Viggen*. The following month, the AJ 37 *Viggen* was demonstrated in Austria. On 21 April, Saab offered 24 Saab 37Ö *Viggens* (similar to the JA 37) to Austria at a price tag of 900 million SEK. Delivery was scheduled in 1980. Until the arrival of the *Viggens*, Austria was offered to lease 15 used Saab J 35B *Drakens*. No deal resulted, though. In 1978, Austria submitted another request. Yet again, no deal. A third request was made in 1983, with a deal being concluded, albeit for 24 35OE *Drakens* (modified former *Flygvapnet* J 35Ds).

By the late 1990s, the question of a new fighter aircraft for Austria became urgent. Saab offered the JAS 39 *Gripen*. Prior to converting from the *Draken* to the *Gripen*, Austrian pilots were offered to fly a number of sorties in JA 37s during "sharp" exercises in Sweden (at F 21). During 1999, Austrian pilots flew both the SK 37 and JA 37 *Viggen* at F 21 during the "Austrian Education Squadron, Project Polar Light". The sale of used JA 37s was discussed. However, the fact that the *Viggen* was about to be phased out in Sweden was considered a drawback. Among other things, maintaining spares, etc., would be expensive. Instead, Austria chose to order the Eurofighter Typhoon. But in the interim, when the *Draken* was phased out, and the Eurofighters had not been delivered, Austria leased a number of F-5 Tigers from Switzerland as a temporary measure...

Chapter 17

Preserved *Viggens*

When the *Viggens* were withdrawn from use in 2005, many aircraft were scrapped by the *Försvarsmaktens Återvinningscentral (FMÅC)* (Defence Forces Recycling Centre) at F 10 and at *Flygvapnets Halmstadsskolor* at Halmstad. Much of the material was recycled. During the final years of service, some *Viggens* were set aside for preservation. At the time of writing (2022), some 35 *Viggens* can be found at aviation museums around Sweden, while a few aircraft have found their way to various European aviation museums (please refer to the tables).

Today (2022), two *Viggens* are airworthy. The first to return to the skies was AJS 37 s/n 37098, now registered as SE-DXN and coded as F 7-52. After being grounded for twelve years, the aircraft was restored to flying condition in 2012. The second one is an SK 37E, s/n 37809, which was flown again in 2018 after being grounded in 2008. It is registered as SE-DXO, being coded F 15-61. Both are based at Såtenäs and operated by the Swedish Air Force Historic Flight (SwAFHF).

AJ 37 s/n 37094, coded F 10-57, on display at Aeroseum, a mountain hangar formerly part of F 9 Säve, north of Gothenburg, Sweden. On these pictures, taken on 6 May 2007, a 30/55 cannon pod is fitted. (Both Mikael Forslund)

(Preserved *Viggen* <u>cockpit/front fuselage</u> **not** showed here. They are written as <u>cockpit</u> in tables)

Version	S/n	Location
Test	37-6	*Västerås Flygmuseum* (at former Wing F 1), Västerås, Sweden
AJS 37	37009	*Söderhamn/F 15 Flygmuseum* (at former Wing F 15), Söderhamn, Sweden
AJS 37	37027	*Stenbäcks Flygmuseum*, Skurup, Sweden
AJ 37	37031	On pole at Söderhamn, Sweden
AJ 37	37034	*Innovantum/Saab bilmuseum*, Trollhättan, Sweden
AJ 37	37050	*F 7 Gårds- och Flottiljmuseum* (at Wing F 7), Såtenäs, Sweden
AJ 37	37056	*Söderhamn/F 15 Flygmuseum* (at former Wing F 15), Söderhamn, Sweden
AJS 37	37057	*Brand- och räddningsskolan (at former Wing F 14)*, Halmstad, Sweden
AJS 37	37058	*Volvo Museum*, Gothenburg, Sweden
AJ 37	37067	*Söderhamn/F 15 Flygmuseum* (at former Wing F 15), Söderhamn, Sweden
AJS 37	37068	*GKN* Aerospace, Trollhättan, Sweden
AJS 37	37072	*Riksväg 44*, Grästorp, Sweden
AJS 37	37074	*Museo del Aire*, Madrid, Spain
AJS 37	37080	*Västerås Flygmuseum* (at former Wing F 1), Västerås, Sweden
AJ 37	37094	*Aeroseum* (at former Wing F 9), Säve, Sweden
AJ 37	37097	*Teknikland*, Optand, Sweden
AJS 37	37098	SwAFHF (flying condition) (at Wing F 7), Såtenäs, Sweden
AJS 37	37108	*Flygvapenmuseum* (at former Wing F 3), Linköping, Sweden
JA 37	37301	*Flygvapenmuseum* (at former Wing F 3), Linköping, Sweden
JA 37	37309	*Combitech*, Arboga, Sweden
JA 37D	37326	*Svedinos Bil- och Flygmuseum*, Ugglarp, Sweden
JA 37Di	37347	*HM Hadtörténeti Intézet* és *Múzeum*, Szolnok, Hungary
JA 37	37362	*Flygmuseet F 21* (at Wing F 21), Luleå, Sweden
JA 37	37366	*F 13 Kamratförening* exhibition (at former Wing F 13), Norrköping, Sweden
JA 37	37367	On pole at *Europaväg 4* (E 4), Linköping, Sweden
JA 37	37378	*RFN Museum*, Vidsel, Sweden
JA 37	37392	*Teknikland*, Optand, Sweden
JA 37	37410	*Österlens flygmuseum*, Östra Wemmerlöv, Sweden
JA 37Di	37412	*Teknikland*, Optand, Sweden
JA 37Di	37415	*Försvarsmaktens Tekniska skola* (at former Wing F 14), Halmstad, Sweden
JA 37	37425	On pole at *F 16 Museum* (at Wing F 16), Uppsala, Sweden
JA 37Di	37428	*Försvarsmaktens Tekniska skola* (at former Wing F 14), Halmstad, Sweden
JA 37Di	37429	*Eesti Lennundusmuuseum*, Tartu, Estonia
JA 37D	37431	*Luftfahrtmuseum*, Graz-Thalerhof, Austria
JA 37	37432	*Bunge Flygmuseum*, Bunge, Sweden
JA 37Di	37440	Gate Guard at *Europaväg 22* (E 22), Sörby, Sweden
JA 37D	37448	*Teknikland*, Optand, Sweden
JA 37Di	37449	*Flygvapenmuseum* (at former Wing F 3), Linköping, Sweden
SK 37	37800	*Stenbäcks Flygmuseum*, Skurup, Sweden
SK 37	37803	*Teknikland*, Optand, Sweden
SK 37	37805	*Söderhamn/F 15 Flygmuseum* (at former Wing F 15), Söderhamn, Sweden
SK 37E	37808	*Musée de l'Air et de l'Espace*, Paris, France
SK 37E	37809	SwAFHF (flying condition) (at Wing F 7), Såtenäs, Sweden
SK 37E	37811	*Musee Europeen de l'aviation de Chasse*, Montélimar, France
SK 37E	37817	*Flygmuseet F 21* (at Wing F 21), Luleå, Sweden
AJSH 37	37901	*Aviodrome*, Lelystad, The Netherlands
AJSH 37	37904	Malmen (at former Wing F 3), Linköping, Sweden
AJSH 37	37911	*Aeroseum* (at former Wing F 9), Säve, Sweden
AJSH 37	37918	Newark Air Museum, Nottingham, UK
AJSH 37	37924	*Visby flygplats*, Visby, Sweden
AJSH 37	37927	Biltema, Luleå, Sweden
AJSF 37	37951	*Slovenské technické múzeum*, Kosice, Slovakia
AJSF 37	37954	*Muzeum Lotnictwa Polskiego*, Kraków, Poland
AJSF 37	37957	*Letecké Muzeum VHU*, Praha-Kbely, Czech Republic
AJSF 37	37961	*F 11 Museum*, (at former Wing F 11), Nyköping, Sweden
AJSF 37	37971	*Museo dell'Aeronautica Gianni Caproni*, Zoppola, Italy

AJSF 37	37972	*Gotlands Försvarsmuseum*, Tingstäde, Sweden
AJSF 37	37974	*Flugausstellung Leo Junior*, Hermeskeil, Germany
AJSF 37	37976	*Ängelholms Flygmuseum* (at former Wing F 10), Ängelholm, Sweden
SF 37	37977	*Flygmuseet F 21* (at Wing F 21), Luleå, Sweden

AJSF 37 s/n 37954, coded F 21-54 is on display at the Muzeum Lotnictwa Polskiego, Cracow, Poland. *Unfortunately, at the time of writing (2022) the aircraft has deteriorated due to having been placed on outdoor display. (Both Bartlomiej Belcarz)*

AJ 37 s/n 37050, coded F 7-50, on display at the F 7 Gårds- och Flottiljmuseum, Såtenäs, Sweden, on 18 May 2008. Two m/70 rocket pods and two RB 74 Sidewinders are fitted to the aircraft. The aircraft has received a coat of varnish to better withstand the harsh Swedish weather. Next to the Viggen is Saab JAS 39 Gripen s/n 39113, coded F 7-13. (Mikael Forslund)

AJ 37 s/n 37050, coded F 7-50, on display at the F 7 Gårds- och Flottiljmuseum, Såtenäs, Sweden, on 18 May 2008. Two m/70 rocket pods and two RB 74 Sidewinders are fitted to the aircraft. The aircraft has received a coat of varnish to better withstand the harsh Swedish weather. Next to the Viggen, is Saab J 32D Lansen, s/n 32603, coded F 16-33. (Mikael Forslund)

The front fuselage of AJSF 37 s/n 37961, coded F 21- , on display at the F 11 Museum at Nyköping, Sweden, photographed on 15 October 2011. Next to the front fuselage is a Viggen ejection seat, and an RM 8 engine. A Scottish Aviation Bulldog (Swedish Army designation FPL 61C), s/n 61061 is hanging from the ceiling. The cockpit of AJSF 37 s/n 37958, coded F 21-(58), can also be found at the F 11 Museum. At the time of writing (2022), this has been converted as a simulator. (Mikael Forslund)

AJ 37 s/n 37009, coded F 15-09, sits outside the Söderhamn/F 15 Flygmuseum at Söderhamn, Sweden. It is framed by a propeller of a Saab J 21A. The photo was taken on 17 October 2010. (Mikael Forslund)

AJ 37 s/n 37056, coded F 15-16, is also preserved with the Söderhamn/F 15 Flygmuseum at Söderhamn, Sweden. The photo was taken on 17 October 2010. SK 37 s/n 37805, coded F 15-65, and the front fuselage of AJS 37 s/n 37081, coded F 15-, are also to be found at the Söderhamn/F 15 Flygmuseum. Another Viggen, AJ 37 s/n 37067, coded F 15-37, sits in a shelter outside the museum. (Mikael Forslund)

Alongside the E 4 highway near Söderhamn, Sweden, pole-mounted AJ 37 s/n 37031, coded F 15-54, has been preserved. The photo was taken on 17 October 2010. (Mikael Forslund)

Among the aircraft preserved at the Flygmuseet F 21 at Luleå, Sweden, is JA 37 s/n 37362, coded F 21-09. The photo was taken on 25 October 2011. Also preserved here are SF 37 s/n 37977, coded F 21-68, SK 37E s/n 37817, coded F 21-75, and the fin (coded 67) of AJSH 37 s/n 37922. A JA 37 simulator is preserved indoors. (Mikael Forslund)

Flygvapenmuseum at Linköping, Sweden has AJS 37 s/n 37108, coded F 10-55, on display. The photo was taken on 1 October 2016. The last production Viggen, *JA 37Di s/n 37449, coded F 4-49, is also preserved by* Flygvapenmuseum, *Linköping, Sweden. (Mikael Forslund)*

For many years, the first Viggen *prototype was on outdoor display at* Flygvapenmuseum, *Linköping, Sweden. Unfortunately, the aircraft suffered much corrosion due to the harsh Swedish weather, being scrapped in 2012. (Mikael Forslund)*

SF 37 s/n 37972, coded F 10-56, preserved outside the Gotlands Flygmuseum *at Visby, Sweden, during the early 2000s. Today (2022), the aircraft can be found at the* Gotlands Försvarsmuseum *at Tingstäde, Gotland, Sweden. (Tor Karlsson)*

Some aircraft have been preserved at the RFN Museum at Vidsel, Sweden, including JA 37 s/n 37378, coded F 4-38. Next to the Viggen is J 35J Draken s/n 35604, coded F 10-04. The photo was taken on 25 October 2011. (Mikael Forslund)

Among the aircraft found at Teknikland *at Optand outside Östersund, Sweden, are JA 37D s/n 37448, coded F 4-04, on outdoor display. The photo was taken on 16 May 2019. (Mikael Forslund)*

Another Viggen *preserved at* Teknikland *at Optand outside Östersund, Sweden, is the Black-painted JA 37Di s/n 37412, coded F 4-12. The photo were taken on 16 May 2019. (Mikael Forslund)*

Also found at Teknikland, located at Optand outside Östersund, Sweden, is this SK 37, s/n 37803, coded F 4-67. The photos were taken on 16 May 2019. (Mikael Forslund)

AJSF 37 s/n 37974, coded F 21-64, is on display at the Flugausstellung Leo Junior, *Hermeskeil, Germany. At the time of writing (2022), the condition of the aircraft has deteriorated due to it being displayed outdoors. (Tomasz Obrębski)*

For many years, the sixth Viggen prototype, 37-6, has been preserved by the Västerås Flygmuseum, Västerås, Sweden. Among the many other aircraft found here is a Saab S 29C Tunnan, coded F 3-20. The photos were taken on 16 April 1991. (Both Mikael Forslund)

JA 37Di s/n 37347 has been preserved with the Magyar Repüléstörténeti Múzeum, Szolnok, Hungary. Unfortunately, at the time of writing (2022), the aircraft has deteriorated due to being on outdoor display. (All Tomasz Obrębski)

Chapter 18
Colours and Markings

When first delivered, the AJ 37s of Wing F 7 and F 15 were overall Natural Metal, with national insignia and Black (FS 27038) numerals. The Black (FS 27038) Wing numeral (7 or 15) was located on the air intakes. The fin code in Black (FS 27038) also appeared on the landing gear doors. The four-colour splinter camouflage was then introduced in 1973 with s/n 37051 (F 7-51) being the first AJ 37 to be painted in this manner, consisting of *ljusgrön 322M* (Light Green, FS 34082), *mörkgrön 326M* (Dark Green, FS 34079), *brun 507M* (Brown, FS 30051) and *svart 093M* (Black, FS 37038), on the upper surfaces and *blågrå 058M* (Blue Grey, FS 35237), on the lower surfaces. The numerals were Yellow (FS 23655). The Wing numeral was subsequently moved to the nose ahead of the national insignia. After a while, the numerals were painted Bright Red (FS 28905). Eventually all *Viggen* variants were finished in the four-colour splinter camouflage.

In 1982, two F 13 JA 37s (s/ns 37347, code F 13-37 and 37348, code F 13-38) were camouflaged overall *vit* (White FS 37925) for trials. This colour turned out to be less suitable. Simultaneously, two other JA 37s (s/ns 37328, code F 13-68 and 37349, code F 13-39) were finished in an overall *mellangrå* (Medium Grey FS 36314) colour scheme, with two additional JA 37s (s/ns 37329, code F 13-69 and 37350, code F 13-40) being painted overall *mörkgrå* (Dark Grey FS 36251). The camouflage tests resulted in a standard two-tone Grey (FS 36251 upper and FS 36463 lower) colour scheme being selected. Initially, a few JA 37s were flown in an overall Natural Metal scheme.

In 1982, a radical departure regarding the camouflage schemes of fighters in particular saw most of the JA 37s finished in a two-tone Grey camouflage scheme. This consisted on *mörkgrå 033M* (Dark Grey FS 36251), on the upper surfaces and *ljusgrå 032M* (Light Grey FS 36463) on the lower surfaces. Initially, the numerals were Black (FS 27038) later being changed to Bright Red (FS 28905). On aircraft retaining the old splinter camouflage, the numerals were Yellow (FS 23655). On some aircraft, a Bright Red (FS 28905) triangle was painted/taped on the upper part of the fin. On many *Viggens*, the last three numerals of the serial number were painted in Yellow (FS 23655) on top of the fin. The reason why some JA 37s retained the old splinter camouflage was that in case of war the enemy would be led to believe that these were AJ 37 variants which, incidentally, retained the splinter camouflage.

The individual aircraft numeral, e.g. 28, was painted in a large angular typeface on the upper surfaces of the wings (one numeral on each wing). Black (FS 27038), White (FS 27875) or Bright Red (FS 28905).

AJ 37 s/n 37051, code F 7-51, was the first operational Viggen *to receive the splinter camouflage.*

AJ 37 s/n 37034, coded F 6-34, seen just after take-off. The upper surfaces are svart (Black) 093M (FS 37038), ljusgrön (Light Green) 322M (FS 34082), mörkgrön (Dark Green) 326M (FS 34079) and brun (Brown) 507M (FS 30051). The lower surfaces are blågrå (Blue Grey) 058M (FS 35237). The nose section is Black (FS 27038), the Wing numeral (6), Yellow (FS 23655) and individual aircraft code numeral (34) lysröd (Bright Red) (FS 23905). (Leif Fredin, via Archives of Mikael Forslund)

The AJSF 37s of F 21 (SWAFRAP) were finished in a similar two-tone camouflage as the JA 37s (upper Light Ghost Grey FS 36375 and lower Light Grey FS 36495). The national insignia appeared in Dark Grey (FS 36176), as did all the numerals. These had a different typeface than before (please refer to the photos). Additionally, one solitary SK 37 s/n 37811 was already finished in such camouflage when serving with F 15. The camouflage was retained when used as an SK 37E at F 4 and F 21.

A large number of special markings and insignia, including Wing, Squadron and Company insignia, were painted on, or as transfers, on many 37 *Viggens*, irrespective of variants (please refer to the photos). Exercise markings in different shapes also appeared (please refer to the photos). A few *Viggens* were also finished in highly imaginative markings. Most of these were applied when the aircraft were due to be phased out by the respective squadron/Wing. Such aircraft were generally only flown on rare occasions before being scrapped. However, other *Viggens* which had special insignia/markings were flown more frequently. A few examples are presented here:

A splinter camouflaged SH 37, s/n 37908, code F 13-15, passing near a West German Navy destroyer in 1976. (Åke Andersson, Saab, via Archives of Swedish Aviation Historical Society)

- 37411, F 16-11, had two lateral Black Grey (FS 37031) stripes on the upper surfaces of the canard wings and the wings. On the fin the numeral 11 and a triangle appeared in Bright Red (FS 28905).

Two JA 37s of F 4, s/n 37353, coded F 3-33, is finished in the four-colour splinter camouflage, with the external fuel tank being Dark Grey (FS 36173), and s/n 37394, coded F 4-64 in Grey air superiority camouflage; the upper surfaces are mörkgrå *(Dark Grey) 032M (FS 36173), with the lower surfaces being* ljusgrå *(Light Grey) 032M (FS 36463). The individual code numeral, 64, is Black (FS 27038). (Photo via* Flygvapnet*)*

The No.3 Sqn/ F 16 insignia appeared in Grey (FS 36251) on the fuselage. The Wing numeral, 16, was Black (FS 27038). A large Black (FS 37038) Mustang (horse) insignia (of No.1 Company/F 16), five metres diameter, was painted on the lower surfaces of the wings. National insignia under the wings was Black Grey (FS 37031). The Mustang insignia (smaller) was also painted on both sides of the rear fuselage. The aircraft was finished in these markings in June 2000 to function as the *Flygvapnet* air display *Viggen* during the type's final years. The last flight was made on 14 October 2003, when the *Viggen* was ferried to Halmstad for scrapping.

- 37347, F 16-47 as a trials aircraft at *FC* had five small White dots superimposed on Black (FS 27875 and FS 27038) squares painted on the right-hand side of the aircraft, a Yellow and Blue (FS 23655 and FS 25095) Swedish flag, the text INTEROPERABILITY JA 37D ED 36 and the code numeral 47 in Black (FS 27038) on the left side of the fin. The insignia of No.2 Sqn/F 16 appeared behind the left side of the canopy. The right side of the fin remained standard, with Bright Red (FS 28905) code numeral, 47, and triangle. The aircraft was finished in this way in 2002 to show it had been upgraded as a JA 37Di. The Black (FS 27875) Wing numeral, 16, was later removed from both sides of the forward fuselage, with a 50 cm wide Orange (FS 22510) band appearing on the nose. Since 1996, this *Viggen* had spent most of its time with *FC*. These markings remained on the aircraft, which made its final flight on 9 May 2005. On this date, s/n 37347 was ferried to *HM Hadtörténeti Intézet és Múzeum* at Szolnok, Hungary, where it remains (2022) on display.

- 37432, F 16-32 was finished overall Blue (FS 25095) with Yellow (FS 23655) stripes, numerals and text. On the top of the fin, P 32 appeared in Black (FS 27038). On both sides of the fuselage and the upper and lower surfaces of the wings, the insignias (three each) of No.2 Sqn/F 16 and No.2 Company/F 16 appeared. The test *Petter Blå* appeared in Yellow (FS 23655) below the left side of the windscreen. The aircraft was adorned in this manner in July 2000 in anticipation of the *Flygvapnet* 75th anniversary airshow, held at F 16 in 2001. The *Viggen* made its final flight on 10 October 2001, its destination being *Gotlands Flygmuseum* at Visby, Sweden. Today (2022), s/n 37432 is on public display at *Bunge Flygmuseum*, Bunge, Sweden.

- 37027, AJS 37 F 10-57 was finished overall Red (FS 11136) in early 2000 in connection with the replacement of the *Viggen* with the JAS 39 *Gripen* at F 10. The nose and top of the fin appeared in Black (FS 37038). The legend THE SHOW MUST GO ON appeared in White (FS 17875) on both sides of the fuselage. The ghost squadron insignia appeared in White (FS 17875) on both sides of the fin, the upper and lower surfaces of the wings and on both sides of the nose section. On the right-hand side of the nose, the Squadron/Company appeared in a refined variant on a Black shield with Golden wings and relevant text. The code numeral, 57, appeared in a small Yellow (FS 23655) variant on both sides of the fin. Additionally, there were three Yellow (FS 23655) crowns on the rear section of the external fuel tank. The aircraft flew in these colours until June

2001. The final flight was into preservation with *Flygvapenmuseum*, Linköping Sweden. Today (2022), this *Viggen* is preserved with *Stenbäcks Flygmuseum*, Skurup, Sweden.

- 37412, F 4-12, was finished overall Black (FS 27038) with numerals, stripes and national insignia in Gold (FS 17043). The No.2 Sqn/F 4 insignia appeared on the left side behind the canopy, with the No.2 Company insignia appearing on the opposite side. These markings were applied in the latter part of 2004 to mark the phasing-out of the *Viggen* from *Flygvapnet* service. On 24 April 2005, the aircraft was ferried to Optand for eventual display along the E 14 highway. It is still (2022) there, functioning as a roadsign for *Teknikland*, Optand, Sweden.

- 37386, F 4-46, the Lake Storsjön beast appearing on the nose section in two Green shades (FS 24190 and FS 24172), Red (FS 21105) and Black (FS 27038) eye. The Regional flag of Jämtland in Blue (FS 25095), White (FS 27875), and Green (FS 24190) representing the sky, snow and forest, appearing on the fin together with the Province of Jämtland Coat of Arms in Black (FS 27038), located on the White section of the flag. The No.1 Sqn/F 4 insignia appeared behind the canopy on the right side of the fuselage and that of No.2 Sqn/F 4 on the opposite side. The Wing numeral, 4, appeared in Black (FS 27038) on the rear section of the air intakes. The aircraft was finished in these markings in late 2004 to mark the phasing-out from F 4 of the *Viggen*. A few flights were subsequently made, with the final flight occurring on 9 December 2004 to Halmstad for scrapping. However, the front fuselage was saved, being transferred to *Svedinos Bil- och Flygmuseum* at Ugglarp, Sweden, where it remains on public display (2022).

- 37950, F 21-48, (essentially painted/marked SWAFRAP in colours), the rear fuselage was finished in different shades of Blue with the Bright Red (FS 28905) legend *AKKTU STAKKI* (Lonely Wolf), a stripe and the code numeral 48 appearing on the fin. A wolf's head appeared on both sides of the fin. The insignia of No.1 Company/F 21 appeared in place of the fuselage national insignia. The fuselage national insignia was repositioned to the air intakes below the canard wings. The *Viggen* was painted in this way in early 2005 to mark the phasing-out of the *Viggen* reconnaissance variant from F 21. The aircraft was flown for the last time on 8 December 2005, the destination being Halmstad for scrapping.

- 37410, F 16-10, Red (FS 21105) fin with Black (FS 27038) "Mustang insignia" (of No.1 Company/F 16) appearing on the fin. Red (FS 21105) P 10 on the Black (FS 37038) upper section of the fin. The insignia of No.3 Sqn/F 16 appeared behind the canopy on both sides of the fuselage. The *Viggen* was painted in this way in August 2003 to mark the phasing-out from F 16 as well

A splinter camouflaged JA 37, code F 17-49, armed with four RB 24J Sidewinders and two RB 71 Sky Flash. (Rune Hedgren, F 17)

as the disbandment of the Wing. The aircraft made its final landing at F 16 on 8 October 2003, subsequently being placed on display at the Wing's museum. In May 2013, s/n 37410 was transported to *Österlens Flygmuseum* at Östra Vemmerlöv, Sweden, where it remains (2022) on display.

- 37083, F 10-07, Red (FS 11136) fin with a White (FS 17875) Santa Claus on the left side, with the No.1 Sqn/F 10 insignia, a White (FS 17875) ghost on the right side. The aircraft was finished in this manner for a 1995 Christmas card. S/n 37083 was scrapped shortly afterwards. The fin was saved, being mounted outside No.1 Sqn/F 10.
- 37304, F 21-01, (based at F 17) Purple (FS 27144) fin with Yellow (FS 23655) roundel upon which the viking Hagbard (the insignia on No.2 Company/F 17) appeared. Yellow (FS 23655) 01 on the fin. The *Viggen* was adorned in this way in June 2000 in connection with No.2 Sqn/F 17 replacing their JA 37s with the JAS 39 *Gripen*. The aircraft was scrapped shortly afterwards.

A Grey camouflaged JA 37, coded F 21-15, at Visby airport, Sweden. (Tor Karlsson)

A Grey camouflaged JA 37 s/n 37425, coded F 16-25, photographed at Rommehed, Borlänge, Sweden, on 22 October 1991. Note that the Light Grey paint on the nose section has partly worn off. (Mikael Forslund)

The front fuselage was subsequently used as a teaching aid at F 17, with the fin being placed outside No.2 Sqn/F 17.

- 37347, F 13-37, Red (FS 21105) legend *GOD JUL* (i.e. Merry Christmas) painted on the upper surfaces of the wings. The aircraft was painted in this way for a December 1987 Christmas card. An unknown number of flights were made during the time these markings were applied.
- 37394, F 17-47, Blue and Yellow (FS 25095 and FS 23655) stripes on fin and forward leading edges, the Swedish flag on the rear part of the external fuel tank and the Black (FS 27038) text 1982 2002 together with a circular Black (FS 27038) insignia in Grey (FS 36251) with the text JA 37 at F 17 on both sides of the fin. Otherwise, the aircraft had standard colours and markings. The *Viggen* was finished in these markings in July 2002 to mark the transition of No.1Sqn/F 17 from the JA 37 to the JAS 39 *Gripen*. On 29 August 2002 this JA 37 was ferried to Halmstad for scrapping.
- 37402, F 21-02, Yellow (FS 23655), Blue (FS 25095) and Black (FS 27038) sun ray stripes on the fin. The insignia of No.3 Sqn/F 21 on both sides of the fuselage. No.1 Sqn/F 21 insignia on both sides behind the canopy. The aircraft was adorned in this manner in June 2004 to mark the phasing-out of the *Viggen* at F 21. On 17 June 2004 the aircraft was ferried to Halmstad for scrapping.
- 37952, F 13-04, No.1 Sqn/F 13, was adorned with a Red and White (FS 21105/FS 27875) shark's mouth for a 1990 Christmas card. It is unclear if the aircraft was flown in these markings.
- 37965, F 21-54 was painted with a Grey (FS 36251) wolf's head, Red (FS 21105) tongue, White (FS 27875) teeth and eye, White and Black (FS 27038) mouth and pupil on the nose. The Wing numeral 21 was Bright Red (FS 28905). The aircraft was flown a number of times in these markings, applied for a 1987 Christmas card.
- 37023, F 6-22, No.1 Sqn/F 6 insignia on the fin in Yellow (FS 23655), the legend GREENPIECE on the fuselage, rainbow colours on the air intake and FOXTROT WARRIOR in Yellow on the nose. The aircraft was painted and marked as described for a 1987 Christmas card. However, s/n 37023 never flew carrying these markings.

To write more comprehensive information is not possible due to space considerations. Instead, the reader is referred to look carefully at the photos of different aircraft contained within these pages.

JA 37 s/n 37321, coded F 16-61, taking off from Gardermoen, Norway, on 14 June 1992. (Mikael Forslund)

175

Chapter 19
Technical Description
JA 37 *Viggen*

The aircraft has a bypass turbine engine and is equipped for all-weather operations.

The aircraft has been designed to meet requirements for high speed at low altitude, good climb performance, good acceleration and good supersonic performance at high altitude, and good low-speed characteristics with STOL (short take off and landing) capabilities.

The flight controls are hydraulically powered. The autopilot provides for fully automatic flight and can also be used for damping in manual mode. The foreplane is equipped with trailing-edge flaps to increase lift at take off and landing.

The pressurized cockpit has a jettisonable canopy and a rocket ejection seat.

The bypass turbine engine is a modified version of the Pratt & Whitney JT8D commercial engine equipped with a three-stage afterburner. To reduce landing distance, a hydraulically powered thrust reverser is provided. The take-off rating is 66,600 N (6,795 kp) without afterburner and 110,300 N (11,250 kp) with max afterburner.

An auxiliary fuel tank (drop tank) can be installed under the fuselage.

The aircraft has an internal 30 mm Oerlikon automatic gun. Other weapons are carried as external stores under the wings and the fuselage.

The aircraft has an extensive electronic system with the main computer as the integrating unit. This is utilized extensively tor navigation and aiming calculations, controlling and switching duties and for systems monitoring.

General
The airframe is mainly of bonded and riveted aluminium stressed-skin construction.
Major sections:
- Nose
- Forward fuselage
- Rear fuselage
- Tail cone
- Main wing
- Canard foreplane
- Tail fin

JA 37 s/n 37331, code F 17-31, taking off from Rörberg airfield, located between Sandviken and Gävle, Sweden, on 18 May 1996. (Mikael Forslund)

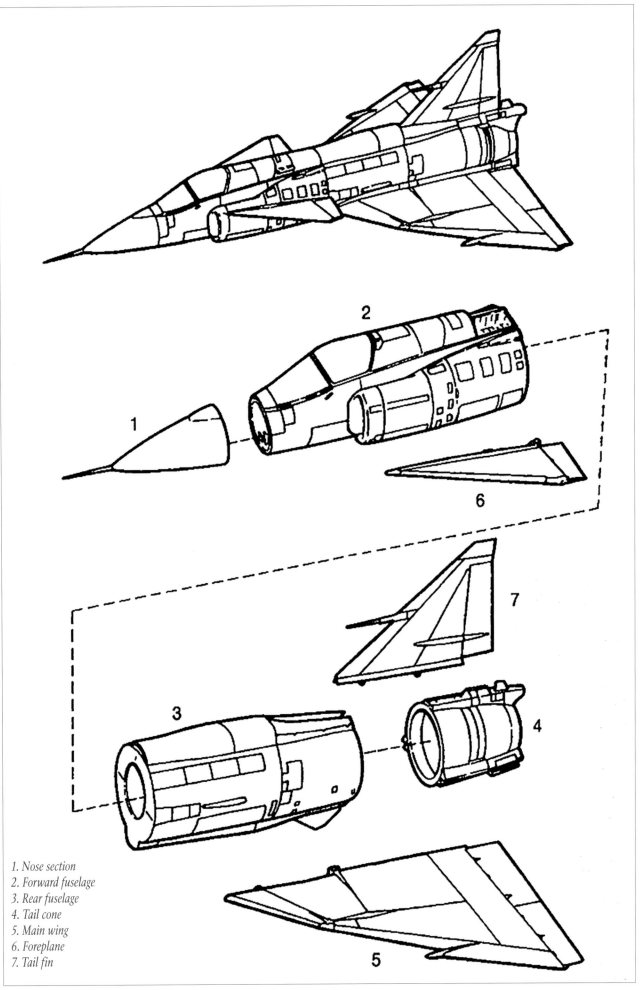

1. Nose section
2. Forward fuselage
3. Rear fuselage
4. Tail cone
5. Main wing
6. Foreplane
7. Tail fin

Nose section

The pressurized nose section, housing the radar, is attached to the forward fuselage with quick-release latches and can be pulled forward to facilitate access to the radar. It can also be completely disconnected.

The radome is made from antistatic laminated glassfibre. The main pitot tube is attached to the nose tip.

The pitot tube is electrically grounded to the aft (metal) part of the nose section to reduce the risk of damage in case of a static discharge/lightning strike.

JA 37 s/n 37392, code F 4-62, photographed at Teknikland, Optand, Sweden, on 20 October 2011. The radar is fitted beneath the nose cone. Two more Viggens, SK 37 s/n 37803, code F 4-67 and AJ 37 s/n 37097, code F 15-29, can be seen in the background. (Mikael Forslund)

JA 37 s/n 37392, code F 4-62, photographed at Teknikland, Optand, Sweden, on 16 May 2019. The nose cone has been fitted. (Mikael Forslund)

Forward fuselage

The forward fuselage contains:
- Cockpit
- Nose landing gear
- Three integral fuel tanks
- The major parts of the hydraulic, air, electric and avionic systems.
- The engine air intakes (one on each side) are removable. They join to a circular duct connected to the engine intake.

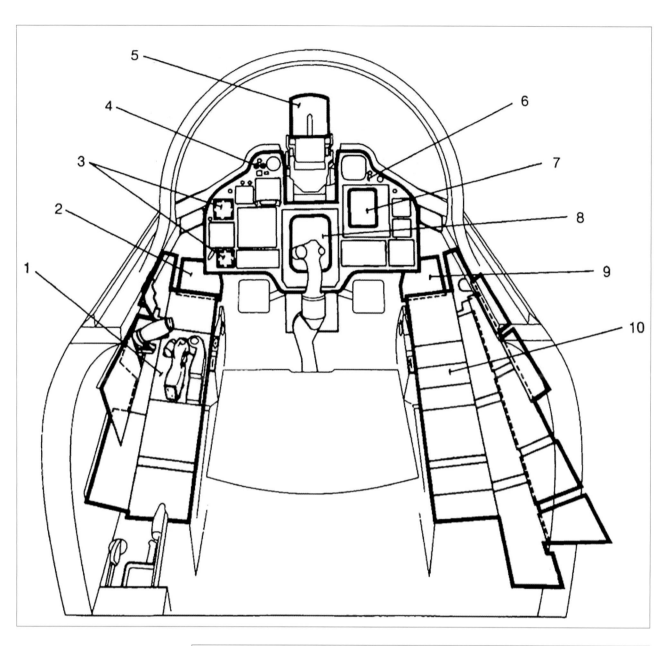

1. Panels, left side
2. Warning panel, left side
3. Standby instruments
4. Master Warning/Caution lights
5. HUD, Head Up Display
6. Front panel
7. HSD, Horizontal Situation Display
8. TD, Target Display
9. Warning panel, right side
10. Panels, right side

1. Trigger button
2. Manoeuver Load Limiter (stick shaker)
3. Safety catch
4. Autopilot quick disengage button
5. IRRB reference / atitude hpld swich
6. Optical aiming mode button
7. PTT button
8. Trim switch
9. IRRBtarget seeker release / automatic aiming switch

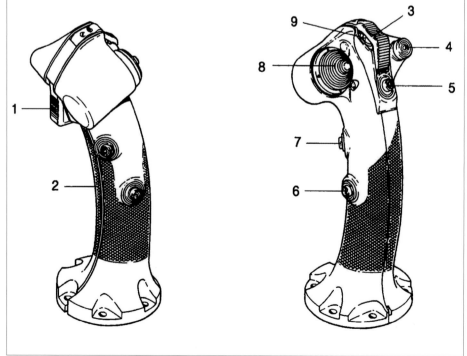

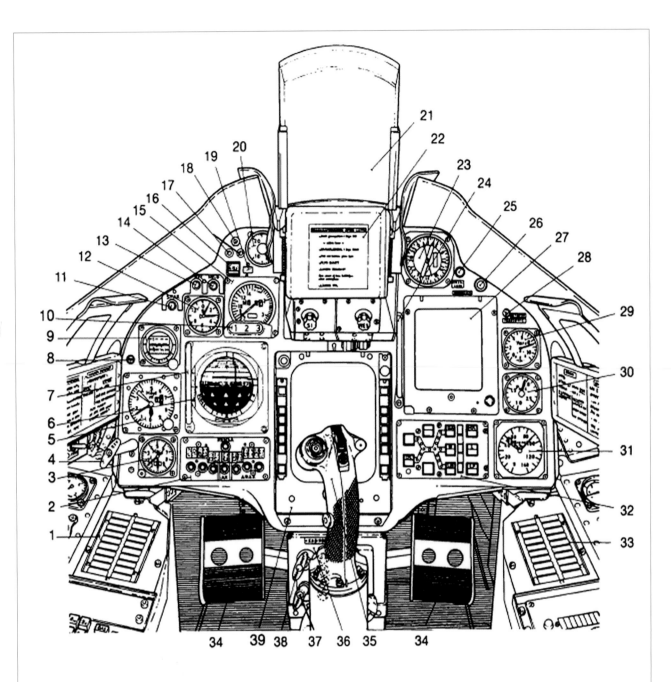

1	Warning panel, left side (see Fig 7)	20	Angle–of–attack indicator
2	Weapons display	21	HUD
3	Standby altimeter	22	Emergency checklist panel (see Fig 10)
4	Thrust reverser handle	23	Heading indicator
5	Altimeter	24	Handle bar
6	Attitude/Director Indicator (ADI)	25	RESERVKURS(standby heading) pushbutton/light
7	Handle bar	26	SNABBRESN (fast–erect) pushbutton/light
8	REV thrust reverser status light	27	HSD, Horizontal Situation Display
9	Standby horizon	28	REVAVDR/TRANSONIC (surge prevention) light
10	Afterburner zone indicator	29	R.P.M. indicator
11	SPAK (CSS) autopilot pushbutton/light	30	EPR indicator
12	G–meter	31	Fuel gauge
13	ATT autopilot pushbutton/light	32	Systems panel
14	HÖJD (ALT) autopilot pushbutton/light	33	Warning panel, right side (see Fig 7)
15	Airspeed/Mach indicator	34	Rudder pedals with toe brakes
16	Alpha 15,5° pushbutton/light	35	Control stick (see Fig 8)
17	Master Warning/Caution lights	36	Cockpit lights panel
18	Master Warning/Caution acknowledge button	37	Parking brake handle
19	AFK (A/T, autothrottle) light	38	Pedal adjustment handle
		39	TD, Target Display

Cockpit — center section

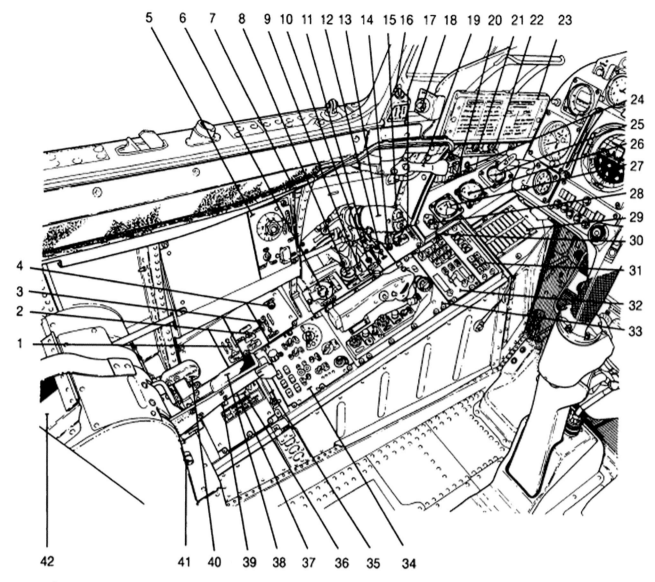

1	NÖDTRIM ROLL switch (standby roll trim)
2	NÖDTRIM TIPP switch (standby pitch trim)
3	SIDTRIM switch (yaw trim)
4	Yaw trim indicator
5	Air conditioning panel
6	RENFLYGN (balanced flight) knob
7	Arm restraining net
8	NÖDSKJUT HUV pushbutton (emergency canopy release)
9	AUT–MAN TÄNDS switch (ignition)
10	ÅTERSTART switch (engine restart)
11	START switch
12	GENERATOR switch
13	Thrust lever
14	LT–KRAN light (LP fuel valve)
15	HUVUDSTRÖM switch (Master) – (not visible in the figure)
16	PTT-switch NÖDS FR 29 (emergency radio)
17	LT–KRAN switch (LP fuel valve)
18	OPT FIX pushbutton
19	Canopy handle
20	IND LAMP HEL HALV switch (bright/dim)
21	STRÅLKAST switch (landing/taxi lights)

22	NÖDBEL switch (emergency lights)
23	Emergency checklist panel (see Fig 10)
24	KONTR LAMPTABLÅ switch (lamp test)
25	Cabin pressure indicator
26	Brake accumulator pressure indicator
27	Pitch trim indicator
28	Roll trim indicator
29	Left Warning panel (see Fig 7)
30	Holder for arm restraining net wire
31	KV3 channel selector (radio)
32	KV1 channel selector (radio)
33	Radar control panel
34	FR29 control panel (radio)
35	Handle bar
36	ALLMÄN BEL light intensity knob (flood lights)
37	PANELBEL light intensity knob (panel lights – not visible in figure)
38	Landing gear handle
39	INSTR BEL light intensity knob (instrument lights – not visible in figure)
40	Thrust lever friction control
41	Landing gear handle emergency release
42	Aircraft technical log stowage

Cockpit — left side

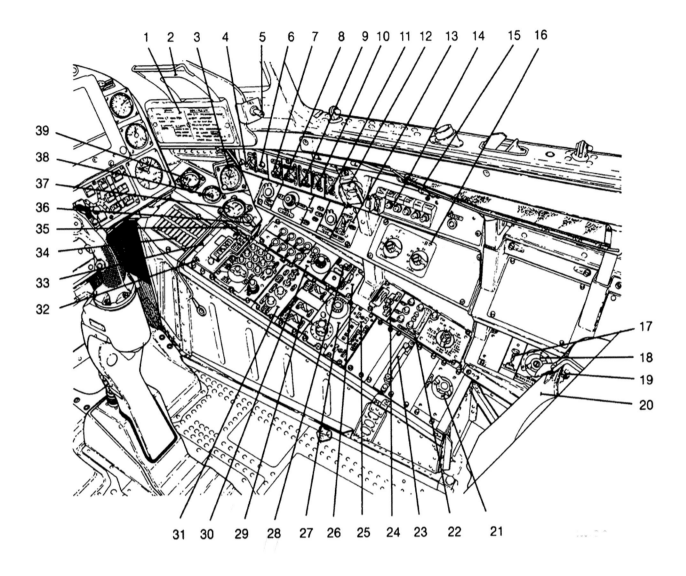

1   Emergency checklist panel (see Fig 10)
2   Map holder
3   Clock
4   BRÄNSLEREGL fuel control switch
5   Light switch, right & left emergency checklist panels
6   KONTROLL test switch
7   TANKPUMP, fuel pump switch
8   LT–KRAN EBK, LP fuel valve switch, afterburner
9   RESERVSTRÖM standby alternator switch
10   TIPPVÄXEL pitch gearing switch
11   AVISN MOTOR engine anti–ice switch
12   Central connection stowage
13   Weapons panel
14   Circuit breaker panel
15   Arm restraining net
16   ECM control panel
17   TÄNDSTIFT ignition switch
18   BRAGG KABINLUFT VENTDRÄKT cooling air control knob
19   RPM indicator test port
20   Protective mask box (may be replaced by holder for hand–held camera)

21   LEDLJUS formation lights intensity knob
22   Test panel
23   Handle bar
24   VARMLUFTSPOLNFRONTRUTA windshield defogging knob
25   SSR PN 865 transponder control panel
26   GPWS selector
27   PN 799 control panel
28   RHM radar altimeter switch
29   External lights panel
30   Navigation panel
31   App 73 (RWR) control panel
32   Data panel
33   Notes tape
34   Warning panel, right side
35   Holder for arm restraining net wire
36   Oxygen on/off selector
37   Oxygen pressure indicator
38   Tailpipe temperature indicator
39   Nozzle position indicator

Cockpit — right side

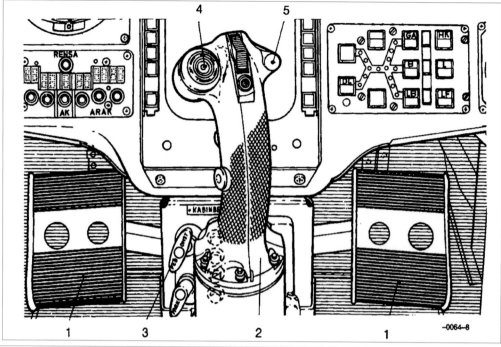

The Viggen control stick and rudder pedals, overview.
1. Rudder pedals
2. Control stick
3. Pedal adjustment handle
4. Trim switch
5. Autopilot quick-disengage switch

Pilot workload was considerably eased with the introduction of various digital displays.

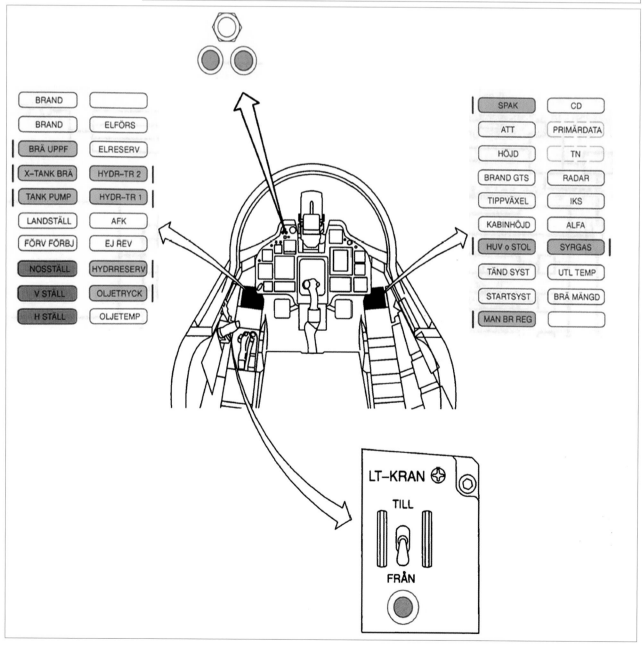

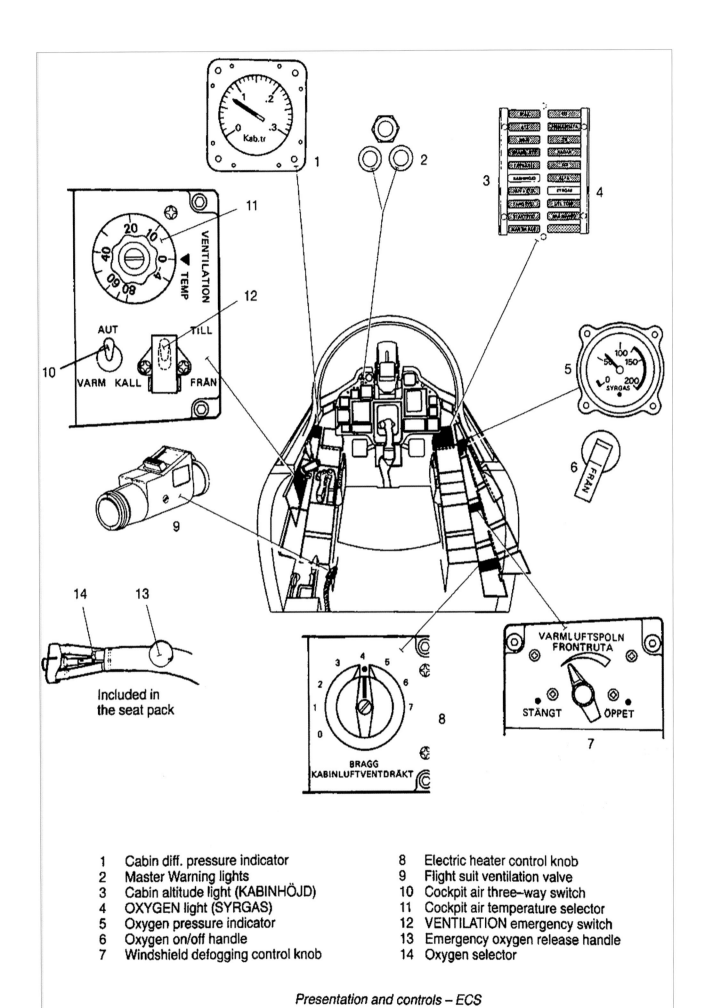

1	Cabin diff. pressure indicator
2	Master Warning lights
3	Cabin altitude light (KABINHÖJD)
4	OXYGEN light (SYRGAS)
5	Oxygen pressure indicator
6	Oxygen on/off handle
7	Windshield defogging control knob
8	Electric heater control knob
9	Flight suit ventilation valve
10	Cockpit air three-way switch
11	Cockpit air temperature selector
12	VENTILATION emergency switch
13	Emergency oxygen release handle
14	Oxygen selector

Presentation and controls – ECS

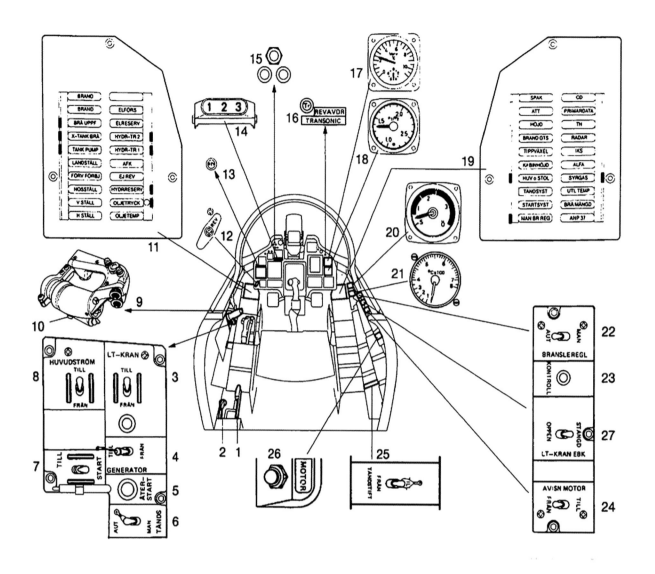

1   Landing gear handle
2   Brake control handle
3   Switch, LT–KRAN (LP cock)
4   Switch, GENERATOR
5   Switch, ÅTERSTART (re–light)
6   Switch, TÄNDS (Ignition system)
7   Switch, START
8   Switch, HUVUDSTRÖM (Master switch)
9   Thrust lever
10 Disengagement pushbutton, AFK (A/T)
11 Warning panel, left
12 Reverse handle
13 REV light
14 a/b zone indicator

15 Master Warning light
16 REV AVDR (TRANSONIC) light
17 R.P.M. indicator
18 EPR indicator
19 Warning panel, right
20 Nozzle position indicator (a/b)
21 EGT indicator
22 Switch, BRÄNSLEREGL (fuel control)
23 Switch, KONTROLL (test)
24 Switch, AVISN MOTOR (engine anti–ice)
25 Switch, TÄNDSTIFT (ignition plug)
26 Circuit breaker, MOTOR, ignition system
27 Switch, LT–KRAN EBK (LP cock, a/b)

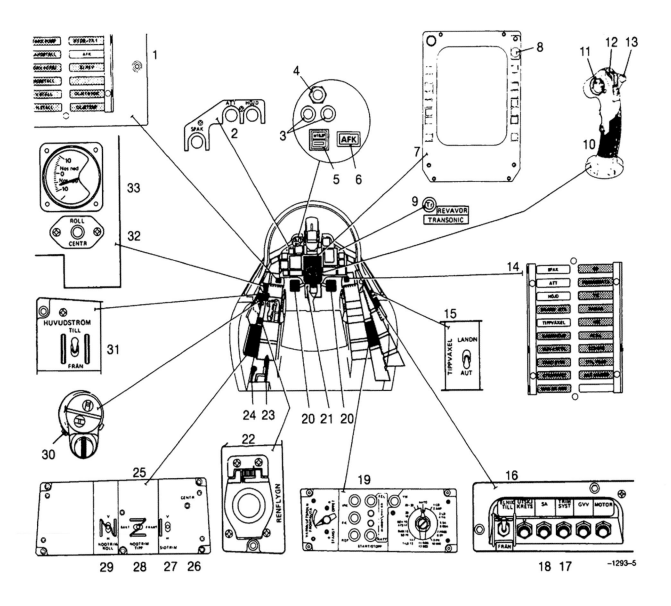

1	Warning panel, left
2	Autopilot mode selector switch with lights
3	Master Warning lights
4	Acknowledge button, Master Warning
5	Reference alpha 15,5° pushbutton
6	A/T engaged light
7	Target Display
8	Altitude warning light
9	TRANSONIC light
10	Control stick grip
11	Trim switch, pitch and roll
12	Release automatic aiming switch
13	Autopilot quick–disengage button
14	Warning panel, right
15	TIPPVÄXEL switch
16	Circuit breaker panel
17	Circuit breaker TRIM SYST
18	Circuit breaker SA (main switch for autopilot)
19	Test panel
20	Rudder pedals
21	Pedal adjustment handle
22	Balanced–flight potentiometer
23	Landing gear handle
24	Friction lever and A/T engagement
25	Trim panel
26	Yaw trim indicator
27	Yaw trim switch
28	Standby trim switch, pitch
29	Standby trim switch, roll
30	A/T Disengage switch
31	Master switch
32	Roll trim indicator
33	Pitch trim indicator

AJ 37 cockpit (simulator), with the circular radar indicator in the centre of the panel.
(Sven Stridsberg, via Archives of Swedish Aviation Historical Society)

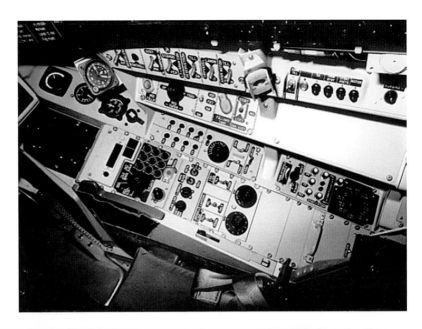

The left, centre and right JA 37 instrument panels.
(Via Archives of Swedish Aviation Historical Society)

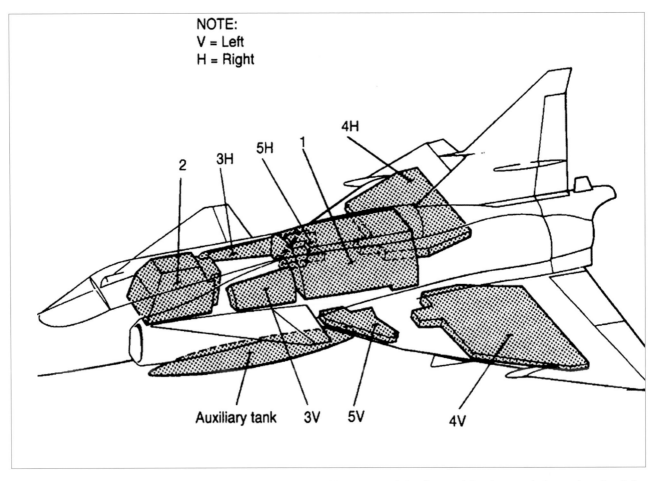

NOTE:
V = Left
H = Right

4H

5H

3H

2

1

Auxiliary tank   3V   5V   4V

Fuel tanks-schematic. The internal tanks are of the integral type and are separated from other areas of the aircraft by double skins as far as possible. The drop tank is a stressed-skin design

The foreplane is fitted to the middle section of the forward fuselage and the underside of the fuselage has hardpoints for weapon pylons.

The pilot's luggage can be stowed and secured inside the lower equipment bay.

The cockpit has a wrap-around single-piece windscreen, a jettisonabie canopy and a rear part to which the canopy is hinged. The canopy opens upwards by an electric actuator.

Rear fuselage

The rear fuselage houses the engine with its afterburner, and a saddle type fuel collector tank. The main wings and the fin are attached to the rear fuselage, where the inner main gear doors are also hinged. The automatic gun is fitted into the lower, forward, section of the rear fuselage. The underside has a glassfibre ventral fin with an integrated radio antenna. The top side has a spine housing control cables, fuel lines, electric cables, an oil cooler and a fuel tank.

AJS 37 s/n 37098, code F 7-52 (registered as SE-DXN), of the Swedish Air Force Historic Flight (SwAFHF), taking off at full afterburner. (Tomasz Obrębski)

Tail cone

The tail cone with ejector, which has secondary exhaust nozzle and reverse-thrust functions, forms the aft part of the rear fuselage. The cone has an annular-shaped tertiary air intake and houses a cylindrical seal and three thrust reverser doors. The doors, when activated, force the engine exhaust forward through the annular air intake, thereby shortening the landing roll.

At low air speeds, air enters this intake, adding some thrust. At high speeds, a cylindrical seal closes the intake.

For reasons of durability and heat resistance, the ejector and the thrust reverser doors are made of titanium.

*The rear section
of AJS 37 s/n 37108,
code F 10-55, with the
Radar Warning Receiver
(RWR) antenna removed.
The picture was taken
at Flygvapenmuseum,
Linköping, Sweden,
on 1 October 2016.
(Mikael Forslund)*

AJS 37 s/n 37098, code F 7-52 (registered as SE-DXN), of the Swedish Air Force Historic Flight (SwAFHF) taking off at full afterburner.
(Both Tomasz Obrębski)

Main wing

The main wing is a delta configuration with compound sweep and a dog tooth on the outer portion. Each half of the wing is fitted to the rear fuselage at ten points. The wing contains four integral fuel tanks and the main landing gear. The elevons (combined ailerons/elevators) are hinged at the trailing edge. The underside has hardpoints for weapon pylons.

AJS 37 s/n 37098, code F 7-52 (registered as SE-DXN), of the Swedish Air Force Historic Flight (SwAFHF) at low altitude. (Tomasz Obrębski)

Foreplane

The two halves of the canard foreplane are fitted to the forward fuselage at five points. The foreplane has trailing edge flaps, primarily used for take-off and landing.

Small photo: *A close-up of the right canard wing with flap on AJS 37 s/n 37108, code F 10-55, preserved by* Flygvapenmuseum, *Linköping, Sweden. (Mikael Forslund)*
Large photo: *Left canard wing with flaps on AJS 37 s/n 37108, code F 10-55, at* Flygvapenmuseum, *Linköping, Sweden. Both pictures was taken on 1 October 2016. (Mikael Forslund)*

The fins of JA 37 s/n 37432, code F 16-32, and s/n 37304, code F 13-44. (Mikael Forslund and Leif Fredin, via Archives of Mikael Forslund)

Tail fin

The fin is located on the centerline on top of the rear fuselage. It may be folded to the left to facilitate hangar storage. A pitot tube is located in the middle of the leading edge, supplying standby instruments, flight control and escape systems. The rear part of the fin carries the rudder hinges. The fin tip incorporates a radio antenna. The fin root houses an underwater locator beacon which automatically activates when immersed in water. (A similar beacon is installed on the ejection seat).

Folding of the fin

The fin folds down and is raised hydraulically with a hand pump. The pump with its pressure gauge is located under the access doors in the spine near the fin.

The fin is kept in the raised position by a double locking mechanism. Locking is correctly done when the doors over the locks can be closed.

A JA 37 in the F 21 workshop on 9 June 1991. (Mikael Forslund)

Electrical system

Most components in the aircraft are electrically controlled and operated. The operation can either be manual or through automatic control circuits, or a combination of both.

The electrical components use AC and/or DC power. Thus the electrical system consists of one AC and one DC system.

The main power supply is an engine-driven AC generator. In normal operation the AC generator supplies the AC systems and the DC system is supplied from two rectifiers, connected in parallel with the AC system.

A ground power unit (GPU) can be connected to the left side of the aircraft below the foreplane. Conditioned air for avionics cooling and cockpit air conditioning is also supplied via the same connection. The external power supply is auto-matically disconnected from the aircraft as soon as the AC generator is on line. The ground power supply can be connected to the aircraft before the engine is stopped and can thus supply AC power to the systems immediately after the AC generator goes off line. The engine is normally started with a GPU, but it is also possible to use the aircraft battery to start the engine.

The aircraft also has a back-up power supply system by means of a ram air turbine. This system partly replaces the functions of the AC generator if there is a failure in the ordinary system. Also, the aircraft battery is a back-up but only for the DC system.

AC system

The AC system mainly comprises a system of busses, an AC generator with a control panel and a ram air turbine (in case of a system failure). The AC system works at a frequency of 400 Hz.

Canopy

General

The canopy assembly consists of a blown acrylic canopy in an aluminium frame. The forward frame has three rear view mirrors. The canopy is hinged at the rear and opens upwards and backwards by an electric actuator, activated by one internal or one external handle on the aircraft's left side.

A tubular seal around the canopy is automatically inflated by the pneumatic system at engine start-up. Similar seals exist at the nose section and the upper equipment bay door. All seals are evacuated when the canopy is opened.

The left periscope on SK 37 s/n 37805, code F 15-65, preserved with Söderhamn/F 15 Flygmuseum at Söderhamn, Sweden. A Saab A 21A-3, s/n 21311, code F 15-Red A, can be seen in the background. The picture was taken on 10 October 2010. (Mikael Forslund)

JA 37 s/n 37392, code F 4-62, photographed at Teknikland, Optand, Sweden, on 16 May 2019. A dummy has replaced the pilot. (Mikael Forslund)

Canopy mechanism

The canopy system comprises an electromechanical system for opening/closing, and an electro/pyrotechnical system for canopy jettisoning at seat ejection or other emergency.

There are two locks, one in each side frame, with associated levers and rods. An electric actuator is located in the cockpit rear bulkhead. One external handle or one internal handle on the left side are used for normal operation.

The canopy locks and actuator can be operated by the handle in the cockpit or by an external handle, which is connected separately. The locks are mechanically operated, while the actuator is electrically operated via two microswitches - one for opening and one for closing - which are triggered by the operating handle.

The rear end of the canopy has a bracket, against which the actuator operates during opening. When the canopy is in the closed position the actuator is disconnected. At opening, the actuator locks on to the canopy by a catch which can be manually disabled with a handle on the inside of the left canopy frame; this makes it possible to manually lift the canopy in case the actuator is inoperative.

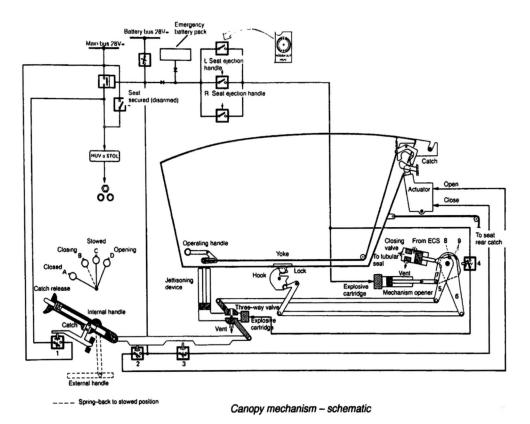

Canopy mechanism – schematic

Ejection seat

General

The rocket ejection seat consists of a seat frame with a vertically adjustable pan. The frame consists of a firing tube and two side beams with sliding shoes. The firing tube surrounds a piston which, together with two guide rails, are attached to the aircraft, thus forming the seat base.

The seat is secured to the piston with a ball lock which opens at ejection.

The rocket motor is attached to the bottom part of the seat base; at the upper part there is a leather covered headrest, filled with energy absorbing material.

A damping device is fitted between the seat and the aircraft structure, which is activated by large upward forces on the seat from below. Damping is achieved by a hole being punched in a dedicated washer, thus smoothing the downward movement of the seat. This minimizes the risk of back injuries to the pilot during, for instance, a belly landing. An activated damper does not prevent seat ejection.

The seat can be adjusted up or down by an electrical actuator, controlled by a spring loaded switch on the seat's left side. The range of travel is limited by two limiter switches.

To prevent rotation after ejection because of centre-of-gravity variations caused by the adjustment of the seat, the rocket motor alignment is automatically adjusted as the seat pan is moved up or down.

An underwater locator beacon (automatic ultrasonic "pinger" transmitter) is attached to the bottom part of the seat. It activates automatically when immersed in water.

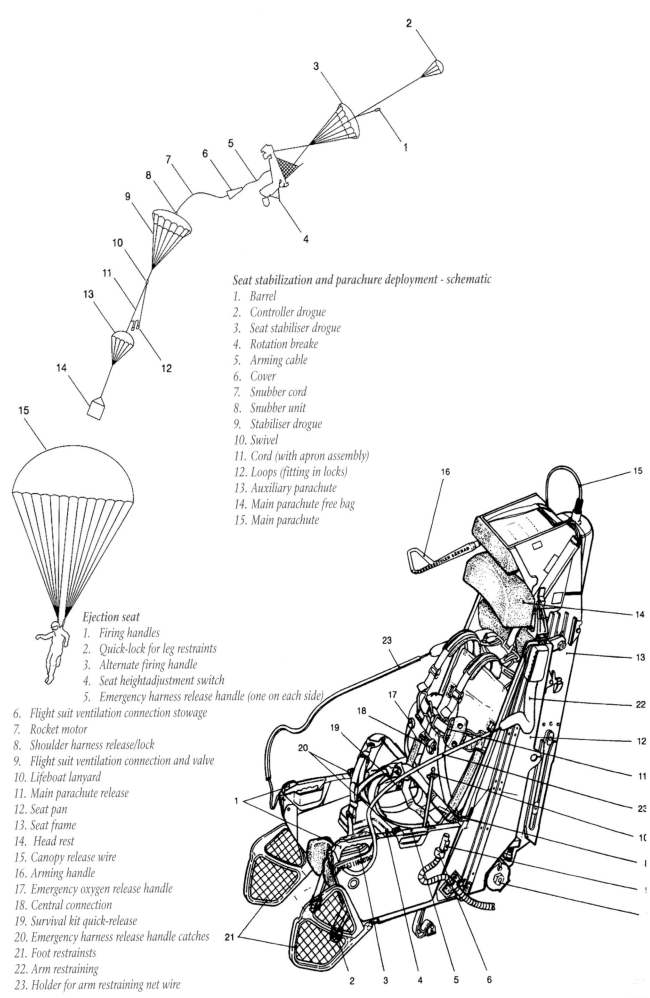

Seat stabilization and parachure deployment - schematic
1. Barrel
2. Controller drogue
3. Seat stabiliser drogue
4. Rotation breake
5. Arming cable
6. Cover
7. Snubber cord
8. Snubber unit
9. Stabiliser drogue
10. Swivel
11. Cord (with apron assembly)
12. Loops (fitting in locks)
13. Auxiliary parachute
14. Main parachute free bag
15. Main parachute

Ejection seat
1. Firing handles
2. Quick-lock for leg restraints
3. Alternate firing handle
4. Seat heightadjustment switch
5. Emergency harness release handle (one on each side)
6. Flight suit ventilation connection stowage
7. Rocket motor
8. Shoulder harness release/lock
9. Flight suit ventilation connection and valve
10. Lifeboat lanyard
11. Main parachute release
12. Seat pan
13. Seat frame
14. Head rest
15. Canopy release wire
16. Arming handle
17. Emergency oxygen release handle
18. Central connection
19. Survival kit quick-release
20. Emergency harness release handle catches
21. Foot restrainsts
22. Arm restraining
23. Holder for arm restraining net wire

Landing gear
General
The landing gear comprises one twin wheel nose landing gear, and two tandem bogie main landing gears. The nose gear retracts forwards into the nose gear bay, and the main gears retract inwards into the main wing.

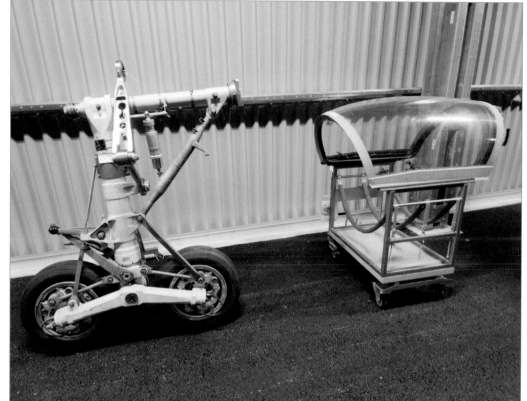

The right main undercarriage and a canopy at Teknikland, Optand, Sweden. (Mikael Forslund)

A close-up of the undercarriage of AJS 37 s/n 37108, code F 10-55, preserved with Flygvapenmuseum, Linköping, Sweden. The picture was taken on 1 October 2016. (Photos: Mikael Forslund)

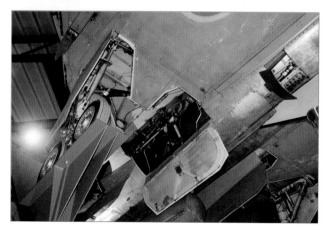

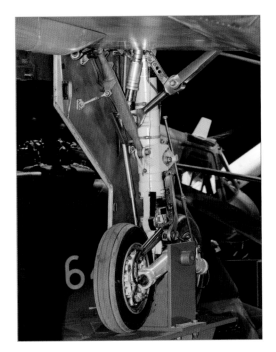 

The left and right main undercarriage. (Photos: Mikael Forslund)

Engine

General

The two main assemblies of the Swedish Air Force adapted Prat & Whitney JT 8D power plant (Swedish Air Force designation *RM 8B*) are the engine and the afterburner (a/b). The engine is of the bypass type, which means that the airflow after passing the first three compressor stages is split in two different streams, an inner stream, gas generator (gg) airflow, and an outer stream, the fan airflow. The gas generator airflow passes through the low-pressure (LP) and high-pressure (HP) compressors, the combustor and the HP and LP turbines. The fan airflow passes through the outer part of the blades in the first three LP compressor stages that form the fan and is then led into an annular duct - the fan duct - surrounding the compressor air stream. After the turbines the inner, hot, air stream unites with the outer fan air stream in the mixing section, or diffuser, that forms the inlet to the afterburner.

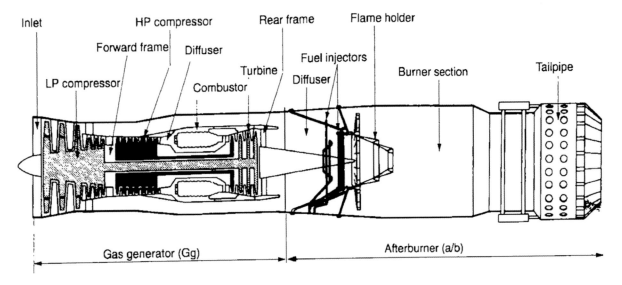

Main assemblies

Seen from the front, the engine can be divided into the following main assemblies.

The inlet frame houses a number of inlet guide vanes. Around its outer front part there is a bay cooling air inlet flap which, on the ground and at low speed - when there is actually a suction pressure in the air inlet - prevents a reversed airflow from the engine bay zone (the area between the engine and the aircraft).

The low-pressure compressor contains six compressor stages. After the first three (fan) stages, which give a pressure ratio of 2,2:1, the airflow splits up into two different flows - the fan airflow and the gas generator airflow. The air mäss ratio between these two flows (the by-pass ratio) is 1,03:1.

The forward frame is the main engine frame and connects the LP compressor with the HP compressor and houses a number of bleed air valves.

The HP compressor consists of seven compressor stages which, together with the LP compressor, gives an overall pressure ratio of 17:1. From the front of the HP compressor there are radial drive shafts for the accessory drives.

From the HP diffuser that connects the HP compressor with the compressor flame tubes, HP air is bled off to the Environmental Control System (ECS).

Afterburner

Main assemblies

The diffuser mixing section has an increasing cross sectional area which reduces the speed of the flow streams from the fan duct and gas generator to a level more suitable for combustion. The diffuser contains the atomizer rings and flame holders for the three zones in the afterburner.

In the burner section the cross sectional area is divided into three concentric zones which are ignited in succession as the thrust lever is advanced.

The exhaust part contains a primary exhaust nozzle with 20 moving petals which centre the outlet area. The petals are mechanically activated by four hydraulic actuators which are powered by fuel pressure from the a/b fuel regulator.

Thrust reverse

By deflecting the jet stream from the engine exhaust forward, the engine thrust can be used to slow down the aircraft during taxiing after touchdown. In this way the landing run for the aircraft can be considerably shortened.

The jet stream is deflected by three butterfly doors in the aft of the tailcone which are extended to turn the jet stream forward in such direction that it exits through the tertiary aircone surrounding the tail cone. The tertiary air cone is so shaped that the lower part of the jet stream is not deflected as much as the upper part. This gives a certain nose-down effect during reverse thrust. To assist the airflow through the tertiary air cone, the primary nozzle is fully opened. Reverse thrust is obtainable from the thrust lever up to max MIL power.

The reversing butterfly doors are hydraulically controlled by pressure from the hydraulic System 1. The extension and retraction of the butterfly doors, which takes approx. 1,5 sec, is electrically controlled from a solenoid valve, which controls the fluid pressure extension and retraction circuit.

The reverse is either automatically initiated at touch down when the right main landing gear is loaded, if there has been a pre selection by the reverse handle being pulled out before touch down, or manually if the handle is pulled out when the nose landing gear is not loaded within one second after the main landing gear is loaded. If the nosewheel is unloaded again, reverse thrust condition is maintained for 30 sec, irrespective of whether initiation was automatic or manual.

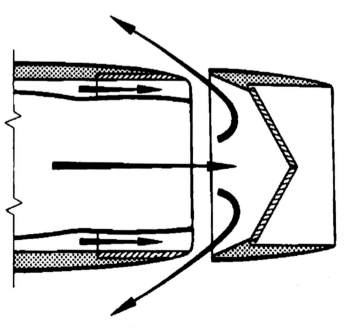

Thrust reverser, principles

Fuel system

General

The fuel system is of the low-pressure type and consists of fuel tanks, fuel lines, and equipment for refuelling, storage and supply of fuel to the high pressure fuel systems of the engine and afterburner.

Fuel quantities and tank volumes are classified information (1999).

Maximum feed capacity to the engine is about 68,000 l/h, of which about 8,000 l/h is to the gas generator and about 60,000 l/h is to the afterburner.

Functionally, the fuel system consists of the following subsystems:

The fuelling system
The feed system
The tank pressurization system

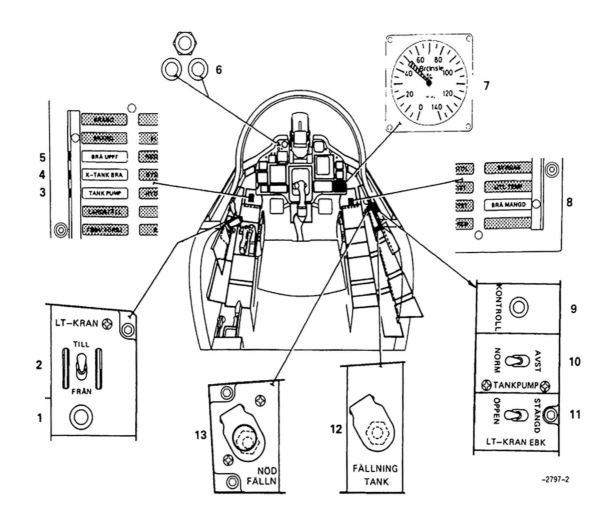

1	LT–KRAN light	8	BRÄMÄNGD light
2	LT–KRAN TILL/FRÅN (on/off) switch	9	KONTROLL pushbutton
3	TANKPUMP light	10	TANKPUMP switch
4	X–TANK BRÄ light	11	LT–KRAN EBK ÖPPEN/STÄNGD (open/closed) switch
5	BRÄ UPPF light	12	FÄLLNING TANK pushbutton
6	Master Warning lights	13	NÖDFÄLLNING pushbutton
7	Fuel indicator		

Figure 4.   Fuel system — presentation and controls

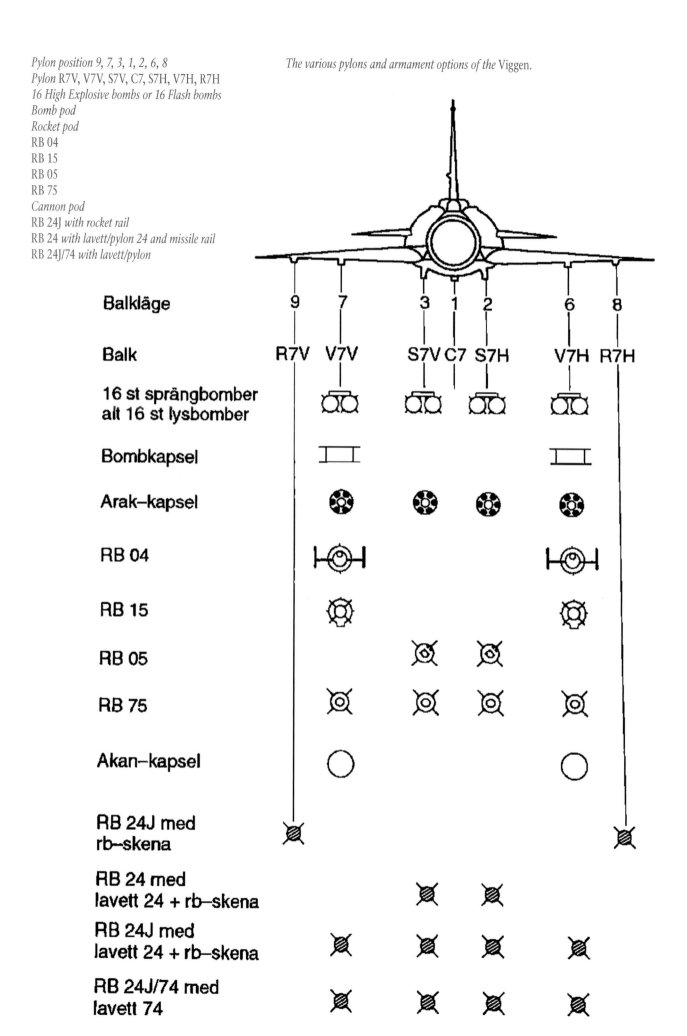

Pylon position 9, 7, 3, 1, 2, 6, 8
Pylon R7V, V7V, S7V, C7, S7H, V7H, R7H
16 High Explosive bombs or 16 Flash bombs
Bomb pod
Rocket pod
RB 04
RB 15
RB 05
RB 75
Cannon pod
RB 24J with rocket rail
RB 24 with lavett/pylon 24 and missile rail
RB 24J/74 with lavett/pylon

The various pylons and armament options of the Viggen.

202

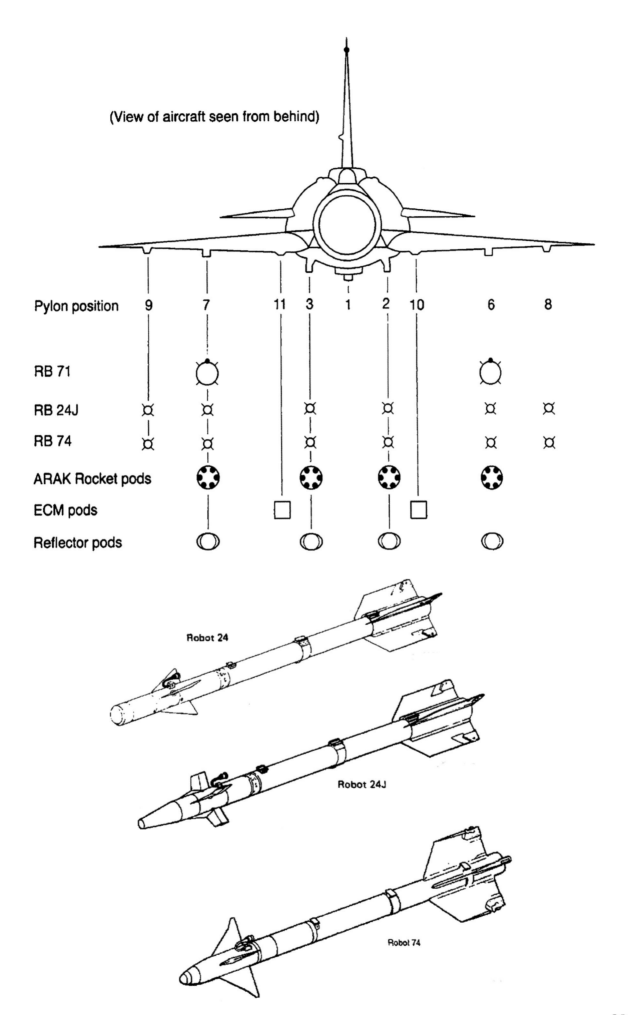

(View of aircraft seen from behind)

Pylon position	9	7	11	3	1	2	10	6	8
RB 71		⬤						⬤	
RB 24J	✕	✕		✕		✕		✕	✕
RB 74	✕	✕		✕		✕		✕	✕
ARAK Rocket pods		✹		✹		✹		✹	
ECM pods			◻				◻		
Reflector pods		◐		◐		◐		◐	

Robot 24

Robot 24J

Robot 74

The KCA Oerlikon 30 mm cannon pod.

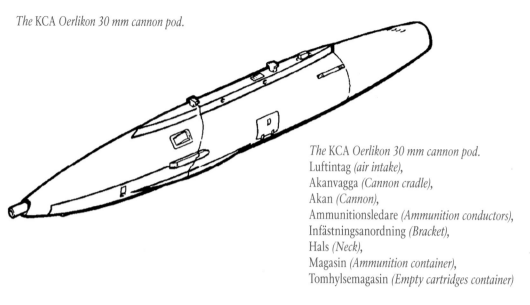

The KCA Oerlikon 30 mm cannon pod.
Luftintag *(air intake)*,
Akanvagga *(Cannon cradle)*,
Akan *(Cannon)*,
Ammunitionsledare *(Ammunition conductors)*,
Infästningsanordning *(Bracket)*,
Hals *(Neck)*,
Magasin *(Ammunition container)*,
Tomhylsemagasin *(Empty cartridges container)*

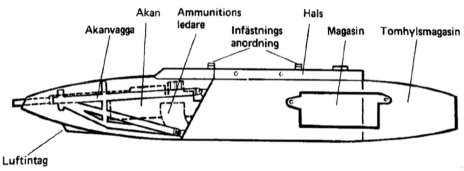

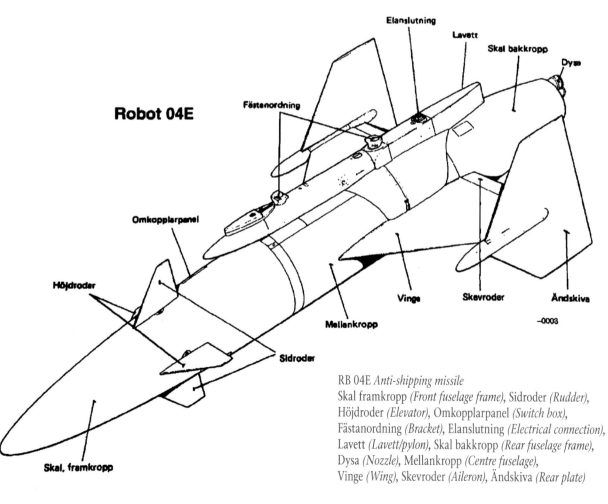

Robot 04E

RB 04E *Anti-shipping missile*
Skal framkropp *(Front fuselage frame)*, Sidroder *(Rudder)*,
Höjdroder *(Elevator)*, Omkopplarpanel *(Switch box)*,
Fästanordning *(Bracket)*, Elanslutning *(Electrical connection)*,
Lavett *(Lavett/pylon)*, Skal bakkropp *(Rear fuselage frame)*,
Dysa *(Nozzle)*, Mellankropp *(Centre fuselage)*,
Vinge *(Wing)*, Skevroder *(Aileron)*, Ändskiva *(Rear plate)*

The RB 24J *Air-to-air missile in its dummy variant, broken down into its various components.*

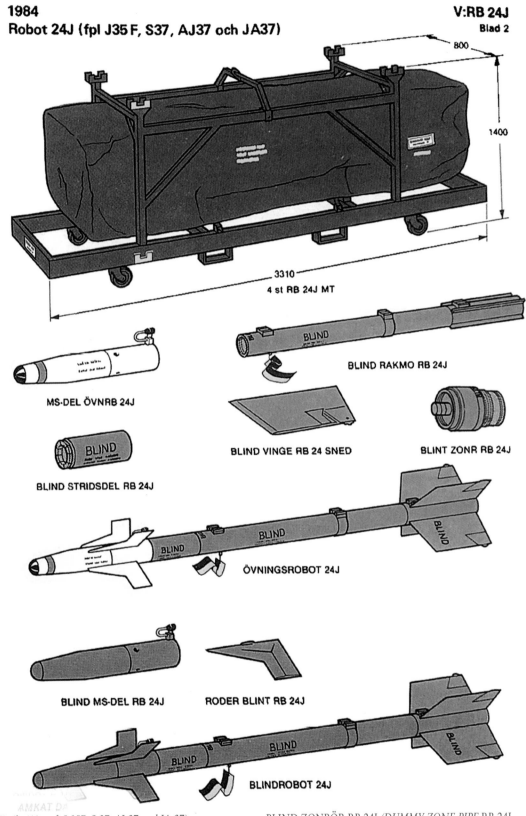

800

1400

3310

4 st RB 24J MT

MS-DEL ÖVNRB 24J

BLIND RAKMO RB 24J

BLIND STRIDSDEL RB 24J

BLIND VINGE RB 24 SNED

BLINT ZONR RB 24J

ÖVNINGSROBOT 24J

BLIND MS-DEL RB 24J

RODER BLINT RB 24J

BLINDROBOT 24J

24J *Missile (Aircraft J 35F, S 37, AJ 37 and JA 37)*
MS-DEL ÖVNINGS-RB 24J *(MS-SECTION DUMMY 24J MISSILE)*
BLIND STRIDSDEL RB 24J *(DUMMY WARHEAD RB 24J MISSILE)*
BLIND RAKMOTOR RB 24J *(DUMMY ROCKET ENGINE RB 24J MISSILE)*
BLINDVINGE RB 24 SNED *(DUMMY WING RB 24 MISSILE OBLIQUE)*

BLIND ZONRÖR RB 24J *(DUMMY ZONE PIPE RB 24J MISSILE)*
ÖVNINGSROBOT 24J *(PRACTICE 24J MISSILE)*
BLIND MS-DEL RB 24J *(DUMMY MS-SECTION RB 24J MISSILE)*
RODER BLINT RB 24J *(DUMMY RUDDER RB 24J MISSILE)*
BLINDROBOT 24J *(DUMMY 24J MISSILE)*

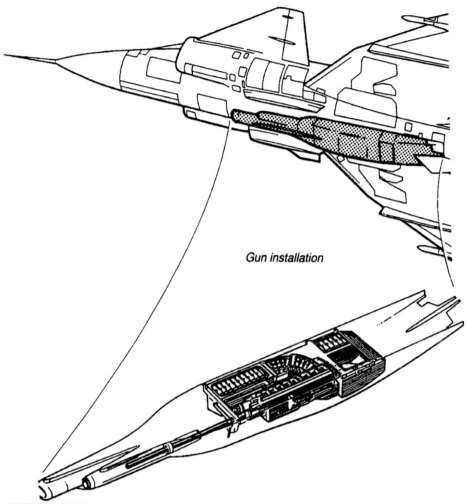

Gun installation

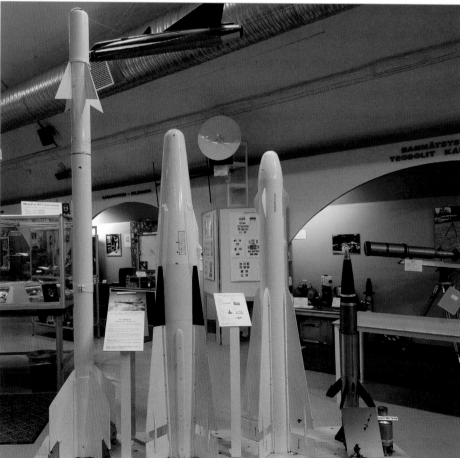

RB 24 Sidewinder, *RB 27* Falcon (radar) *and* RB 28 Falcon *(infra red), on display at the* RFN *Museum at Vidsel, Sweden, on 25 October 2011. The* RB 28 *was considered as part of the* Viggen *armament, but these plans did not reach fruition. (Mikael Forslund)*

Rocket installation. Air–to–surface rockets

The aircraft can carry four pods of rockets. Each pod can be loaded with six 13,5 cm rockets, giving a total of 24 rockets.

The rocket pods can be installed in pylon positions 2, 3, 6 and 7. See Fig 1.

Rocket pod m/70B

The rocket pod contains the mechanical and electrical devices for rocket firing.

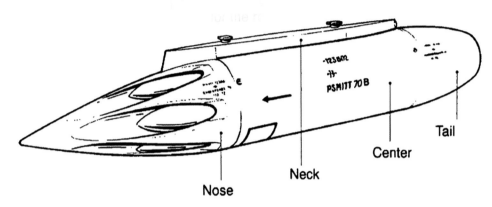

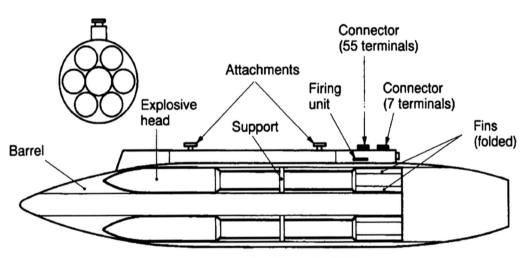

Figure 4.   Rocket pod m/70B

The 13,5 cm rocket m/70 consists of a head with a fuze and a rocket motor with a fin holder.

The head is available in two different versions, high–explosive and armor–piercing. The heads accomodate impact fuses or proximity fuses.

When the rocket leaves the barrel the six fins are unfolded for stabilization.

Note

The training rocket pod m/70B, the blind pod m/70 and the 6,3 cm training rocket are described in Volume 3, a/c Description.

ARMAMENT (Self defence and jamming pods not shown here. See relevant chapters)		
Version	Rockets and guns	Bombs
AJ 37	RB 04E RB 05A RB 24B RB 24J RB 74 RB 75 30 mm *gun (pod) (12,7 mm/practice)* *Attack rocket (135 mm)*	*Bomb (120 kg)* *Flash bomb (80 kg)*
AJS 37	RB 04E RB 05A RB 15F RB 24B RB 24J RB 74 RB 75 30 mm *gun (pod) (12,7 mm/practice)* *Attack rockets (135 mm)*	*Bomb (120 kg)* *Flash bomb (80 kg)* *Bomb pod (650 kg)*
SK 37	*None*	*None*
SK 37E	*None*	*None*
SH 37	RB 04E RB 24J	
AJSH 37	RB 04E RB 15F RB 24B RB 24J RB 74	*Bomb pod (650 kg)*
SF 37	*RB 24B* *RB 24J*	
AJSF 37	*RB 24B* *RB 24J* *RB 74*	
JA 37	30 mm *gun* RB 24J RB 71 RB 74 *Attack rocket (135 mm)*	
JA 37D/Di	30 mm *gun* RB 24J RB 71 RB 74 RB 99 *Attack rocket (135 mm)*	